THE
CAREER FITNESS
PROGRAM

EXERCISING YOUR OPTIONS

Diane Sukiennik
Lisa Raufman
William Bendat

GSP

Gorsuch Scarisbrick, Publishers
SCOTTSDALE, ARIZONA

Publisher: John W. Gorsuch
Editor: Nils Anderson
Developmental Editor: Gay L. Pauley
Production Coordinator: A. Colette Kelly
Copyediting: Paula Williams
Illustrations: Joan Marlowe
Cover Design: Maliwauki Graphic Design
Typesetting: The Image Makers
Printing & Binding: Edwards Brothers

Gorsuch Scarisbrick, Publishers
8233 Via Paseo del Norte, Suite F-400
Scottsdale, AZ 85258

10 9 8 7 6 5 4 3 2 1

ISBN 0-89787-816-7

Printed in the United States of America.

Acknowledgments

We are indebted to our friend and publisher, John Gorsuch, for his encouragement throughout our many years of association. We also appreciate the input of professional contacts and colleagues throughout the country and the stimulating opportunities to share ideas. These have served to influence and enhance this third edition of the *Career Fitness Program*. Thanks also to the reviewers who read part or all of the manuscript for this new edition and offered suggestions for its improvements. We are grateful for their ideas and assistance.

About the Authors

Dr. Diane Sukiennik is a career counselor; a licensed marriage, family, and child counselor; and a nationally recognized lecturer and workshop facilitator in the field of career planning. She holds advanced degrees from Columbia and Nova universities as well as extensive postgraduate training in industrial psychology, management, and organizational development. Currently Dr. Sukiennik is on the faculty of Moorpark College, where her areas of expertise are career development, personal and professional presentation skills, and managerial effectiveness. She is also an industry consultant and has a private practice.

Dr. Bill Bendat is Dean of Student Services at Moorpark College, with responsibility for a comprehensive counseling network. He attended the University of California at Berkeley and Los Angeles as well as San Diego State University, earning graduate degrees in counseling psychology. Dr. Bendat has taught and counseled at all academic levels from elementary through higher education. As an early contributor to career guidance in California, he has continually interacted with college programs and private industry. As a grant writer and consultant, Dr. Bendat has directed a host of projects and consulted with state agencies.

Dr. Lisa Raufman is a career counselor as well as a licensed marriage, family, and child counselor. Her master's degree is in counseling, with specialization in community college counseling and vocational rehabilitation. Her doctoral degree from the University of California, Los Angeles, is in higher education, work, and adult development. Dr. Raufman is a counselor at Moorpark College, specializing in advising business majors. She has served as president of the Los Padres Chapter of the American Society for Training and Development and as an industry consultant in career and life planning. She is actively involved in statewide counseling associations and currently serves as president of the California Community College Counselors Association.

Contents

7 Sizing Up Your Options   139

Decision Making □ Overcoming Barriers to Decision Making □ Decision-Making Strategies □ Decision-Making Model □ Rational/Linear Decision Making □ Intuitive Decision Making □ Goal Setting □ Moving Toward a Decision □ Deciding on Training

Part II
JOB SEARCH STRATEGY: MAINTAINING MOMENTUM   171

8 Focusing in on Your Target   173

Designing a Comprehensive Job Search Strategy □ The Traditional Job Search □ Want Ads □ Understanding Want-Ad Headings □ Direct Mail □ Employment Agencies □ Employment Agencies—Temporary □ The Nontraditional Job Search □ Volunteering □ Starting Your Own Business □ Job Search While Unemployed □ College Seniors □ Action Plan and Organization □ Information Interviewing and Networking □ Information Interviewing—The Purpose □ Information Interviewing—The Process □ Information Interviewing Outline □ Practice Information Interviews □ Networking

9 Preparing Your Resume   197

Resumes □ Purpose □ Resume Review □ Preparation for Composing Your Resume □ Guidelines for the Resume □ Action Words □ References □ Types of Resumes □ The Functional Resume □ Suggestions for Job Descriptions □ Creative Functional Resume □ Pros and Cons □ The Chronological Resume □ Pros and Cons □ The Combination Resume □ Cover Letter Guidelines □ Application Forms □ Neatness Counts □ Filling Out Application Forms

Tables

Exhibits

Introduction

On Your Mark...Get Set...

Modern life is filled with changes and choices. An immense rainbow of possibilities makes this the most exciting time in history. Yet many of us are overwhelmed by our lack of knowledge about our choices and our place and purpose in the world. The only thing that is certain is change. It is essential to prepare ourselves to expect change, accept it, and plan for it. We can best prepare for it by learning "who we are" in terms of lifetime goals and by taking responsibility for shaping our lives. As we gain information about ourselves and as we begin to make our own decisions, we gain self-confidence. In a deep, personal way we begin to believe that no matter how drastically the world changes, we can deal with it.

The Career Fitness Program is designed to assist you in this process of self-discovery and realization. The main goal of this book is to lead you through the process of career planning, which includes self-assessment, decision making, and job search strategy; our primary objective is to assist you in making satisfactory career choices. By following our chapter-by-chapter program, you will learn more about yourself and how this self-knowledge relates to your emerging career plan.

Let's review the contents of this book to see how it will help you achieve your career goals. The career-planning process is divided into two main parts: personal assessment, Chapters 1–7 and job search strategy, Chapters 8–10.

Chapter 1   Identifies reasons for planning your career and some personal and social background factors to be considered in your career planning.

Chapter 2   Helps you to understand the important effect your attitude has on your actions and to develop a positive approach to life and career planning.

Chapter 3   Helps you to identify your needs, wants, and values, as well as what they mean to you and how they influence your career choices.

Chapter 4   Helps you to assess your skills and how they relate to your career decision.

Understanding the process of career planning

1

Chapter 5   Highlights the societal and cultural biases that subtly or blatantly affect your choice of careers and identifies trends in the workplace.

Chapter 6   Helps you to identify your interests and learn how your interests are related to careers. Written information sources are highlighted and information about local, state, and federal job markets is included.

Chapter 7   The first part of this chapter explains how people make decisions and helps you to identify and improve your own decision-making skills. The second part helps you to integrate your attitudes, values, life-style preferences, cultural biases, interests, skills, and aptitudes into a tentative career plan.

Chapter 8   Helps you to systematically and assertively gather information about possible careers by learning the traditional and nontraditional approaches to job search so that you can decide whether they are viable options for you.

Chapter 9   Helps you to write a resume and cover letter and to fill out application forms. Sample resumes and cover letters are included.

Chapter 10   Covers all aspects of the interview process in order to complete the book's objective of providing you with all the strategies necessary to compete in today's job market.

Process

Meeting the challenges

In many ways, the process of preparing to meet job and career challenges is much like the process by which athletes prepare to meet the challenges of competition in their particular sport. Basically, it involves establishing a fitness program in which the competitor sharpens existing skills, adds needed new skills, and, most important, develops a mental attitude of success.

Theory

Any good fitness program is a combination of theory and exercise, and our career fitness program has this balance. For each step of the planning process, we will explain the theory why we are taking that step, how it relates to the previous step, how it connects to the next step, and how it moves us closer to our final goal of identifying career options.

Exercises

There are exercises at the end of each chapter. These exercise components are designed to bring each step to life. They will serve to make you more aware of your strengths, weaknesses, attitudes, and stereotypes, and they will also help you to summarize what you think is important to remember after each chapter. Remember that reading a chapter or a book is a passive activity. However, responding to questions makes you an active participant in the career exploration process. You may find that it helps to share your answers with at least one other person; a classroom setting where group discussion is encouraged is even better and adds to your own awareness and perspective. It is very easy for anyone to sit back and read about career planning or fitness and agree totally with all of the text and with all of the theories and with all of the exercises. But until you make the commitment to throw yourself into the process, to actually get involved, to participate, and to experience the progress and occasional discomfort along the way, you will not be able to reap the benefits of the process.

Becoming an active participant: with commitment

Discomfort

Yes, we did mention the word *discomfort*. What do we mean by that? Anytime you start out on a new physical exercise program, even if you start gingerly and sensibly in relation to your level of past activity, new muscles are being stretched. In the process of doing so, you feel them. They feel awkward. They ache. You become aware of parts of your body that you may never have noticed before. You can also expect this to happen in the process of career planning. Along the way, confusion and some discomfort may occur. We are going to be asking questions and helping you to dig deep into yourself to pull out the answers. In this process of self-awareness, you are going to discover a lot of things about yourself that you like and maybe some things that you would like to change.

The process of change and personal growth

Because of this process of self-discovery, at certain points along the way in our fitness plan you may feel a bit confused, a bit anxious, a bit impatient. All of these feelings are normal. When you start out on a physical fitness program you idealistically hope that in a week or two you will have the body that you are imagining in your mind even though you know realistically that developing a good physique is going to take a lot longer. And so too, with your career plan, you may begin to feel impatient and want things to move along more quickly or more clearly. It is important to remember that any kind of change, any kind of growth typically includes a bit of discomfort, uneasiness, and anxiety. Frankly, if you begin to experience some of those feelings, it is a good sign! It is a sign that you are stretching, that you are growing, and that you are moving toward a newly developed awareness of who you are and how you relate to the world of work.

Typically, when you are feeling anxious, you try to do anything and everything in your power to get rid of the discomfort. This reaction to anxiety causes many people to make career decisions prematurely, without really examining themselves and their options and then taking care to make a considered decision about their future. Instead they simply take the first thing or the quickest thing that comes along so that they can tell themselves and other people that they have chosen a career. In many cases, this impatient, impulsive, quick decision making really does not pan out very well in the long run. People who have made quick career decisions often live to regret their haste, and making a career transition later on is much more difficult for them because of financial commitments and life-style responsibilities.

Commitment

Benefits of perseverance and belief

Those of you who are taking the time at the beginning of your adult career to carefully and thoroughly examine your options will reap tremendous benefits in the future. The benefits you experience "at the finish line" will be directly proportional to your willingness and ability to deal with the anxiety and uncertainty you will experience at some points in the career planning process. In essence, the more you put into any activity, the more you are likely to get out of it. Stories that we have heard and read about our cultural heroes and heroines, whether they be athletes, performers, renowned scientists, or political figures, tell us that the end results, which look so easy and sound so glamorous, are always and only the reward of tremendous sustained effort, commitment, and perseverance. A quote attributed to the famous artist Michelangelo seems to say it all: "If people knew how hard I had to work to gain my mastery, it wouldn't seem so wonderful after all."

Your career search requires a similar commitment. It requires the willingness to go with the process; to trust specialized assistance; and to move through points of frustration, uncertainty, and confusion in the belief that you will come out with more awareness and a good sense of the next steps to take along your career path. We invite you to participate in an adventure and endeavor that are every bit as exciting and every bit as rewarding as preparing for the Olympics. You are identifying your own mountain peaks and are setting out to climb them. Among your resources is the assistance of this career-planning textbook, which incorporates the wisdom and experience of the authors and of successful career planners over the past decade. Most of all, the special attributes of your own spirit, vitality, and intuition, together with the desire to improve yourself will serve you well through your search. This career fitness program will help you deal with the inevitable changes that occur within yourself, within your evolving career choices, and in the work world. It will help you identify options that are consistent with who you are. It will enable you to be the champion of your own career.

PART ONE

Personal Assessment

Taking Stock 1

> My life is my message.
> *Mahatma Gandhi*

LEARNING OBJECTIVES AT THE END OF THE CHAPTER YOU WILL BE ABLE TO:

Differentiate between a job and a career

Identify life stages as they relate to career planning

Understand that personal assessment is the key factor leading to career satisfaction

Do you hope to have a career that meets your needs, complements your personality, and inspires you to develop your potential? Are you someone who wants to choose the type of life you want to live? If so, you need to set goals that will take you from where you are now to where you want to be. However, such goals are products of your past experiences, desires, needs, interests, values, and vision of the future.

Empowerment = choice, not chance

PERSONAL ASSESSMENT

This first chapter examines your past experiences, who you are right now, your stages of career and life development, and your ability to deal with new information. Once you begin to identify what energizes you about life, you can then begin to incorporate those insights into a career. Self-awareness composes the first stage of the career-planning process. Donald Super, a renowned psychologist from Columbia University, is credited with developing the theory that a career makes it possible for you to actualize or express your self-concept (Super, 1957). Your self-concept is in essence how you see yourself. Consider the following principles of Super's theory on career development and think about how they relate to you.

Super's Self-Concept Theory

1. We differ in abilities, interests, and personalities.

2. Every occupation requires a characteristic pattern of abilities, interests, and personality traits. Within each occupation are workers with varying degrees of these characteristics.

3. Each of us is qualified for a number of occupations.

People are motivated by self-concepts, needs, and drives

4. Vocational preferences and skills, the situations in which we live and work, and our self-concepts change with time and experience. These factors make choice and adjustment a continuous process based on our maturity and life-style.

5. Selecting a career involves the following pattern:

   a. GROWTH: This involves your physical and emotional growth when you are forming attitudes and behaviors that relate to your self-concept. Think about what you learned about yourself from childhood games or family roles. For example, "I am a team player," "I am an individualist," "I am a mediator," or "I would rather read than play games." A child begins having fantasies at this period, e.g., a child's dream of becoming a doctor.

   b. EXPLORATION: This is divided into *fantasy* (e.g., a child's dream of becoming a doctor), *tentative* (e.g., high school and post–high school periods of exploration in which ideas are narrowed down), and *reality testing* (e.g., in high school or early college, working part-time or volunteering in a hospital and taking math and science classes).

   c. ESTABLISHMENT: This includes initial work experience that may have started only as a job to earn a living but that offers experiences for growth such that it becomes a part of a person's self-concept. For example, "I am an assistant manager, I am responsible for the bookkeeping, and I look forward to becoming the manager," rather than "This is just a job, and I will be doing bookkeeping until I can finish my bachelor's degree and get into law school." Very often several changes in jobs will occur over a few years.

   d. MAINTENANCE: This is a time when we maintain or improve in our career area. Advancement can be to higher levels or laterally across fields. For example, "I am extremely competent," "I can compete with others," "I can cooperate and share my knowledge," or "I can train others."

   e. DISENGAGEMENT: This is the stage just before retirement or when we see no new challenges or chances for mobility. This phase is also known as "decline." It actually becomes a time when there is a shift in the amount of emphasis you place on a career. You may even seek a reduction in the hours that you work.

6. The nature of any career pattern is sometimes determined by parental socioeconomic level, mental ability, personality characteristics, and the opportunities to which the worker is exposed. Both limits and opportunities may be apparent as a result of these factors. People are affected by the realities

of everyday life. For example, a teenager living in an affluent suburb may have the opportunity to focus on high school classwork because of ample financial support. On the other hand, a teenager living in the inner city with seven siblings may work 20 hours or more each week to help the family financially. Such limitations may be overcome only with great effort and perseverance.

7. The process of career development is essentially that of developing and implementing a self-concept. All of us try to maintain a favorable picture of ourselves.

8. Work satisfactions and life satisfactions depend on the extent to which we find adequate outlets for our abilities, interests, personality traits, and values.

What has influenced your self-concept? Do you have an accurate view of your likes and dislikes, desires, attributes, limitations, needs, wants, and values? An accurate self-assessment will enable you to make better career decisions by increasing your personal awareness and understanding. Self-awareness improves the probability of seeking and selecting jobs that fit your unique self-concept.

Job vs. Career

We will be using the words *job* and *career* throughout this book, so let's define them. There is an important difference between them. Basically, a job is a series of tasks or activities that are performed within the scope of what we call work. These tasks relate to a career in that a career is a series of jobs. But more than jobs, a career is a sequence of attitudes and behaviors that are associated with work and that relate to our total life experience. A career is really an integration of our personality with our job activities. Therefore, our career becomes a primary part of our identity or our self-concept.

A career is the integration of personality with work activities

In the past, people chose a career early in life, and they tended to stay in it most of their life. Farmers worked on their farm, secretaries stayed in the office, and teachers taught in their school until retirement. More recently the trend in America is toward multiple careers. We can now expect to have two, three, or more careers in our life. With the rapid changes in society and with new economic conditions, new jobs, and new technologies, many traditional jobs are becoming obsolete. More than ever it is important to know what you want to do so that your training and education can be relevant both to your interests and to new trends in the job market. You also need to assess your skills so that you will know which are transferable from an original career to a newly emerging field with a minimum amount of retraining. Knowing yourself and developing a plan of action based on both your needs and the needs of the job market will help you get into the career most satisfying for you rather than just following the latest trends in newly opened fields.

Trends in the marketplace come and go rather rapidly. Several years ago, teachers were in demand. Then for about a decade, there was a glut of teachers on the market. Now again, there seems to be a renewed need for teachers in the

Follow intuitions, not trends

work force. The same is true in engineering. Even today the demand for computer programmers, which was once thought to be inexhaustible, may be reaching saturation. If you base your career decision primarily on current trends, it is quite possible that by the time you obtain the training necessary to get into the "hot" field, it may well have cooled down. This strategy leaves you with slim prospects for a job that can lead to a career, and quite possibly with skills and training in a field that you weren't terribly excited about in the first place except as a quick opportunity.

Super's theory assures us that each of us is qualified for any number of occupations. Getting to know yourself better through self-assessment will help you identify careers that will be best suited to your personality. People who are not prepared for change wait until others make decisions for them. They are often frustrated and unhappy because they are forced to take whatever they can get.

Be prepared for change

They were never told that they have a choice. They haven't taken the time or energy to become aware of their preferences. They settle for less than what might be best for them. Dad says, "get a job in business" even though his child has a special talent in art. The senior high school adviser recommends engineering because scholarships are available. The employment department directs the unemployed into an electronics assembly training program because there's an opening. By knowing your own preferences you will be ready to manage your career change instead of following others' suggestions regarding jobs that happen to be available at the time.

Job Satisfaction

No wonder that survey after survey on job satisfaction among American workers indicates that well over 50 percent of workers are dissatisfied with their job. Because people may be changing jobs and careers several times in their life, there is more need than ever before to have accurate knowledge about oneself and the

Keep your work options open

world of work. Two thirds of a group of adults surveyed (Gallup Organization, 1990) said that if they were starting all over they would try to get more information about their career options. Chances are, in ten or fifteen years, you will face the need to reevaluate yourself relative to your work, and you may quite possibly choose a very different career. It is useful to know about the changing world of work and to know which occupations allow you to express your highest self, your greatest talents. When analyzing your assets, it is to your advantage to ultimately think about the total job market. We want you to search for jobs that will lead you into a career. You will benefit greatly from identifying a variety of alternatives that allow you to express your personality. Once you have looked within yourself and identified what you want and need in a job, future changes will be easier to make because you'll know when you have outgrown one job and need a new one.

What does this really mean? Well, for most of us, career planning is not a simple, straightforward linear process in which we follow certain prescribed steps, end up at a specific destination, and live happily after. It is instead a cyclical feedback loop that continues to self-correct as we add information about our changing self and the world around us. We are constantly revising our career plan as we grow and change. This means that there isn't any one "right" career. Instead, there are many careers in which we could be equally happy, equally successful, equally satisfied.

We are looking, then, not for the *one* right career but for the series of alternatives and career options that seem to make sense to us given our background, our personality, and our career and life stages. Super's theory briefly mentioned the general career stages that many people have experienced. These were identified as Growth, Exploration, Establishment, Maintenance, and Disengagement. Since many of you are currently between the stages of Exploration and Maintenance, it is useful to understand that you are also experiencing the transitional stages that relate to your age and affect your career planning.

OVERVIEW OF LIFE STAGES

The following life stage descriptions suggest that we emphasize different needs at different times of our life. Planning a career involves thinking about the past, present, and future. The following overview summarizes what researchers know about adult life stages (Levinson, Sheehy, Gould, Erikson, 1978). This research is based on the studies of Daniel Levinson, Gail Sheehy, Roger Gould, and Erik Erikson. Reviewing life stage information allows a career searcher or changer to gain and accept insight regarding certain personal and emotional issues that tend to influence values, future planning, and goal setting.

Needs will change throughout life

☐ *Ages 16–22—Late Adolescence*

Leaving parents' world, independence being established but not stable, unsure of ability to make it in the adult world, open to new ideas.

☐ *Ages 22–28—Provisional Adulthood*

Gaining independence in work, marriage, or intimate relationships, testing all of the parental shoulds and oughts, and choosing which to retain in adulthood. Still proving competence to parents, more self-reliant, building for the future, marriage and family considerations.

☐ *Ages 28–32—The Thirties Transition*

Questioning the early commitments to marriage and relationships, family and career, reassessments and changes that may take place. A particularly vulnerable stage for continuity, although many choose to continue their earlier choices.

☐ *Ages 32–39—The Time of Rooting*

Dealing with established lives, children growing and/or last chance to have children being considered, no longer proving self to parents but blaming parents for personality problems; acceptance of the choices made and a buckling down to business, reputation established, until about age 35, when the question "Will I have time to do it all?" begins to arise; time running out;

weary of being what one is supposed to be; asking "What do I really want to be?"

☐ *Ages 39–43—The Turning Point Years*

Experiencing a period of great upheaval and mid-life crisis when it becomes obvious that earlier dreams may not be attainable; wondering "Why am I here, where am I going—I'm in a rut"; radical life-style changes, often without adequate forethought; feeling that there must be something else to life; final thoughts about raising a family.

☐ *Ages 43–50—Restabilization/Bearing Fruit*

Feeling settled with questions of mortality, career, and life-style transitions, children leaving the nest, parental regrets for any errors in raising kids, careers blossoming; attending more to inner development, being a mentor for young people; intimacy needs changing as your children become adults.

☐ *Ages 50–65—Renewal*

Enjoying a time of relative calm, boredom, or acceptance and enjoyment of life, planning for retirement; physical energy and strength may decline, spouses and/or friends die; new life structure emerges, and risk taking seems less likely to occur; acceptance of parents' role in one's life; spiritual questioning; potential for creative growth, disengaging from concept of "work," though some people will start a new career at this time.

☐ *Ages 65 and up—Retirement*

As life is extended and retirement is not mandatory, this period may become the true "golden years" of continued usefulness to society and growth for oneself.

Remember that these life stages are based on social norms of the past and present. The world is changing at such a rapid pace that social norms may be different in future studies. For example, two-career families, single parents, people living alone, later marriages, alternative life-styles, people living longer, fewer entry-level jobs, need for more people with technical skills, and need for lifelong learning may appear as trends in future studies.

Here are some examples of the kinds of career selection we've been discussing.

Sample career changers

Professor Nguyen had reached his life goal or so he thought. He was one of the chosen few to be a professor of religion at a small Catholic college in the San Francisco area. One day he woke up with stomach pains and body aches and had little energy. He had to drag himself out of bed. When the pains lasted longer than three days, he visited his family physician only to find that there was no medical reason for his discomfort. He then realized he had to do some soul searching. His pains and nightmares were continuing over a period of months and seemed to occur only during the work week. On weekends when he was with his family or volunteering at a hospital, he was energetic and healthy. Soon he took a leave of absence from his job and devoted more time to his hospital avocation. The physical ailments mysteriously disap-

peared. He spent one year examining his needs, consulting with a career counselor, and talking things over with friends. He found that his real satisfaction came from helping people in the hospital rather than from teaching religion. Shortly thereafter, a friend told him about a job opening as an ombudsman in a hospital. He got the job and now lectures to local classes in career development on the hazards of keeping a job that is making you ill! Professor Nguyen needed to reexamine his original goals to discover why his career as a professor wasn't meeting his needs.

Jerry was a bottled water distributor for more than ten years. He earned over $30,000 annually. With overtime he could earn about $40,000. However, by the time he was 30, he had become tired of lifting heavy bottles. Jerry started taking a computer course at the local college and found he enjoyed the academic environment. He continued studying and completed the necessary courses for a certificate in information systems. By the time he was 35, he transferred to the data processing department of his company. He is continuing his course work with the goal of completing an evening bachelor's degree program. Jerry found that as he grew older, mental activity was more enjoyable than physical activity, no matter what the pay.

Meanwhile, Maria spent five years in college completing a bachelor's degree program in teaching with an emphasis in special education. After 2 ½ years working in the field she decided that she needed a change; the school system was no longer challenging. She found a job as a stockbroker trainee. Within six months she was a full-fledged stockbroker. Now she's a corporate financial adviser.

Then there's Bob. He was a successful accountant for nine years. Now he's a professional comedian and is able to support himself financially in his new career.

As there is no crystal ball that will predict the one right career for you, you need to consider several options while you are in the exploration stage of career development. The previous examples illustrated people who reassessed their needs and changed fields. However, it is possible to survey your needs, values, interests, skills, aptitudes, and sources of information about the world of work in order to create a broader career objective. Some careers do have career paths. In teaching, one often starts out as a tutor, works up to student-teacher, and then becomes an assistant teacher before becoming a full-time teacher. In the marketing profession, people often start in sales. Therefore we need to think about careers in the sense of their being both short term and long term. A short-term career goal is one that can be rather quickly attained. It might be, for instance, that in the process of career planning, you discover you want to be a lawyer. We would normally consider law a long-term career option because it generally takes many years of study and preparation. However, a short-term career goal that relates to law might be a job as a legal secretary or a paralegal. Either of these would give you the opportunity to be involved in an environment that excites and

Preparation = short- and long-term goals

energizes you without having to postpone the experience until you actually achieve your final and ultimate career goal.

> *Sandra was 17 when she started her first secretarial job. By luck, it was in a legal office. For ten years she was happy being a secretary involved with the legal profession. This left her time to raise her family. But her employers encouraged her to continue her education. Not only did she attend evening courses, but she also became involved with the Professional Secretaries' Association. By the time her children were grown, she had completed a two-year college degree program, had been president of her association, had started a training course to become a paralegal, had been promoted to legal assistant, and was teaching legal terminology at a local community college.*

If you examine enough options during the career-planning process, you may be able to use past career experiences to move into future related career areas just as Sandra did. Subsequent chapters in this book will help you identify your related options.

There is a final very important reason why this effort at personal assessment is crucial as the first step in your career-planning process. Once you know who you are and what your preferences and talents are, you can better make sense of the information that continually bombards you regarding the world of work. It's almost impossible to read a newspaper, listen to a news broadcast, or watch a television show that does not have some implication for you and your career. Quite frequently you may suffer from information overload. Looking at the want ads and reading about employment projections and future trends can cause confusion, frustration, and very often discouragement about what place you might have in this elusive job market.

Self-knowledge helps decision making

One of the best ways to achieve a sense of control and perspective on this constant stream of information is to know who you are so that when you are listening, reading, watching, and experiencing, you will have a means of processing information through your consciousness, through your set of preferences, and through your values and skills. Eventually, you will be able both to recognize and reject information that does not apply to you and to internalize and add to your career plan that information that does apply to you. If a group setting such as a career class is available to you, all the better! The opportunity to discover yourself and expand your horizons is multiplied by the added benefit of group interaction.

SUMMARY

The best approach to the process of career planning is first to examine who you are and what you know about yourself and what you need and want and then to mesh that information with the world of work. You then have the distinct advantage of training to do something about which you are truly excited and enthusiastic. These two qualities are probably among the most important to potential employers. Even if the job market for the field in which you have trained is extremely competitive,

Programming Yourself for Success 2

> If you think you are beaten, you are;
> If you think you dare not, you don't;
> If you like to win, but you think you can't,
> It is almost certain you won't.
>
> If you think you'll lose, you've lost,
> For out of the world we find
> Success begins with a person's will;
> It's all in the state of mind.
>
> If you think you are outclassed, you are;
> You've got to think high to rise.
> You've got to be sure of yourself before
> You can even win a prize.
>
> Life's battles don't always go
> To the stronger or faster man,
> But sooner or later, the person who wins
> Is the person who thinks, "I can!"
>
> *Anonymous*

LEARNING OBJECTIVES AT THE END OF THE CHAPTER YOU WILL BE ABLE TO:

Understand the importance of a positive attitude
in developing a successful career plan

Identify specific components of "the success profile"

Recognize approaches and techniques for creating
success in your career planning

ATTITUDE

During the process of career planning, you are going to learn how to take what you've got (values, skills, interests, aptitudes, qualities, limitations) and do what it takes (job search strategy) to reach your career goal. Satisfactory progress in your career is attainable if you decide you want it. We are beginning the process

Assessing your attitude

of career planning with an assessment of your attitudes, because your mental outlook is the crucial variable that will move you toward or keep you from identifying and achieving your career goals. There is no book, set of exercises, system, or counselor that will affect your success as much as your own belief system and your own commitment to achieving success. Your beliefs are reflected by your actions. How many times have you told yourself, "I'm going to start on a new exercise program today"? How easy it is to find a "legitimate" excuse to postpone your efforts. Are you really ready to work on your career fitness? If so, let's examine some of the beliefs and attitudes that can assist you with your plan.

SUCCESS

Although the word *success* means many things to many people, success in general usually means the progressive external demonstration of internalized life goals. In other words, success refers to the step-by-step movement toward the attainment of an object, quality, or state of mind that we value and wish to possess.

Develop your own definition of success

Slowly, during the last decade, the American concept of personal success has changed. Old symbols of success like money, large homes, and luxury cars have lost their prominent place. According to a 1983 Gallup poll, good health was the number one criteria for success, with an enjoyable job rated as number two, and a happy family, good education, peace of mind, and good friends, in that order, as the most important criteria of success.

Do you have your own personal definition of success for the 1990s? Regardless of the particular goals you have in mind, you need to think positively to attain them.

MAINTAINING A POSITIVE OUTLOOK

Have you ever heard the saying, "It's all in your head"? People who say this believe that our mind and mental attitudes have control over our body and our life and can, therefore, program our success or failure. Although many of our attitudes and beliefs come from early messages we received from our parents and teachers, as adults we can choose to keep or change these messages depending on how helpful they are to us in achieving success and satisfaction in life.

Therefore, one might say, "Believing is seeing." To have a concept of what could be better, try examining your philosophy of life. How you see life in general is how you lead your life. A quick way to identify your philosophy is to visualize how you see the future.

Read the following scenarios and select the one that best relates to your point of view (Kauffman, 1976).

1. The future is *a great roller coaster* on a moonless night. It exists, twisting ahead of us in the dark, although we can see each part only as we come to it. We can make estimates about where we are headed and sometimes see around

a bend to another section of track, but it doesn't do us any real good because the future is fixed and determined. We are locked in our seats, and nothing we may know or do will change the course that is laid out for us.

2. The future is *a mighty river*. The great force of history flows inexorably along, carrying us with it. Most of our attempts to change its course are mere pebbles thrown into the river: they cause a momentary splash and a few ripples, but they make no difference. The river's course can be changed, but only by natural disasters like earthquakes and landslides or by massive, concerted human efforts on a similar scale. On the other hand, we are free as individuals to adapt to the course of history either well or poorly. By looking ahead, we can avoid sandbars and whirlpools and pick the best path through any rapids.

3. The future is *a great ocean*. There are many possible destinations, and many different paths to each destination. A good navigator takes advantage of the main currents of change, adapts the course to the capricious winds of chance, keeps a sharp lookout posted, and moves carefully in fog or uncharted waters. Doing these things will get the navigator safely to a destination (barring a typhoon or other disaster that one can neither predict nor avoid).

4. The future is entirely random, *a colossal dice game*. Every second, millions of things happen that could have happened another way and produced a different future. A bullet is deflected by a twig and kills one person instead of another. A scientist checks a spoiled culture and throws it away or looks more closely at it and discovers penicillin. A spy at the Watergate Hotel removes the tape from a door and gets away safely or forgets to remove the tape and changes American political history. Since everything is chance, all we can do is play the game, pray to the gods of fortune, and enjoy what good luck comes our way.

These scenarios are timely today and may reflect your attitude about life. Is your life a roller coaster, out of control; a mighty river to which you must adapt; a great ocean with many directions and options; or just a game of chance? Are you a positive thinker or a negative thinker? The second and third scenarios tend to be the positive reflections. Your belief system will affect how you see life. Have you ever noticed how your most dominant thoughts reinforce what happens to you? This phenomenon is sometimes called the "self-fulfilling prophecy." Remember the times you've thought the following:

Develop the mindset for success

"That's just the way I am."

"I can't control what I do."

"I just can't seem to finish anything I start."

"I would like to do that differently, but it's just too hard to change."

"Yep, it happened again."

"I've never been good at that."

If you reinforce the negative, you will act negatively. If you affirm your limitations, you will be limited. Mark Twain once observed, "It ain't the things I don't know that gets me in trouble, it's the things I know for sure." Thus, your mind tends to believe what you tell it. And, yes, you can, if you *think* you can.

Cultivating a positive, assertive outlook on life is the most crucial factor that makes the difference between those people who have a successful, satisfying life/career and those who don't. Let's examine some of the aspects of this positive, assertive outlook so that we can get into the mind-set for success.

The Assertive Attitude

One of the most basic choices we make on a moment-to-moment basis is whether to be assertive, aggressive, or passive in response to life situations. Basically, being assertive means being the ultimate judge of our own behavior, feelings, and actions and being responsible for the initiation and consequence of those actions. In essence, assertive people choose for themselves and put themselves up *without* putting others down. Aggressive people choose for themselves and others; they put themselves up *by* putting others down. Passive people allow *others* to choose *for them;* they put themselves down or allow others to do so.

Assertive attitudes help to maintain control

You need to develop an assertive attitude in order to maintain some control over today's tight job market. An assertive outlook enables you to be persistent, to seek more information when you run out of leads, to weigh all alternatives equally (incorporating both your logic and your intuition), to be willing to revise your goals when necessary, and to pursue your goals with commitment and purpose. Assertiveness specifically enables you to say what you feel, think, and want. It allows you to be expressive, open, and clear in communication. You are able to say no under pressure, recognize and deal with manipulation, and stand up for your rights in negative, confrontational situations. You gain the ability to become a better listener. Others appreciate your directness and ability to hear them. You enjoy more positive interactions with people and feel more positive about being able to handle life situations.

Assertive personal traits include body language as well as words. Studies indicate that more than 90 percent of the meaning of any message is nonverbal. Look at yourself and think about your typical physical stance when you are feeling assertive compared with when you are feeling passive. What does your style of dress say about you? Can changing the color of your outfit change the mood you project to others? Did you ever notice your gesturing? Assertiveness is often associated with expansive gestures rather than limited ones. Finally, how do you deal with touch or physical closeness? Being assertive means feeling comfortable within your own body space.

Positive, assertive behavior shows self-confidence

Most important, positive assertive behavior suggests that you really have confidence in yourself. This behavior conveys verbally and nonverbally that you have confidence in your abilities and that you believe in your own worth. That positive, confident, and enthusiastic self will set you apart, make people take notice of you, and ultimately enable you to exercise control over your career and your life.

Self-Confidence

Self-confidence, perhaps more than any other factor, is the secret to success and happiness. It is the ability to recognize that even though you are imperfect, you are a unique, worthwhile, and lovable person who deserves and can attain the best things in life. You project a sense of self-confidence by your body language, your dress, your pace, your ability to take pride in your accomplishments, your ability to learn from your mistakes, and your ability to accept suggestions and praise from others. Because you believe you deserve the career of your choice, you can attain it.

Discover your own self-worth

You can begin to develop more self-confidence by remembering and rewarding yourself for something you did *well* each day. You may automatically seem to review, in great detail, each and every negative event that has occurred. This is indeed a common, natural, understandable human reaction that can be neutralized by deliberate positive thinking. You may have to literally force yourself to think of something positive and give yourself a "pat on the back" or a gold star. Better yet, make it a point to share the good news with a friend, a support person, someone who you know will delight in your small personal achievement. In fact, think about starting a support group consisting of individuals who want to share their personal victories with each other. The reinforcement and support of others are powerful tools in our personal quest for success. Start small, remembering that an Olympic gold medal, just like self-confidence, is built on hours, days, weeks, months, and years of small personal victories!

Personal Enthusiasm

You can always identify achievers by their consistent posture of optimism and enthusiasm. They know that life is a self-fulfilling prophecy, that people usually get what they actively imagine and expect. They choose to start the day on a positive note by listening to music, singing in the shower, or telling themselves that this will be a good day. They view problems as opportunities to be creative. They learn to stay relaxed and calm under stress. They associate with people who share their optimism about life and who support each other through praise, encouragement, and networking. When asked about their career goals, instead of saying, "I don't know," they say, "I'm in the process of discovering my career goals."

When employers are asked what traits they look for in prospective employees, enthusiasm is always at the top of the list. What kind of people do you want as friends, associates, and colleagues? Chances are you want people who are optimistic and have a zest for life. You can become more enthusiastic by getting involved in something that has meaning for you. A hobby, volunteer work, mastery of a skill, a new relationship all provide opportunities to experience and express your enthusiasm. On the job, a professional attitude includes your ability to act as if things are fine even when you feel upset or depressed. At work, acting positive and up pays off. Not only do you come across as mature and professional,

Employers rate enthusiasm highly

but as you begin to "act" enthusiastically you receive positive feedback from others. The smiles, nods, and positive words of others begin to make you feel enthusiastic. You discover you are no longer acting, you genuinely feel better!

One of the most effective ways to improve your self-image is the deliberate use of positive self-talk. You already talk to yourself; we all do constantly! But we usually do not consciously listen to our internal dialogue, and consequently we often allow ourselves to listen to negative, self-defeating messages that create and reinforce a low self-image. Once you decide to take charge of your self-talk, you can begin to repeat positive messages that will reinforce a positive self-image. This process is commonly called creating affirmations.

Positive self-talk improves self-image

Affirmation is a statement or assertion that something is already so (Sunshine, 1975). It is an existing seed or thought in the here and now that will grow as life unfolds. It is not intended to change what already exists but to create new, desired outcomes. Remember, all events begin with a thought. If you think you can, you can! Anything a person can conceive can be achieved. Good gardeners cultivate not only flowers but also soil. The thoughts you are thinking and sending out are the "soil" of your life. If you are constantly projecting thoughts of lack, you will have barren soil. If you project thoughts of prosperity, your soil will be rich. Therefore, any career you can conceive of in which you can imagine yourself being happy and successful can be achieved.

However, when thinking about your own affirmations, remember that you are planting a seed and that the seed must carry the exact information you want so it may grow into the result you desire. When you become specific about what you want, you are focusing the power of your mind's energies (your thoughts) on your desires. The more specific you are about your goals, the more focused you become about what must be done to reach them. You know you are being specific enough when you can visualize details about what you want. For example, if you are a student and you want to become a college professor, you must be able to see yourself on a college campus, in a specific classroom, standing before a room of students, lecturing, interacting with other professors, and correcting papers!

Here are some hints to follow when writing down your own affirmations.

1. Always write the affirmation in the present, never in the future; otherwise it may remain in the future. If you wanted a job for yourself, you would write, "I now have the most appropriate, satisfying job for me."

2. Phrase your affirmation in the positive rather than the negative. In other words, avoid affirming what you don't want. Instead of writing "My present job doesn't bother me anymore," it would be much more effective to write, "My work is wonderful" or "I enjoy my job."

3. Maintain the attitude that you are creating something new and fresh. You are not trying to manipulate, redo, or change an existing thing or condition.

Let's experience this technique in action. Think of a quality that you want to develop in yourself. Let's use enthusiasm as an example. Your first instinct might be to say or think, "I'm not very enthusiastic." As soon as this thought comes to mind, replace it with the opposite thought, "I am enthusiastic." Repeat the phrase over and over, day and night, until you feel you own it; it soon will feel comfortable. At the same time, picture yourself doing something enthusiastically, such as explaining to your boss why you deserve a day off, starting a conversation with a stranger, or honestly disagreeing with an instructor during a class. Picture yourself making your statement and being positively reinforced. Your boss says yes, you deserve it; the stranger becomes a friend; the instructor praises you for your insight.

Even before you actually do something enthusiastically, you have prepared yourself mentally for a positive outcome. Your chances of experiencing the outcome improve because you are projecting a positive self-image. Try it!

Self-Image

Not only do successful people like themselves, but they also visualize themselves at their best and monitor their self-talk to reinforce their images of success in word and action. They know that self-image acts as a regulator, an unconscious thermostat. If you cannot picture yourself doing, being, or achieving something, you literally cannot do, be, or achieve it! Your self-image absorbs information, memorizes it, and acts accordingly. Every time you say, "I can't," you are creating a negative self-image. Every time you say, "I can and will," you are giving yourself permission to be your best self. Successful people recognize how potent their beliefs are, and they take responsibility for shaping their own self-image rather than allowing others' opinions to limit them.

Role Models

So far we have been exploring ways of developing a personal and positive self-image. Now it's time to look outside yourself at the people who display the qualities of success that you want to cultivate. Think about whom you admire, and begin to make a list. First, think globally about prominent individuals on the national and international scene. Then, think locally about people with whom you work and individuals who are part of your community, your neighborhood, your religious affiliation, your school, your hobbies. Finally, think personally of the people you admire who are nearest and dearest to you—your family and friends. Which of their qualities do you admire? In what ways do you want to be more like them?

Start observing them in action, consider telling them just what you admire about them, and ask them to tell you how they developed those qualities. Ask them for insights and suggestions that you might use in developing your own success profile. Make these people a part of your network of contacts. You may find that even the most successful people have struggled with moments of self-doubt or a crisis of self-confidence. Ask them what they do when the going gets rough.

First steps in networking and information interviewing

Just as you choose your friends and associates deliberately and with care, knowing that you are influenced by the attitudes of the company you keep, be aware that each time you seek out individuals and acknowledge the qualities you admire in them, you are giving them the gift of recognition and appreciation, a valuable commodity in today's fast-paced, all too impersonal world. Be aware also that by speaking with your role models, you are practicing information interviewing (to be discussed in Chapter 8) and taking the first steps in developing the art of networking. You are making connections that can later assist you in the job search process. Of course, you are also projecting the positive self-image that you are cultivating.

Self-Initiation

Successful people realize that goals activate people and that fears stop people. If you dwell on your fears, whether real or imagined, you will be immobilized in the pursuit of your goals. If you concentrate on your goals, you will move toward them. People who are afraid to tell the world what they want don't get it. The difference between those who are successful and those who are not is attitude. What side of the coin do you choose to look at—fears or goals? In what direction are you going—away from or toward your goals?

Goals activate people

> *Allan had been laid off after working for a company for twelve years. After the shock and disbelief of his involuntary career change had passed, he began to ask himself what he would really enjoy doing. He realized that the hours he spent in the library provided some of his most rewarding experiences. Because he was not a librarian, he could not imagine himself working in a library in any capacity and could not even bring himself to volunteer his services in a library. His fears about lacking the qualifications to become a librarian (fear of inadequacy) prevented him from moving in the direction of his desire (to work in a library). After many months of fruitless job hunting, he finally mustered up the courage to become a volunteer at the library. In less than two months, the staff recognized his valuable contributions, and he was offered the next paid position that became available.*

Imagine yourself in your ideal or dream job, your fantasy career, the kind of job you would pay to do. Take the job of cruise ship director, for example. Now identify someone who has that occupation. If you don't know of anyone, ask your friends, relatives, neighbors, and classmates, all of whom are part of your extended network (see page 192 for an extended list of people who make up your network). Ask if they know someone who actually has your dream job. Next, contact that individual in person, if possible, and arrange a brief information interview. Read the section in Chapter 8 on information interviewing, and plan to ask the sample questions.

After you have gathered some facts about your fantasy career, ask yourself if it still holds its appeal for you. If so, you may wish to talk to others in the same field to further develop an even more accurate and detailed assessment. If not, you may want to choose another fantasy career to investigate.

Persistence

Successful people take full responsibility for the initiation and consequences of their actions. They know that life is full of choices, not chances. They realize they personally have the power to take control of their life, both physical and mental. They know that trying to blame Mother Nature for a less than perfect body or calling it fate when they don't get the job is simply "copping out." Successful people really do make things happen for themselves. What might appear to be luck really is opportunity meeting preparation.

Through persistence, determination, and consistent effort, much can be achieved. There are countless examples of individuals with talent and education who are surprisingly unsuccessful in their career. Remember, nothing can take the place of persistence and enthusiasm.

Luck = opportunity and preparation

Self-Discipline

Self-discipline is the conscious implanting of specific thoughts and emotions that will, through repetition, become part of our unconscious and then our conscious mind, resulting in the creation of new habits and a new self-concept. While it is easy to marvel at the mastery of an expert, we often assume that the person was born with superhuman talents or skills. We forget that every champion athlete, every great performer, every skilled surgeon, and every professional developed their expertise by endless hours of physical and mental practice. They visualize their performance, they engage in positive self-talk ("I can," "I'll do better next time"), and, through repetition, they become more and more of what they desire to be. This self-talk is also known as practicing both *mental imagery and mental rehearsal*. Golfer Jack Nicklaus, for example, attributes 10 percent of his success to his setup, 40 percent to his stance and swing, and 50 percent to the mental imagery he uses before he takes each stroke (Murphy, 1978). The gold and silver medalists in the slalom at the 1984 Olympics were seen on television visualizing their runs as they waited in the starting line (Kreiger and Kreiger, 1984). Equally dramatic are the results of a study using three groups of students chosen at random who were shooting basketball foul shots. One group visualized itself shooting foul shots for 30 minutes a day. At the end of twenty days the first group, which had practiced every day, improved 24 percent. The second group, which had done nothing, showed no improvement. The third group, which had only visualized itself shooting fouls, improved 23 percent (Samuels and Samuels, 1975).

Use mental rehearsal for success

All of the people in the cited examples used visualization regularly over a period of time. This is the key to the success of mental rehearsal. Experts estimate that a goal must be visualized 30 minutes a day for at least a month to obtain results. This discipline distinguishes visualization from random daydreaming, an effortless activity we all engage in periodically.

GOAL IDENTIFICATION

Successful people have clearly defined plans and objectives that they refer to daily to keep in mind their lifetime goals and to order their daily priorities. Clearly defined, written goals help to move us to completion. The reason most people don't reach their goals is that they don't identify them (Waitley, 1984). They don't know what they want.

Knowing what you want is step number one

If you don't know where you are going, you probably won't get there. Even though you are just embarking on your career fitness plan and you probably don't have a specific career in mind as yet, you can still begin the process of goal setting. Your first goal might be to read this book with purpose, one chapter a week, and complete all the exercises after each chapter with attention and the intent of learning more about yourself so you can make appropriate career choices when the times are right. Ideally, you should set aside a specific time and place each week so that you will get into the habit of working on your career fitness plan in the same way that you would work on a physical fitness plan—with consistency and commitment.

EXHIBIT 2.A

What makes workers succeed.
Executives say these personality traits are most important:

Enthusiasm	**80.6%**
"Can Do" Attitude	**65.1%**
Loyalty	**62.6%**
High Energy	**40.3%**
Assertiveness	**30.5%**

Source: Management Dimensions Inc.; Survey of 241 executives from all types of companies. Elys McLean-Ibrahim, *USA Today.*

SUMMARY

Programming yourself and "psyching yourself up" for success compose the first step of your personal assessment program. Getting into a positive frame of mind on a daily basis is just as important as a regular round of calisthenics to "rev up" your internal engine and start the day off right. Once you begin to develop a positive outlook, you are ready for step number two of the personal assessment program—values clarification.

1) deserve
2) desire
3) dream
4) discipline
5) demention

?? WRITTEN
EXERCISES

These exercises are designed to review your attitude and assertion skills. Try to answer the first set of questions as quickly and spontaneously as possible. Do not censor your answers. These are called open-ended questions. Open-ended questions sometimes make people think about different responses each time they see them. Therefore it's all right to have more than one answer as well as to change an answer whenever you review the questions. These questions will also cause you to review your past actions so that you can better identify how such past actions reflect who you are today. Answer the questions in the rest of the exercises to reflect your ideal environment and how you see yourself.

2.1 PAST ACTIONS AND INFLUENCES

Fill in each blank carefully and honestly. Be true to yourself; don't try to please anyone else with your answers.

a. I am proud that _____

_____

b. One thing I can do that I couldn't do a few years ago is _____

_____

c. Name the person you most admire. This person can be living, historical, or fictional. Write down the specific characteristics that you admire in this person (e.g., smart, famous, rich, loving, generous). _____

_____

_____

d. Write the name of the person you least admire and why. _____

_____

_____

e. Name a person who is like you, and describe him or her. _____

_____

_____

f. In the last two weeks what activities or people gave you a feeling of being energized? _____

_____

_____

_____

g. What have you always wanted to do in your life? What's keeping you from doing it? What action could you take in the next year to get closer to this goal? _____

_____

_____

_____

h. What habit have you successfully attempted to change? _____

_____

_____

i. What three words would you like others to use in describing you? _____

_____

2.2 TWO PERFECT DAYS

a. *Written description*

In order to be clear about what you want in your life, write a one-page description of two ideal days in your future. One day should be related to leisure, and one day should be related to work. Think about where you would be, what you'd be doing, who, if anyone, would be with you, if your major activity would be work or leisure, etc. Try to be as detailed as possible. Use this space for notes:

_____

_____

_____

_____

b. *Summary in two or three words*

Write down two or three words or phrases that would capture the *essence of the quality of these two days,* e.g., peaceful, challenging, fun, harmonious, exciting, restful, productive. You may summarize each day separately if you wish.

_____

_____

2.3 ASSERTIVENESS AND ATTITUDE CHECKLIST

Answering the following questions will give you a better idea about how your attitude is reflected by your actions. Consider also asking several important people in your life to respond to these questions about you. Compare their answers with yours. Choose two or three areas to work on to improve your attitude and assertiveness skills.

	Satisfied	Need to Improve
a. Do I always do my best?		
b. Do I tend to look at the bright side of things?		
c. Am I friendly and cooperative?		
d. Am I prompt and dependable?		
e. Do I do more than my share?		
f. Do I appear to be confident?		
g. Am I believable?		
h. Do people ask my opinion of things?		
i. Do I appear to be trustworthy, intelligent?		
j. Am I poised, well-mannered, tactful, considerate of others?		
k. Do I dress appropriately?		
l. Do I put others before myself? To what extent?		
m. Can I accept compliments?		
n. Do I give compliments?		
o. Do I make suggestions?		
p. Can I say no?		
q. Do I wait for others to decide for me?		

2.4 AFFIRMATIONS

a. Write six affirmations related to being successful in your career and life planning. Put them on 3 x 5 cards (one per card). Some examples:

1. *I am a confident and competent person.*
2. *I have many transferable skills.*
3. *I am a valuable employee.*
4. *I am a risk taker.*
5. *I am a skilled networker.*
6. *I enjoy talking to people about their careers.*

1. _____

2. _____

3. _____

4. _____

5. _____

6. _____

b. Read your affirmations to yourself two times during the day, once in the morning as you awake and once just before going to sleep.

c. To accelerate their effectiveness, try the following suggestions.

1. *Write your affirmations in longhand while speaking them aloud to yourself ten, twenty, or more times.*
2. *When writing affirmations, try writing in different persons, such as "I, Marilyn, am highly employable." "You, Marilyn, are highly employable." "She, Marilyn, is highly employable."*
3. *Record your affirmations on a cassette tape recorder and listen to them as you drive or while doing chores around the house.*
4. *Before going to sleep at night or upon arising in the morning, visualize yourself as you are becoming. For example, see yourself as more assertive, loving, social, enthusiastic.*
5. *Chant or sing your affirmations aloud while driving or during any appropriate activity.*
6. *Meditate on your affirmations.*
7. *Tape them up around the house, on the telephone, on the mirrors, on the refrigerator, on the ceiling above your bed, on the dashboard of your car, in your dresser drawers.*
8. *Use affirmations as bookmarks.*

d. It has been said that three conditions must be present to create change: First, there must be real dissatisfaction with what is, then there must be a concept of what would be better, and, last, there must be a belief that there is a way to get there. This whole process must support the idea that the benefits of the change outweigh the costs of making the change. Affirmations help you believe that there is a way.

    The following questions relate to *obstacles* that may be interfering with the achievement of your desires.

1. How much intention do you really have?
2. What identity would be threatened by achieving your goal? For example, would a better job make you too independent or enable you to earn more than your mate?
3. Do you secretly feel you don't deserve to attain your desires?
4. Are you proving to anyone else that you can't change?
5. Is it worth it to you? (The work, concentration, time.)
6. Are you following all the steps suggested?
7. Is it what you really want? George Bernard Shaw once commented that "The only thing worse than not getting what you want is getting what you want!" In other words, "Many go fishing all their life, only to realize later that it wasn't the fish they wanted."

2.5 YOUR FANTASY CAREERS: *"Wouldn't it be great to be . . ."*

List your current fantasy careers below. Then think back chronologically from an earlier age and try to recall some of your past fantasy careers; list them as well. We develop fantasy careers at a very young age. Most children see cartoons, television dramas, and movies about doctors, lawyers, police officers, firefighters, astronauts, teachers, and scientists, to name a few popular careers. Books about solving mysteries create an image of excitement about being a detective. Current movies influence many to dream of being a jet pilot or gifted performer. What have you read about or seen in the movies or dreamed about doing?

a. For each career on your list, ask yourself this question: "What about this career is or was appealing to me?" Many of us might have the same fantasy career but for different reasons.

Current	*What about this career appeals(ed) to me?*
1. _____	_____
2. _____	_____
3. _____	_____
4. _____	_____

Chronological Past (in five-year increments)	*What appealed most to me about this fantasy career?*
1–5 _____	_____
_____	_____
_____	_____
6–10 _____	_____
_____	_____
_____	_____
11–15 _____	_____
_____	_____
_____	_____
16–20 _____	_____
_____	_____
_____	_____

b. Now choose the one fantasy career that is most appealing. Try to locate someone who is doing it for a living. If you are part of a class, ask your instructor and classmates if they can refer you to someone. Otherwise, try to make a connection by asking people you know at school, work, and social gatherings. Read the information in Chapter 8 on information interviewing. Arrange an interview, preferably in person, and ask the questions in the sample list of typical questions under Information Interviewing Outline.

EXERCISE SUMMARY

What have I learned about myself? _____

_____

I want to improve _____

_____

I admire the following qualities in people: _____

_____

My affirmations are _____

_____

_____

_____

_____

What can I do in the next two weeks to improve my self-confidence? _____

_____

_____

What lies behind us and what
lies before us are tiny matters
compared to what lies within us.
—Ralph Waldo Emerson

Part I

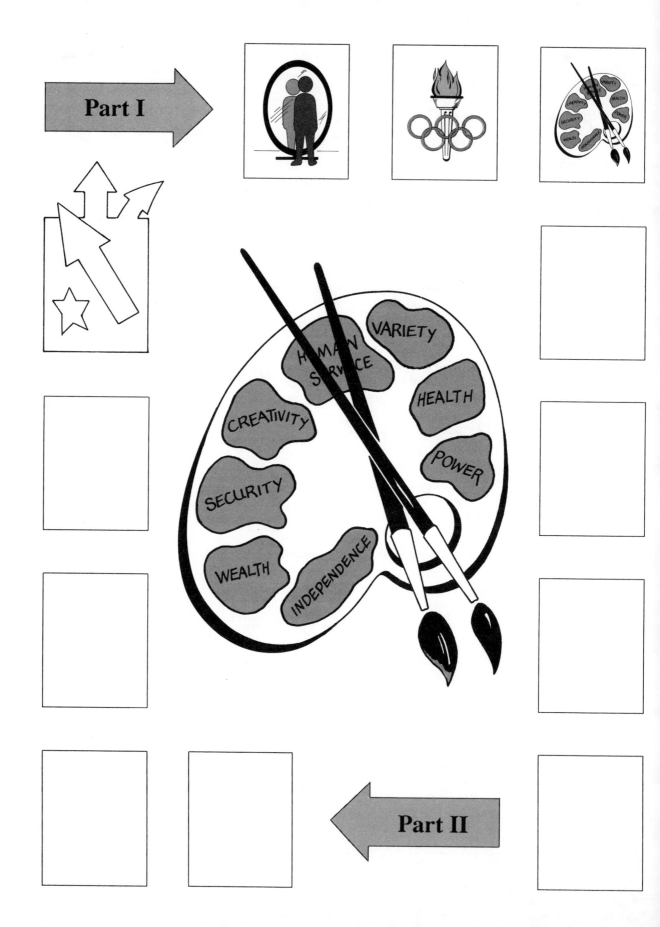

Part II

Values Clarification 3

He who has a why to live can bear with almost any how.

Nietzsche

LEARNING OBJECTIVES AT THE END OF THE CHAPTER YOU WILL BE ABLE TO:

Define and clarify your values

Understand how your values motivate you

Demonstrate how your values affect your career decisions

IMPORTANCE OF VALUES

What is it that causes someone to study for years before entering a career such as medicine or law while others are looking for the quickest, easiest way to make a buck? What causes someone to switch careers midstream after spending years developing mastery and a reputation in a field? The answer to these questions is *values*. Your values are the often unidentified, but nevertheless all-pervasive, forces that guide and influence your decisions throughout your life. If you value fitness and good health, you make time for daily exercise, positive self-talk, and proper nutrition. If you value career satisfaction, you will take the time to examine your values and begin to make choices consistent with your values.

Values as the basis for decisions

DEFINITIONS

Values are the self-motivators that indicate what is important in your life. Values are reflected in what you actually do with your time. They indicate what you consider most important in your life. This chapter will help you identify what is needed in your work environment to make you feel satisfied with your job. You may discover that the reason you are dissatisfied with your present job is that it

Values as self-motivators

contains few of your values. People often settle for a job just to bring in money, and then feel empty, frustrated, and unfulfilled. Once you become aware of your values, you can make meaningful and satisfying decisions about jobs. In other words, your decisions can be based on what's really important to you.

CLARIFICATION

Now that you have begun to take charge of your mental attitude, identifying your values becomes the next step in your personal assessment program. By the age of 10, most of us have unconsciously adopted the values of our parents, teachers, and friends. By adolescence, we have begun to sort out which of these adopted values we want to freely choose as our own. This process is often generalized as "teenage rebellion." Parents, in particular, often take offense when you question or reject a value that they hold dear. In fact, this process of values clarification is an essential part of growing up. Mature, independent, successful individuals typically act upon their own values rather than those of others.

Review your values

This frees them from unnecessary guilt ("What would my mother say if . . .?") and indecision ("What would Dad do in this situation?") and fosters satisfaction and self-confidence ("Regardless of the outcome, I'm in control of my life"). Many adults fail to reassess their values as life goes on. Research about life stages indicates that adults can and do make dramatic changes in their personal and career life based on changes in values. This process of change can be less traumatic for all of the individuals involved if, as adults, we periodically review and reassess what is important to us.

> *Mary was one such individual who benefited from reviewing her values. A secretary, she was delighted that her company, an air freight carrier, had contracted for the services of a career counselor. She couldn't wait to get some help in choosing a new job. She felt bored and stagnated where she was. As the counselor helped her to identify her values, Mary realized that she liked security and didn't mind routine, structure, or taking orders. As she further explored her feelings of boredom, she remembered that the main reason she chose to work at an airline was for the travel privileges. Yet it was years since she had actually taken advantage of the travel opportunity. Once she remembered and reevaluated her desire for travel, she began to utilize this benefit and was quite content to continue working with her current employer.*

EVALUATING YOURSELF

Recognizing your values

By this time, you are probably wondering how you can recognize your values. The more intense your favorable feelings are about some activity or social condition, the more you value it. Is there anything in the current news that excites you or makes you angry? Are there certain activities that energize you? Are there circumstances in your life that lead you to certain activities? All of these indicators reflect your values.

More specifically, the following criteria will help you determine your values. Values that are alive and an active part of you have the following qualities (Raths, Simon & Harmin, 1966):

1. *Prized and cherished.* When you cherish something, you exude enthusiasm and enjoyment about it. You are proud to display it and use it.

2. *Publicly affirmed.* This involves being willing to and even wanting to state your values in public.

3. *Chosen freely.* No one else is pressuring you to act in a certain way. You own these values. They feel like a part of you.

4. *Chosen from alternatives.* When given a choice whether to play a leading role in a Hollywood film or to be provided with a full scholarship to study at Harvard Business School, which would you choose? Acting in Hollywood would highlight such values as creativity, prestige, glamour, possible monetary returns, and high risk taking, whereas acquiring a Harvard M.B.A. would suggest such values as prestige, monetary returns, education, intellectual stimulation, and security.

5. *Chosen after consideration of consequences.* You tend to consider the consequences when you have to make a decision that is very important. Consider the immediate impressions that arise with the idea of either relocating to a job that is 2,000 miles from where you've lived all your life, or marrying someone who is 30 years older than you, or buying a car from a used car salesman. What values come into play?

6. *Acted upon.* Again, values are reflected by what you do with your time and your life; they are more than wishful thinking or romantic ideals about how you should lead your life.

7. *Acted upon repeatedly and consistently to form a definite pattern.* The main idea is that you repeatedly engage in activities that relate to your highest values. For example, complete the Life and Personal Values Grid in the exercise section that follows this chapter. List five to ten aspirations or goals you have achieved in your lifetime, e.g., finished high school, member of debate team, planned a surprise party, found a job. Check the values that you use repeatedly.

As you begin to think about it, you will come to realize how much you rely on your values to make decisions. People facing career planning often wonder how they will ever choose any one career when they have so many possibilities in mind. This is precisely the time when knowing your values is important. Let's say you've discovered that economic return, helping others, and security are your three top values. You are thinking about becoming an artist, an actor, or a speech teacher. You might well be able to do all three, even simultaneously! However, in order to choose one career direction, try deciding which career would best satisfy your top three values. You are likely to experience the most success and happiness from this kind of choice. In this case, speech teacher most closely incorporates the values mentioned.

NEEDS AND MOTIVATORS

So far we have discussed self-motivation based on successful attitudes and values. In addition, inner drives or needs also influence how you choose a career. People experience psychological discomfort when their needs are unmet. We best meet our needs by identifying them and then setting goals to meet those needs. Once our needs are met, tension and discomfort are reduced. There are five primary needs as identified by Maslow, a famous psychologist (Maslow, 1970):

1. *Physiological needs:* basic survival needs such as food and water.
2. *Safety needs:* both physical (security, shelter, protection, law and order, health insurance, pension plans, secure job) and psychological (freedom from fear and anxiety).
3. *Belongingness and love:* friends, affiliation, affection, relationships, love.
4. *Self-esteem/ego status:* prestige, self-respect, competence, self-confidence, sense of self-worth.
5. *Self-actualization:* achieving one's potential, being creative, serving a cause, contributing to society.

As you can see, these needs progress from the most basic and biologically oriented (survival needs) to the more complex and socially oriented level of needs. When people are preoccupied with finding ways to put food on the table (physiological needs), they have little time or desire to work on developing relationships or to search for a job that can utilize their talents. Rather, they work at any job that will immediately bring in money. A person becomes aware of a higher-order need only when a lower-order need has been met. Although these needs seem to move from "lower to higher," in actuality people address their various needs at all levels throughout their lives. These needs are such primary and intense self-motivators that your *values* may be eclipsed while you are being influenced to meet primary *needs*.

It is also important to assess needs from a cultural perspective and to realize that individuals may function and see things differently depending on the cultural context. For example, recent immigrants need time to adapt or adjust to a new environment. Even if their survival needs for food, clothing, and shelter are met in the new culture, their lack of familiarity with local customs and their home-sickness for familiar people and customs may diminish a sense of security, psychological well-being, and competence as outlined by Maslow.

Once you have stabilized your ability to meet your physiological and safety needs, you may find that you demand more feedback (satisfaction of social needs) in your work environment. A researcher, Frederick Herzberg, has examined what creates job satisfaction for most workers (Herzberg, 1966). We have already explained that being in a job that reflects your top values results in job satisfaction. However, Herzberg has also found that we have both external motivators and internal motivators. External motivators include salary, working conditions, company policy, and possibility for advancement. These just happen to fulfill physiological and safety needs. Meanwhile, internal motivators involving the amount of responsibility, type of work accomplished, recognition, and achievement all contribute to job satisfaction. These motivators appear to be most important for people who value and need status and self-actualization. People do not necessarily respond to each need with identical intensities of desire. For your own benefit, it would be useful to examine what brings satisfaction to you on the job. Figure 3.A illustrates how Herzberg's research on job satisfaction overlaps with Maslow's list of needs.

Job satisfaction: internal vs. external motivators

FIGURE 3.A
Needs and motivators.

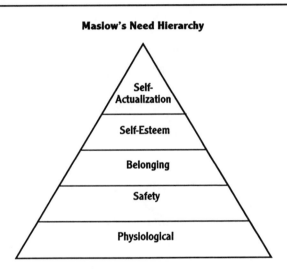

Maslow's Need Hierarchy

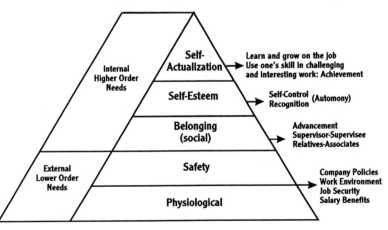

Herzberg's Theory of Motivation

BALANCE

Balance is the ability to include all your top priorities and values in your career life plan. Although people who live to work (workaholics) may say they are happy, they are certainly not experiencing balance.

As we move further into the 1990s, people in all age groups seem to value balance, and as a result they are making tough career and life-style decisions that use the balance factor as a prime consideration. In a recent survey by the Roper Organization, 41 percent of those surveyed said that leisure is the most important factor in their life; 36 percent cited work as the most important factor. According to *U.S. News & World Report,* consultants and career counselors have contact with a greater number of burned-out 30- and 40-year-olds who want to trade their fast-track corporate career for a job that offers a more balanced life-style.

As the survey indicated, more and more individuals are passing up otherwise attractive career opportunities that are not compatible with a balanced life-style. Corporate interviewers and selection committees choosing among candidates with professional degrees in law, medicine, or business use balance as an important selection criterion, and they look for candidates who are well-rounded. Those individuals who have addressed their physical, emotional, spiritual, social, and educational needs will have a competitive edge in today's market. It pays to demonstrate a diversified set of interests and values.

SUMMARY

In Chapters 2 and 3, we have discussed forces that propel you to act on your goals, attitudes, values, and needs. In the next chapter, we will focus on the skills you possess and the skills you need in order to get you where you want to go. Once you know what skills you have, which you need to develop, and which you most want to use in the future, you will be well on your way to making some intelligent career plans.

?? WRITTEN EXERCISES

The following exercises will help to identify your own specific values. As you complete the exercises, look for the values that occur repeatedly in your answers. By the end of the exercises you will have identified the five values that come up most often. These are your primary work values. Note them in the exercise summary at the end of the chapter.

The exercises are divided into six parts. Exercise 3.1 is called the Life and Personal Values Grid. It will demonstrate how activities that you consider accomplishments or aspirations contain your values. It also shows how your highest values recur and are implemented repeatedly in a variety of activities. Exercise 3.2 seeks to clarify what is important to you in all aspects of your life, from hobbies to work environments. The job descriptions are actually general descriptions of both jobs and values. Try guessing the name of the value and jobs described. The answers can be found at the end of this chapter. Exercise 3.3 asks you to rank your values in the order of what is most important to you in four different situations. Often, in our career decisions and in life in general, we do not get all that we want and must give up something desirable to get something more desirable. Exercise 3.4 asks you to examine what you say you want to do in your life. If you haven't taken any actions to get what you want, your goals need to be reevaluated. The premise is that what is really valued serves as a driving force that motivates you to take action. Exercise 3.5 asks you to identify the types of careers that would utilize the values you hold dear. Exercise 3.6 asks you to identify some of your fantasy careers and what about them appeals to you. You will be introduced to the research technique called *practice interviewing,* and you will be asked to gather information on one of your fantasy careers. As you continue to identify possible career options, you will be doing more practice interviewing to gather firsthand, real-life information so that your career decisions are based on facts.

3.1 LIFE AND PERSONAL VALUES GRID

Above the numbers 1 through 5, <u>list</u> five aspirations or goals you have achieved in your lifetime. Use only a key word or two to represent the goal. <u>Check</u> the values that were involved in each goal.

VALUE	DEFINITION	GOALS 1 (perform)	2 (school)	3 (talked/conflict)	4	5	Total checks
accomplishment	knowing you've done well	✓	✓	✓			
aesthetics	caring about beauty and harmony			✓			
altruism	helping others	✓		✓			
cooperation	living in harmony with others	✓		✓			
creativity	developing new ideas or things	✓	✓				
education	appreciating learning	✓	✓				
equality	equal opportunity for all			✓			
faith	loyalty to one's beliefs			✓			
family	caring about parents, children, and relatives			✓			
freedom	free choice of thoughts and actions		✓	✓			
health	emotional/physical/spiritual well-being	✓					
integrity	behavior consistent with beliefs			✓			
justice	fair treatment for all			✓			
love	strong personal attachment			✓			
loyalty	devotion to someone or something	✓		✓			
pleasure	seeking enjoyment or gratification	✓	✓				
power	having influence and the ability to act on it			✓			
prestige	becoming well-known and respected	✓					
recognition	gaining respect and admiration	✓	✓				
security	being certain, sure of something		✓	✓			
wealth	accumulating items of value			✓			
wisdom	mature understanding of life			✓			

List the top five values (#1 is the value that received the greatest number of checks).

_____

_____

Using the Life and Personal Values Grid and the list of values at the end of the chapter, identify five jobs that best express your values, then those that least express your values.

Best Express Values	*Least Express Values*
1. _____	1. _____
2. _____	2. _____
3. _____	3. _____
4. _____	4. _____
5. _____	5. _____

3.2 SEARCH YOUR SOUL

a. List five things you love to do. What values are reflected in these activities? (See Life and Personal Values Grid for ideas.) _____

_____

_____

b. What is one thing you would change in the world? In your town? About yourself? _____

_____

c. What is something you really want to learn before you die?

_____

_____

d. List several things that are most important to you in your job (e.g., independence, creativity, working outdoors, environment). _____

_____

_____

e. Work environments are people environments. Some people add to your energy, productivity, and self-esteem; others drain you. Write the names of three people and itemize why they were positive or negative influences. _____

_____

_____

f. If you had unlimited funds so that you would not have to work:

1. How would you spend your time? (Try to think beyond "summer vacation," into a daily lifestyle.) _____

_____

2. To what charities or causes would you contribute? _____

_____

g. Choose the three job descriptions you find most interesting as career possibilities from the following list of fifteen, and then list what values you think each of those three job descriptions imply. Some possible answers follow the exercise summary at the end of the chapter.

Job Descriptions

_____ 1. An opportunity to help people in a personal way. Meet and deal with the public in a meaningful relationship. Help to make the world a better place to live. Pay and benefits in accordance with experience.

_____ 2. Do your own thing! Work with abstract ideas. Develop new ideas and things. Non-routine. A chance to work on your own or as a member of a creative team. Flexible working conditions.

_____ 3. A professional position. Position of responsibility. Secretarial assistance provided. Pay dependent on experience and initiative. Position requires a high level of education and training. Job benefits are high pay and public recognition.

_____ 4. A job with a guaranteed annual salary in a permanent position with a secure, stable company. Supervisory assistance is available. Minimum educational requirement is high school. Slightly better pay with one or two years of college or vocational training. Position guarantees cost-of-living pay increases annually. Retirement benefits.

_____ 5. Looking for an interesting job? One that requires research, thinking, and problem solving? Do you like to deal with theoretical concepts? This job demands constant updating of information and ability to deal with new ideas. An opportunity to work with creative and intellectually stimulating people.

_____ 6. This job requires an extraordinary person. The job demands risk and daring. Ability to deal with exciting tasks. Excellent physical health a necessity. You must be willing to travel.

_____ 7. An ideal place to work. An opportunity to work with people you really like, and, just as important, who really like you. A friendly, congenial atmosphere. Get to know your coworkers as friends. Pay and benefits dependent on training and/or experience.

_____ 8. Work in a young fast-growing company. Great opportunities for advancement. Starting pay is low, but rapid promotion to mid-management. From this position, there are many opportunities and directions for further advancement. Your only limitations are your own energy and initiative. Pay and benefits related to level of responsibility.

_____ 9. Set your own pace! Set your own working conditions. Flexible hours. Choose your own team or work alone. Salary based on your own initiative and time on the job.

_____ 10. Start at the bottom and work your way up. You can become president of the firm. You should have the ability to learn while you work. Quality and productivity will be rewarded by rapid advancement and recognition for a job well done. Salary contingent on rate of advancement.

_____ 11. Ability to direct work tasks of others in a variety of activities. Leadership qualities in controlling work force and maintaining production schedules. Ability to maintain a stable work force. Coordinate work of large management team. Instruct work force. Evaluate work completed. Hiring and firing responsibilities.

_____ 12. Great opportunity for money! High salary, elaborate expense accounts, stock options, extra pay for extra work. Christmas bonus. All fringe benefits paid by company. High pay for the work you do.

_____ 13. Are you tired of a dull, routine job? Try your hand at many tasks, meet new people, work in different situations and settings. Be a jack-of-all-trades.

_____ 14. Does the thought of a desk job turn you off? This job is for the active person who enjoys using energy and physical abilities, since it requires brisk and lively movement.

_____ 15. Opportunity to express your personal convictions in all phases of your job. Devote your life-style to your work.

3.3 YOUR VALUES—SOME HARD CHOICES

In this exercise you are asked to choose the best and worst among sets of options, all of which are more or less unpleasant. Rank the situations and individuals, however unpleasant, that you could best and most easily accept as number one, and the "worst bad case," the situations you would find hardest to accept, as number five, with the intervening cases ranked accordingly.

Job Situations

_____ To work for a boss who knows less than you do about your work and over whom you have no influence.

_____ To be the key person in a job, while someone else gets better paid and all the credit for what you do.

_____ To work with a group where trust is very low.

_____ To work in an organization whose job is to serve the poor but which instead wastes huge amounts of its resources on red tape.

_____ To work day-to-day with someone who is always putting in really second-rate work.

People

_____ The industrialist who in public gives lip service to antipollution concerns but orders the factory to emit heavy pollutants at night to avoid detection.

_____ The person who blatantly ignores the obvious no smoking sign and blows cigarette smoke in your face.

_____ The parent who, on finding the 2-year-old playing with matches, slaps the child across the face and says, "Don't you know any better?"

_____ The college student who sells drugs to high school students at cost, because of a sincere belief that they should have a chance to experience them.

_____ The worker at a neutron bomb manufacturing company who, when confronted by his college-age child about taking part in such an industry, snaps back, "Shut up! The money I make there is putting you through college!"

Environment

_____ In the Arabian desert (120 degrees F.) with a well-paying job.

_____ On a small subsistence-level farm in Appalachia.

_____ In an efficiency apartment in New York on a tight budget.

_____ In a commune where all resources are shared.

_____ In a middle-income suburban housing development, with an hour commute (one way), totally dependent on a freeway route.

Risks

_____ Bet $10,000 in a gamble.

_____ Put $10,000 into a new and uncertain business venture.

_____ Go into business for yourself, with minimum resources.

_____ Without an assured job, move to a place where you always wanted to live.

_____ Risk arrest in a public demonstration for or against something about which you feel strongly.

3.4 TOP FIVE

List five things you want in life. Examine each of these to see what is most important to you. What have you done to support or express these values? What actions have you taken or do you need to take to move toward what you most want in life? What you say is important and what you are actually willing to do deserves close examination.

1. _____
2. _____
3. _____
4. _____
5. _____

3.5 VALUES RELATED TO CAREERS

List (A) your top five values and (B) careers that you believe would allow you to fulfill many of those values. For example, creativity, prestige, variety, money, and independence might all be associated with a career as a lawyer.

Values

1. _____
2. _____
3. _____
4. _____
5. _____

Careers

1. _____
2. _____
3. _____
4. _____
5. _____

3.6 VALUES RELATED TO ETHICS

a. In a class or group setting, discuss how values affect ethical behavior. Consider current events and prominent figures in the worlds of:

     government
     business
     athletics
     entertainment
     science
     education

b. List one example from a newspaper article or magazine article, and explain how you would have acted if you were in the same situation—for example, an athlete takes steroids to be competitive and to win. What values are reflected in your actions?

EXERCISE SUMMARY

1. List the values that are reflected by your answers to this chapter's exercises.

    a. _____
    b. _____
    c. _____
    d. _____
    e. _____

2. Rank the values listed above into your top five.

    a. _____
    b. _____

c. _____

d. _____

e. _____

3. List the top values that could most likely be satisfied by a future career.

_____

_____

_____

_____

4. What I have learned from reading and answering the exercises:

_____

_____

_____

5. I feel _____ after completing this chapter (e.g., more aware, confused, satisfied).

6. I am energized by the following types of activities (use values grid, past jobs, or hobbies):

a. _____

b. _____

c. _____

Job Description Answers

(for pages 52 and 53)

Job Number	Value
1	Altruism
2	Creativity
3	Prestige
4	Security
5	Intellect
6	Adventure
7	Association
8	Advancement
9	Independence
10	Productivity
11	Power
12	Money
13	Variety
14	Physical Activity
15	Life-style

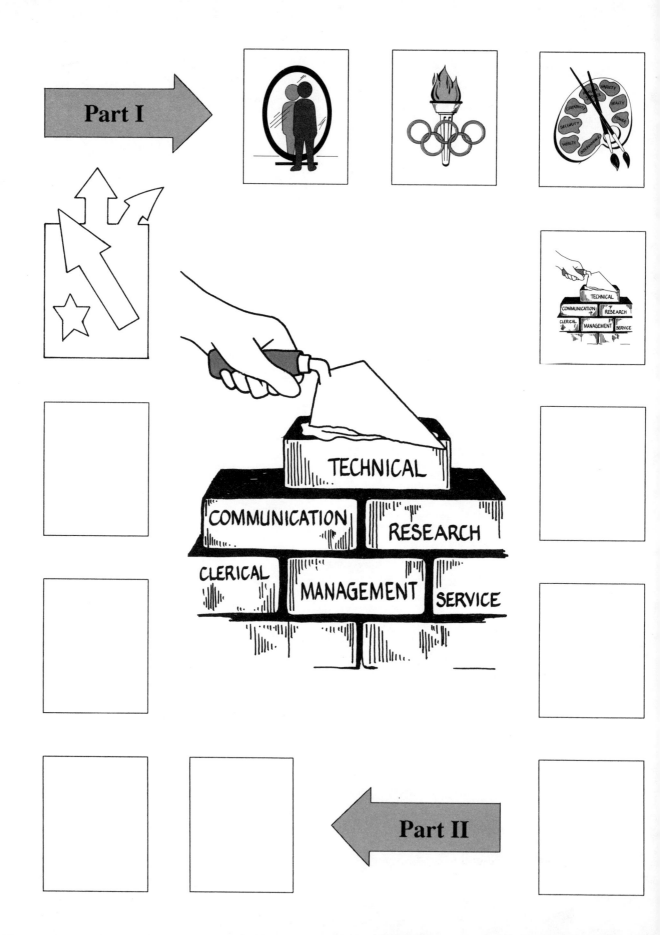

Part I

TECHNICAL

COMMUNICATION

RESEARCH

CLERICAL

MANAGEMENT

SERVICE

Part II

Skills Assessment 4

To find out what one is fitted to do and to secure an
opportunity to do it is the key to happiness.

John Dewey

LEARNING OBJECTIVES   AT THE END OF THE CHAPTER YOU WILL BE ABLE TO:

Understand the importance of skills
in your career search

Define and identify your skills

Recognize the power of the transferability
of your skills

Use the language of skills in writing your
resume and preparing for an interview

SKILLS

The next step in the career-planning process is to identify your skills. Skills are
the building blocks of your future career just as muscles are the building blocks
of your future body shape. A career fitness program helps you to identify your
current skills and the new skills you want to develop. A thorough skills analysis
is a critical component of the career-planning process.

Definitions of Skills

Skills include the specific attributes, talents, and personal qualities that we bring
to a job as well as the learned procedures that a job teaches us. Every job requires
skills. We also develop skills in the process of living, interacting with others, and
going through our daily routines. Your personal preferences often affect your
skills and abilities. You tend to be motivated to repeatedly use skills that are a

**Motivated
skills: those
you enjoy and
do well**

part of enjoyable activities. Your repeated use of and success with certain preferred skills identifies them as your *self-motivators* (also known as your *motivated skills*). Self-motivators are skills you enjoy and do well.

By learning the vocabulary of skills you can recognize the hundreds of skills that may be within your grasp. Skills are generally divided into three types: functional, work content, and adaptive. *Functional skills* are those that may or may not be associated with a specific job, such as answering a telephone, maintaining schedules, collecting data, diagnosing and responding to problems, and measuring productivity. They are called functional skills because they are tasks or functions of a job. *Work-content skills* are specific and specialized to one job, e.g., bookkeeping is done by bookkeepers, assigning grades is done by teachers, interpreting an electrocardiogram is done by specific medical practitioners. *Adaptive skills* are personal attributes; they might also be described as personality traits. The ability to learn quickly, the ability to pay close attention to detail, task orientation, self-direction, congeniality, and cooperativeness are some examples of adaptive skills.

Learn to identify and categorize your skills

Importance of Skills

Basically, the job market pays for skills; the more skills you have, the more valuable you are, and the more you are paid. Individuals who can describe themselves to a potential employer in terms of their skills are the people most likely to enjoy such a career. People who enjoy their work tend to be more productive and healthy. After completing this chapter, you will be able to analyze a potential job on the basis of how the skills the job requires compare with both the skills you possess and enjoy using (your motivated skills) and the skills you want to develop. Furthermore, you will have an improved vocabulary to use in describing your strengths when writing your resume and in future job interviews.

ASSESSING SKILLS

If you were asked right now to enumerate your skills, what would your list look like? It might be a pretty short list, not because you do not have skills, but simply because you are not accustomed to thinking and talking about your skills. Reflecting on your own skills is difficult, because most of us have been taught to be modest and not to brag. It is difficult to recognize that we possess hundreds of skills just by virtue of our life experiences. This chapter seeks to help you learn the vocabulary of skills and acknowledge the skills you possess.

Can you list your skills?

Implications

Once you have begun to recognize your skills, you will become aware that your own identity extends beyond the narrow limits you tend to apply to yourself. We all tend unconsciously to categorize ourselves too narrowly. For instance, you might typically answer the question "Who are you?" with statements like "I am a student," "I am a history major," "I am a teacher," or "I am a conservative." The problem with these labels is that they tend to stereotype you. This is especially true when you are interviewing for a job. If you say you are a student, the interviewer might stereotype you as not having enough experience. If you say you are a secretary, the interviewer may consider you only for a secretarial job or may insist that you start as a secretary. But suppose you say your experience has involved public speaking, organizational work, coordinating schedules, managing budgets, researching needs, problem solving, following through with details, motivating others, resolving problems caused by low morale and lack of cooperation, and establishing priorities for allocation of available time, resources, and funds. Sounds impressive! (See Chapter 9 for the "creative resume" that incorporates these skills into the resume.)

Employers look for employees who are task oriented and who think and talk in terms of what they as employees can do for the employer to make the employer's operation easier, better, and more efficient. The best way to describe what you can do for an employer is to develop the ability to talk about your skills.

Can you talk about your skills?

Unfortunately, not only have most of us been raised to be modest ("It's impolite to brag or boast"), but also once we accomplish a task we tend to discount the worth of our skill development. Most people tend to deny that they have done much of anything. They say, "I haven't climbed the highest mountain," or "I can't run a 4-minute mile," or "I haven't been president of the student body," or "I haven't been elected to public office." Yes, those are accomplishments, but so are the following:

babysitting	getting into college
delivering on a paper route	using a word processing program
riding a bicycle	repairing a car
designing a costume	completing a computer course
planning a surprise party	raising money
giving a speech	writing a term paper
getting a first job	consoling a child
graduating from high school	planning a trip and traveling

Sample accomplishments

In reviewing this list, you may be thinking that some of these activities are simple, "no big deal." Some tend to be activities that you can do without much thought or preparation. However, just because they don't take much preparation does not mean they aren't accomplishments. Start thinking of goals that you have set and then later met as accomplishments!

IDENTIFYING SKILLS

You can begin to recognize your skills by identifying and examining your most satisfying accomplishments. Your skills led you to achieve these accomplish-

Analyzing accomplishments

ments. The analysis of these accomplishments is likely to reveal a pattern of skills (your self-motivators) that you repeatedly utilize and enjoy using. Again, accomplishments are simply completed activities, goals, projects, or actual jobs held.

There are several ways to analyze accomplishments. *One way* is first to describe to someone something that you are proud of having completed and then to list the skills that were required to complete it. Let's look at John as an example.

> *John, an 18-year-old freshman, planned a surprise party for his girlfriend by persuading several friends to contribute decorations and assist in decorating her house. Then he had a few other friends divert the girlfriend from arriving home until everything was in place. Additionally, he arranged for entertainment and party food. In discussing his completed goal (to surprise his girlfriend), he discounted his efforts, saying "Anyone could do it." However, in analyzing this accomplishment, he identified the following skills: organization, persuasiveness, thoroughness, leadership, creativity, communication skills, determination, drive, persistence, dependability, courage, attentiveness to detail, and supervisory ability.*

Can you think of any that he missed? We all have many more skills than we ever credit ourselves with.

Another method used to identify skills is to write a story about one of your accomplishments and then list the skills used. Richard Bolles has popularized this approach in his *Quick Job Hunting Map,* a booklet that lists hundreds of skills (Bolles, 1988).

The following is an example of one student's story and how a group of classmates helped her to list her skills. Her classmates listened to her read her story and were able to identify twenty skills. The list follows the story.

Typing My Term Paper on a Word Processor

It was necessary for me to learn how to use the word processor at a simple level to complete my term paper.

I knew the traditional keyboard and could type. I went to our campus computer center for instruction on how to use all the additional keys. I wrote down on paper all the key functions I had to use in order to give the correct commands to the machine. I got a minioperations course. I learned the following:

1. *Find any page.*
2. *Enter the file.*
3. *Transfer material to different pages.*
4. *Type simple graphs.*
5. *Print out on printer.*
6. *Make corrections.*
7. *Delete and insert characters.*

I proofread, corrected, and typed sixty pages in three weeks, then edited it down to 35 pages.

The paper received an A. Since the experience, I am taking a class in word processing.

List of Skills

1. learns quickly	11. works in a team
2. displays flexibility	12. displays patience
3. meets challenges	13. attends to detail
4. helps others	14. overcomes obstacles
5. follows through	15. communicates clearly
6. faces new situations	16. works under stress
7. proofs and edits	17. displays persistence
8. translates concepts	18. asks questions
9. types	19. gets the job done
10. organizes	20. directs self

Note that the list includes a combination of all three kinds of skills—adaptive, functional, and work content.

A final method can be used if you have had several jobs. You can research the skills associated with these jobs by reading the job descriptions usually located in the personnel office of any company or by researching the job in the *Dictionary of Occupational Titles* (referred to as "the *DOT*"). The *DOT* is an excellent reference source for identifying skills required in over 20,000 different occupations. Here are two examples.

Research skills in the DOT.

131.067.014 COPY WRITER (Profess. & Kin.)

Writes advertising copy for use by publication or broadcast media to promote sale of goods and services: Consults with sales media and marketing representatives to obtain information on product or service and discuss style and length of advertising copy. Obtains additional background and current development information through research and interview. Reviews advertising trends, consumer surveys, and other data regarding marketing of specific and related goods and services to formulate presentation approach. Writes preliminary draft of copy and sends to supervisor for approval. Corrects and revises copy as necessary. May write articles, bulletins, sales letters, speeches, and other related informative and promotional material.

241.267.030 INVESTIGATOR (Clerical)

Investigates persons or business establishments applying for credit, employment, insurance, loans, or settlement of claims: Contacts former employers, neighbors, trade associations, and others by telephone to verify employment record and to obtain health history and history of moral and social behavior. Examines city directories and public records to verify residence history, convictions and arrests, property ownership, bankruptcies, liens, and unpaid taxes of applicant. Obtains credit rating from banks and credit concerns. Analyzes information gathered by investigation and prepares reports of findings and recommendations. May interview applicant on telephone or in person to obtain other financial and personal data for completeness of report. When specializing in certain types of investigations, may be designated CREDIT RE-PORTER (bus. ser.); INSURANCE-APPLICATION INVESTIGATOR (insurance).

In addition to defining specific skills for each job, the DOT divides all jobs into skills relating to the three broad categories of DATA (instructions and information), PEOPLE (supervisors, coworkers, or the public), and THINGS (materials, equipment, or products) as shown in Table 4.A.

TABLE 4.A

Skills relationships of jobs to data, people, and things as identified in the *Dictionary of Occupational Titles (DOT)*.

DATA (4th Digit)	PEOPLE (5th Digit)	THINGS (6th Digit)
0 Synthesizing	0 Mentoring	0 Setting-Up
1 Coordinating	1 Negotiating	1 Precision Working
2 Analyzing	2 Instructing	2 Operating-Controlling
3 Compiling	3 Supervising	3 Driving-Operating
4 Computing	4 Diverting	4 Manipulating
5 Copying	5 Persuading	5 Tending
6 Comparing	6 Speaking-Signaling	6 Feeding-Offbearing
7 No significant relationship	7 Serving	7 Handling
	8 No significant relationship	8 No significant relationship

Skills clusters

In addition to analyzing your skills by examining your completed projects and goals, a list such as the one in Table 4.B can help you become aware of some of the skills that you possess. In Table 4.B we have listed almost 200 skills in twelve different categories. The categories mentioned are useful because they're familiar to employment counselors and often show up in job announcements. Read the items in Table 4.B, considering carefully how each applies to you as a unique person.

Table 4.C demonstrates how the tasks or functions of one occupation, teaching, can be translated into skills that apply to many other occupations. This awareness opens up options and expands individuals' choices (Elliot, 1982).

Instructions for Table 4.B (on the following page): For each item in Table 4.B, mark an "X" next to each activity that you enjoy doing. Then go over the list again and mark a check next to each activity that you do well. Underline any skills that you have ever used. Note that these categories contain work-content, functional, and adaptive skills.

TABLE 4.B
Assessing your skills.

MANAGEMENT SKILLS	COMMUNICATION SKILLS	RESEARCH SKILLS
_____ Planning	_____ Reasoning	_____ Recognizing problems
_____ Organizing	_____ Organizing	_____ Interviewing
_____ Scheduling	_____ Defining	_____ Developing questions
_____ Assigning/Delegating	_____ Writing	_____ Synthesizing
_____ Directing	_____ Listening	_____ Writing
_____ Hiring	_____ Explaining	_____ Diagnosing
_____ Measuring production	_____ Interpreting ideas	_____ Collecting data
_____ Setting standards	_____ Reading	_____ Extrapolating
_____ Working under stress	_____ Handling precise work	_____ Reviewing
_____ Working with people	_____ Working with committees	_____ Working without direction
_____ Traveling frequently	_____ Public speaking	_____ Working very long hours
_____ Negotiating strategies	_____ Correct English usage	_____ Research design
_____ Personnel practices	_____ Subject knowledge	_____ Statistics
_____ Time management	_____ Good sense of timing	_____ Algebra
_____ Working as a team member	_____ Operating communication systems	_____ Working on long-term projects

FINANCIAL SKILLS	MANUAL SKILLS	SERVICE SKILLS
_____ Calculating	_____ Operating	_____ Counseling
_____ Projecting	_____ Monitoring	_____ Guiding
_____ Budgeting	_____ Controlling	_____ Leading
_____ Recognizing problems	_____ Setting up	_____ Listening
_____ Solving problems	_____ Driving	_____ Coordinating
_____ Finger dexterity	_____ Cutting	_____ Working under stress
_____ Concentrating	_____ Doing heavy work	_____ Responding to emergencies
_____ Handling detail work	_____ Knowledge of tools	_____ Agencies' policies
_____ Working under stress	_____ Working on assembly line	_____ Working on weekends
_____ Orderly thinking	_____ Working independently	_____ Working nightshifts
_____ Accounting procedures	_____ Electronic principles	_____ Knowledge of a subject
_____ Data processing	_____ Safety rules	_____ Human behavior principles
_____ Investment principles	_____ Basic mechanics	_____ Community resources
_____ Financial concepts	_____ Basic plumbing	_____ Working under hazardous conditions
_____ Operating business machines	_____ Doing precise machine work	

TABLE 4.B
Assessing your skills (continued).

CLERICAL SKILLS	TECHNICAL SKILLS	PUBLIC RELATIONS SKILLS
_____ Examining	_____ Financing	_____ Planning
_____ Evaluating	_____ Evaluating data	_____ Conducting
_____ Filing	_____ Calculating	_____ Human relations
_____ Developing methods	_____ Adjusting controls	_____ Informing the public
_____ Improving methods	_____ Aligning fixtures	_____ Consulting
_____ Recording	_____ Following specifications	_____ Writing news releases
_____ Computing	_____ Observing indicators	_____ Researching
_____ Recommending	_____ Verifying	_____ Representing
_____ Working as team member	_____ Drafting	_____ Working with people
_____ Working in office	_____ Designing	_____ Working under stress
_____ Following directions	_____ Balancing principles	_____ Working very long hours
_____ Doing routine office work	_____ Working in small studios	_____ Working odd hours
_____ Basic clerical skills	_____ Odd hours	_____ Negotiating principles
_____ Bookkeeping	_____ Economics	_____ Media process
_____ Data-entry operations	_____ Investigation principles	_____ Maintaining favorable image
_____ Telephone protocol	_____ Working in an office/outdoors	

AGRICULTURAL SKILLS	SELLING SKILLS	MAINTENANCE SKILLS
_____ Diagnosing malfunctions	_____ Contacting	_____ Repairing equipment
_____ Repairing engines	_____ Persuading	_____ Maintaining equipment
_____ Maintaining machinery	_____ Reviewing products	_____ Operating tools
_____ Packing	_____ Inspecting products	_____ Dismantling
_____ Replacing defective parts	_____ Determining value	_____ Removing parts
_____ Woodworking	_____ Informing buyers	_____ Adjusting functional parts
_____ Constructing buildings	_____ Promoting sales	_____ Lubricating/cleaning parts
_____ Hitching	_____ Working outdoors/indoors	_____ Purchasing/ordering parts
_____ Working outdoors	_____ Working with people	_____ Climbing
_____ Working in varied climate	_____ Working under stress	_____ Working indoors/outdoors
_____ Manual work	_____ Working long hours	_____ Lifting heavy equipment
_____ Doing heavy work	_____ Knowledge of products	_____ Plumbing principles
_____ Operating basic machinery	_____ Human relations	_____ Basic mechanics
_____ Safety rules	_____ Financing	_____ Electrical principles
_____ Welding	_____ Budgeting	_____ Working as a team member
_____ Horticultural procedures		

TABLE 4.C
Identifying transferable skills for teachers.

TASKS	FUNCTIONAL SKILLS
Teaching	Training, coordinating, communicating, arbitrating, coaching, group facilitating.
Making lesson plans	Designing curricula, incorporating learning strategies, problem solving, developing rapport.
Assigning grades	Evaluating, examining, assessing performance, interpreting test results, determining potential of individuals, monitoring progress.
Writing proposals	Assessing needs, identifying targets, setting priorities, designing evaluation models, identifying relevant information, making hypotheses about unknown phenomena, designing a process, judging likely costs of a project, researching funding sources.
Advising the yearbook staff	Planning, promoting, fund-raising, group facilitating, handling detail work, meeting deadlines, assembling items of information into a coherent whole, classifying information, coordinating, creating, dealing with pressure, delegating tasks, displaying ideas in artistic form, editing, making layouts.
Supervising teacher interns	Training, evaluating, mentoring, monitoring progress, diagnosing problem areas, inspiring, counseling, guiding.
Interpreting diagnostic tests	Screening, placing, identifying needs, diagnosing.
Interacting with students, parents, and administration	Confronting, resolving conflicts, establishing rapport, conveying warmth and caring, drawing out people, offering support, motivating, negotiating, persuading, handling complaints, mediating, organizing, questioning, troubleshooting.
Chairing a department	Administering, anticipating needs or issues, arranging meetings, creating and implementing committee structures, coordinating, delegating tasks, guiding activities of a team, having responsibility for meeting objectives of a department, negotiating, organizing, promoting.

SUMMARY

Past accomplishments reveal skills

We each have our own special excellence. This excellence is most likely to be demonstrated in experiences that you consider to be achievements or life satisfactions. Your most memorable achievements usually indicate where your greatest concentration of motivated skills exists. Analyzing several such achievements is likely to reveal a pattern of skills used repeatedly in making such accomplishments occur. The more you know about your motivated skills, the better you will be able to choose careers that require the use of these skills. Using these skills gives you a sense of satisfaction. You will be happier, more productive, and more successful if you can incorporate your motivated skills into your life work. You may also find that your skills transfer to many different jobs.

If you have started reading about occupations by visiting a local library or college career center, you may find that some occupational information sources list the skills related to the specific career described. There are also computer programs such as EUREKA in California and SIGI Plus (System of Interactive Guidance and Information) and CIS (Career Information System) in many other states that include lists of skills that correlate with job descriptions. Check with your local college or computer store to learn about other skill analysis software.

?? WRITTEN EXERCISES

The following exercises will assist you in identifying your personal constellation of skills. Exercise 4.1 asks you to write about several major experiences in your life with enough detail so that you will be able to analyze each experience for particular skills utilized. Exercises 4.2 and 4.3 ask you to list ten accomplishments and then to describe them in detail. Exercise 4.4 asks that you identify the skills used in the accomplishments described in Exercises 4.2 and 4.3. Exercise 4.5 helps you to distinguish between the work-content, adaptive, and functional skills that you possess. Exercise 4.6 identifies your favorite cluster of skills. Exercise 4.7 helps you to identify whether or not you've developed experiences related to the job responsibilities of your ideal job. Exercise 4.8 serves to review and summarize your most often used and most preferred skills.

4.1 EXPERIOGRAPHY

In order to be able to explore your past experiences and relate them to your career plan, we'd like you to write an account of the significant experiences in your life; in other words, write an *experiography*. The best way to go about this task is to think of three or four major experiences in each of the following categories and then describe each of them in writing in as much detail as you can. It is important to describe not only what happened but also your feelings (good or bad) about the experience or person and what you learned from the experience. The categories to include are:

a. work experience

b. activity experience—school, clubs, etc.

c. important life events

d. leisure time

e. important people in your life

f. life's frustrations

g. life's rewards

Remember, neither the chronology nor the order of significance is important. What is important is that you describe people or events that have had an impact on who you are right now. Keep in mind that the writing needs to be specific enough so you will be able to analyze these experiences for particular skills you have demonstrated.

4.2 ACCOMPLISHMENTS

Write a list of ten accomplishments. You may find that you have already listed some in the Life and Personal Values Grid in the exercise section of Chapter 3.

1. _____

2. _____

3. _____

4. _____

5. _____

6. _____

7. _____

8. _____

9. _____

10. _____

4.3 DESCRIPTION OF ACCOMPLISHMENTS

Select one or two of the accomplishments listed above, and describe each of them. Use one sheet of paper for each. In order to be as detailed as possible in your description of the event, try to elaborate on *who* influenced you, *what* you did, *where* it happened, *when* it occurred, *why* you did it, and *how* you did it.

4.4 THE SKILLS

List the skills you used in your story (you may refer to Table 4.B in this chapter).

_____

_____

_____

4.5 CATEGORIZING SKILLS

As a starting point for analyzing your skills, let's look at you and your work experience. You may choose to look at present employment, either full- or part-time, or volunteer experience, past or present. With that experience in mind, review the definitions and examples of work-content, adaptive, and functional skills at the beginning of this chapter, and then complete this exercise.

Name three specific *work-content* skills you used in that experience; list three *adaptive* skills; and list three *functional* skills.

Work-Content	*Adaptive*	*Functional*
_____	_____	_____
_____	_____	_____
_____	_____	_____

4.6 YOUR FAVORITE SKILLS

Rank the following skills categories as you feel they reflect your favorite skills. (1 = most favorite; 6 = least favorite.)

_____ a. Help people, be of service, be kind.

_____ b. Write, read, talk, speak, teach.

_____ c. Analyze, systemize, research.

_____ d. Invent, create, develop, imagine.

_____ e. Persuade, sell, influence, negotiate.

_____ f. Build, plant crops, use hand-eye coordination, operate machinery.

4.7 IDEAL JOB

Write five ideal job responsibilities. Next to each one write two or more experiences that illustrate your background in each of these areas (e.g., "writing"—I wrote a twenty-page report that was used to justify a grant application). In areas where you have not developed numerous experiences, you may want to create additional learning experiences for yourself to make yourself eligible for your ideal jobs. You may create learning experiences or gain experience by taking classes, by volunteering for extra work in your present job, or by finding another job more closely related to your ideal jobs.

4.8 SKILLS REVIEW

Identify the skills that you most often use and enjoy. _____

_____

_____

Review your responses to Table 4.B, Skills. What skills would you most like to use in your future career? _____

_____

_____

Which of the above skills do you need to develop? _____

_____

_____

How will you develop these? _____

_____

_____

_____

You have now identified your foundation—where you have been most effective and successful in your life. By examining these successes or achievements, you now know what you can handle and what motivates you. It is especially important that you focus on skills you use and enjoy.

EXERCISE SUMMARY

Write a Brief Paragraph Answering These Questions

What did you learn about yourself? How does this knowledge relate to your career/life planning? How do you feel?

_____

_____

_____

_____

_____

_____

_____

_____

_____

_____

_____

_____

_____

_____

_____

_____

_____

_____

_____

_____

_____

_____

_____

_____

_____

_____

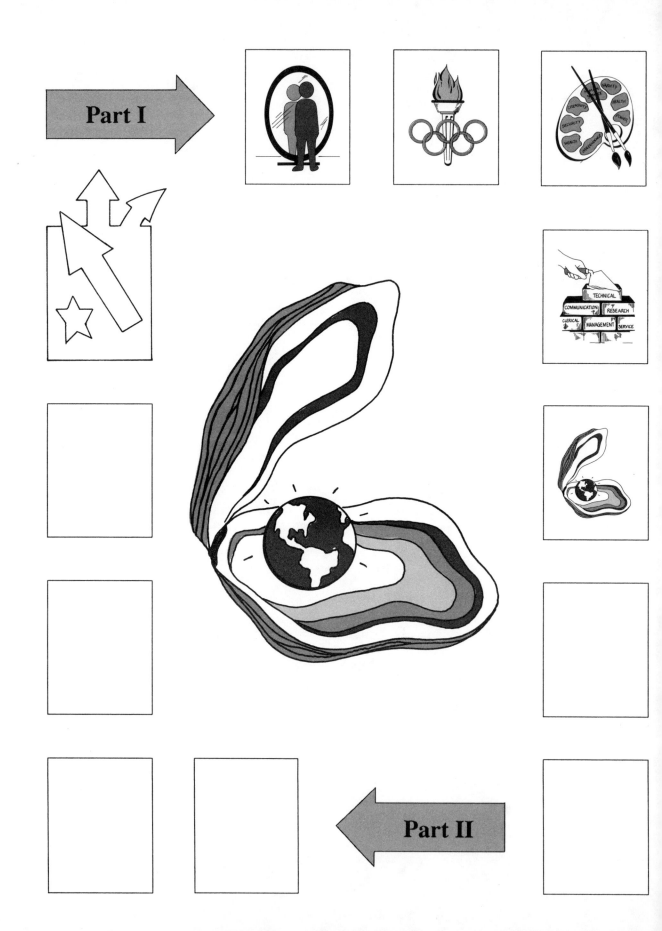

Part I

Part II

The World and You 5

People are lonely because they build walls instead of bridges.

John Newton

LEARNING OBJECTIVES   AT THE END OF THE CHAPTER YOU WILL BE ABLE TO:

Recognize how social and cultural conditioning influence your career choice

Identify trends that will affect your career planning through the 1990s

Understand that options are available for the nontechnical, liberal arts graduate

Your assumptions, limitations, aspirations, dreams, and fantasies are all shaped by the spoken and unspoken rules and norms of the society in which you live. Career choice does not exist in some countries because in those societies the government tells the people what their career will be. It is common to see women in construction work and the medical profession in the Soviet Union even though many Americans still consider these areas to be "men's work." Such facts may seem strange if you take for granted all of the physical, social, and cultural traditions of our own society.

The next step in the career-planning process is to examine the societal and cultural factors that subtly or blatantly affect your career choice. The goal is to heighten your awareness of the biases, beliefs, and assumptions that influence your choice of possible occupations. It is important to analyze these cultural norms because they are often limiting. It is in your best interest to examine your own belief system as it relates to improved opportunity in gender equity, cultural diversity, and future trends in the work force, the main topics of this chapter. As you come to terms with your own feelings about these issues, you can decide whether you want to stick to the norms or strive for success in a nontraditional

Society's norms influence your career choice

75

profession. Every person in a nontraditional occupation, such as female fire-fighters and male nurses, has had to resolve this same issue before embarking upon a chosen path.

INFLUENCES

Career planning does not happen in a vacuum. Your life situation influences what decisions you make and how you make them. The society in which you grow up, your background, your family, your peers, and the way you feel about yourself are all influences on the decisions that you make. Sometimes these factors make satisfying decision making easier. For instance, a friend who encourages you may help to build your confidence and, therefore, make a final decision less difficult.

Common obstacles to decision making

However, social and cultural considerations, family, peers, and feelings about yourself can also act as obstacles to making satisfying decisions. For example, many women are eager to return to school or to work. But they may avoid confronting this decision due to family and peer pressure and certain feelings about themselves, such as lack of self-confidence, fear of failure, age, race, and sex role stereotyping.

> *"Sure, I'd like to go back to school, but how could I get all the cooking, laundry, and shopping done, and who would look after the kids?"*
>
> *"I don't really know what I want to do. Besides, I'm too old to start anything now."*
>
> *"What I would really like to be is an engineer, but I've given up on that because I know it's so hard for Latinos to succeed in that field."*
>
> *"I don't know whether I'm going to apply for that job or not. Besides, they're not going to hire an ethnic minority."*
>
> *"I'm not really qualified to do that kind of job, and my high school grades were weak. I was never good at school work."*

Do any of the preceding statements describe something you have heard people say or maybe even something you yourself have said or felt? It is also possible that you may identify with a number of these statements. They represent some of the most common obstacles that people face when making academic and career decisions. An obstacle to a satisfying decision is anything or anyone that prevents you from adequately considering all the possible alternatives. For example, someone said, "I'm too old to start something new." When looking for a job, such people would miss out by not even considering some positions for which they may be well qualified. Age stereotyping prevents these people from considering all the possible alternatives.

Social and cultural conditioning

This chapter will focus on some of the social and cultural conditioning affecting the roles people play in the job market, with examples related to changing roles in our society. Next, we will discuss occupational trends in order to inform you about predictable changes in society. The section after future trends includes a discussion of the current job market and how ethnic minorities and nontechnical and liberal arts–oriented people are finding employment.

Finally, we provide some written exercises so you may identify your own barriers, attitudes, and biases and predict your own future.

Social Conditioning—Sexism as One Example

Compare your own experiences with these three different advisers' career advice to a woman student.

☐ *Your scores in math and science are excellent. Why don't you get your degree in math education? That would take only four years, whereas medicine would take many more—probably longer than you want to wait before marrying. Furthermore, teaching, unlike other jobs, will let you be home at three o'clock, when your children return home from school.*

☐ *Your scores in math and science are excellent. Perhaps you want to consider a career in medicine. You might almost be a pioneer. There aren't too many brain surgeons who are women. And brain surgeons, of course, can pretty much set their own schedule, so you could plan to be home at three o'clock, when your children return home from school.*

Sex role stereotyping

☐ *Your scores in math and science are excellent. Perhaps you want to consider a career in medicine. You might almost be a pioneer. There aren't too many brain surgeons who are women. Not only could it be an immensely rewarding profession financially, but it could also bring you power, prestige, and honor.*

As recently as twenty-five years ago, most women typically heard advice similar to the first example. About fifteen years ago, counselors started appreciating the fact that female roles in society were expanding and, yes, women could even be surgeons. Yet there was still a basic belief that women should be home when the children came home from school. Now more academic guidance counselors are trying to be sex fair (see definitions in Table 5.D at the end of this chapter). That is, they are treating both males and females similarly. In the context of this chapter, the term sex roles relates to social behavior that is prescribed and defined only by tradition. Unfortunately, past practices have suggested that there are "men's jobs" and "women's jobs." Table 5.A reflects the percentages of occupational roles that have been assigned to women in the past; Table 5.B reflects the pay inequities in selected occupations between women and men; and Table 5.C shows the average annual earnings for women by race and age.

Sex equity in employment standards

In an ideally unbiased society that has 50 percent men and 50 percent women, it would be assumed that there would be 50 percent women and 50 percent men in most occupations. Yet these statistics illustrate an unequal distribution of jobs. Many of our past biases have been based on the social custom that the man in a typical four-member family was the principal wage earner and that the wife was responsible primarily for raising the children. Since society was composed principally of families, women were socially restricted to the role of homemaker. Sexism is only one form of stereotype.

TABLE 5.A
Percentage of selected minority groups in selected occupations in the United States.

OCCUPATION	1989 TOTAL EMPLOYED (THOUSANDS)	PERCENTAGE OF WOMEN	PERCENTAGE OF AFRICAN AMERICANS	PERCENTAGE OF LATINOS
Law				
Lawyers	741	22.2	3.0	3.4
Education				
Teachers, College and University	709	38.7	4.3	2.4
Elementary School Teachers	1489	84.7	11.0	3.5
Secondary School Teachers	1220	52.6	7.7	3.4
Education and Related	585	53.4	9.9	4.0
Health				
Physicians	548	17.9	3.3	5.4
Dentists	170	8.6	4.3	2.9
Pharmacists	174	32.3	4.7	2.2
Registered Nurses	1599	94.2	7.2	3.0
Health Administrators	188	67.6	6.7	3.1
Social Science				
Economists	122	41.3	4.4	3.5
Psychologists	210	54.0	7.7	2.5
Engineering and Science				
Electrical and Electronics Engineers	571	8.5	3.2	2.2
Civil Engineers	249	5.4	4.2	3.6
Industrial Engineers	199	11.5	4.9	1.1
Mechanical Engineers	310	4.9	3.2	1.6
Chemists	122	27.8	5.9	5.2
Arts				
Writers, Artists, Entertainers, and Athletes	1921	46.0	4.5	3.9
Designers	534	51.5	2.8	4.3
Musicians and Composers	170	31.5	7.0	5.3
Photographers	112	30.3	4.8	7.6
Religion				
Clergy	336	7.8	7.2	1.8
Protective Service				
Firefighters	188	3.5	12.0	4.4
Police and Detectives	461	10.2	13.1	4.7
Sheriffs and Bailiffs	112	12.8	7.3	4.5
"Traditional" Female Occupations				
Bank Tellers	503	91.0	9.9	6.9
Billing Clerks	159	90.6	9.6	6.8
Bookkeepers	1926	91.7	5.1	4.6
Office Clerks	810	81.9	12.8	7.1
Secretaries	4010	99.1	7.3	4.6
"Nontraditional" Male Occupations				
Airplane Pilots	109	2.8	.2	2.7
Electricians	702	1.8	7.0	5.3
Auto Mechanics	880	.7	8.2	11.6
Truck Drivers (Heavy)	1850	1.9	14.2	6.5

Source: *Employment and Earnings*, U.S. Department of Labor, Bureau of Labor Statistics, 1989.

TABLE 5.B
Pay inequity: The top-paying jobs for men and women based on 1988 median weekly salaries.

	1988 SALARY	PERCENTAGE CHANGE 1983—88
MEN		
Lawyer	$ 930	42%
Airplane pilot	$ 823	33%
Aerospace engineer	$ 820	29%
Physician	$ 815	58%
Financial manager	$ 788	37%
Chemical engineer	$ 785	24%
Personnel and labor relations manager	$ 785	30%
Securities and financial services salesman	$ 768	25%
Education administrator	$ 757	30%
College professor	$ 752	46%
Electrical engineer	$ 749	21%
Civil engineer	$ 734	27%
Mathematical and computer specialist	$ 733	23%
Pharmacist	$ 720	37%
Economist	$ 719	3%
WOMEN		
Lawyer	$ 774	33%
Engineer	$ 639	28%
Mathematical and computer specialist	$ 575	29%
Personnel and labor relations manager	$ 563	NA
College professor	$ 555	39%
Physician	$ 553	33%
Natural scientist	$ 540	30%
Urban planner	$ 531	39%
Guidance counselor	$ 522	37%
Registered nurse	$ 515	30%
Education administrator	$ 499	28%
Computer programmer	$ 497	21%
High school teacher	$ 491	35%
Librarian	$ 465	25%

NA = Not available.
Note: Figures exclude people who are self-employed or in private practice. Percentage change for airline pilot represents increase since 1984.

Basic data: U.S. Dept. of Labor; *U.S. News & World Report*, September 25, 1989, p. 68.

Social and Cultural Considerations

Statistics from the Department of Labor and Census Bureau show that society is changing radically. Consider the following major shifts.

Marriage. Twenty-five years ago, 28 percent of women aged 20–24 had not yet married; today, that figure is close to 50 percent. Fifteen years ago, the number of unmarried couples living together totaled half a million. Today there are more than two million.

Divorce. The divorce rate is currently 40 percent, but of the couples getting married today, it is projected that half will get divorced.

Birthrate. In 1965, the overall birthrate per 1,000 population was 19.4. By 1976, it had fallen to 14.7, the lowest ever recorded. Since then, it has edged up over 15.0 per 1,000, with the average family size expected to remain around 2.1 children per family. Teenage mothers give birth to 1 out of every 5 babies.

Children. Between 1960 and 1980, the number of children living with only one parent, usually their mother, increased from 1 in 9 to 1 in 5. In the 1990s, that figure is closer to 1 out of every 2 children.

TABLE 5.C
Median annual earnings of women by race and age (1988), which drop steadily after the age of 44.

AGE	AFRICAN AMERICAN	WHITE	LATINO
25-34	$15,903	$17,403	$15,304
35-44	$17,361	$19,611	$16,396
45-54	$17,206	$18,569	$14,370
55-64	$14,485	$17,024	$14,509

Source: Fact Sheet on Women, Work and Age from the National Commission on Working Women of Wider Opportunities for Women, 1325 G Street NW, Washington, DC 20005, 202-737-5764.

Working Women. During the 1970s, more than a million women a year entered the work force. That trend continued in the 1980s but is predicted to stabilize in the 1990s. Nonetheless, in certain geographical areas, the majority of all new entrants into the workplace will be women, ethnic minorities, or immigrants.

☐ Women have made up 60 percent of the net additions in the work force since World War II. In 1970, only 1 in every 4 women aged 16 and over was in the labor force. Today, it is 1 in every 2. In 1990, 55 percent of all women aged 16 and over were working.

☐ Today more than 55 million women are employed in the United States, compared with 26.2 million in 1970. Of the 120 million people working last year, 43.7 percent were women, up from 38.4 percent of a total of 85 million workers a decade ago. By 1995, 80 percent of women between 25 and 44 will be in the work force. In 1970, 30 percent of all mothers with children under 6 years old worked. That figure has now increased to over 50 percent. Since 1970, households headed by women increased 70 percent. Women are the sole earners in more than 15 percent of families.

☐ Three quarters of all women work 35 hours a week or more, and two thirds of married women work full-time. In the 1950s women earned 63 cents for every dollar earned by a man. Today, that figure has increased only to 72 cents for every dollar. Of women working full-time, 66 percent earn less than $10,000 annually, compared to 20 percent of men.

☐ Low income is related to the fact that *two thirds* of employed women now hold clerical, service, nursing, and education jobs; these are traditionally low-paying occupations. Ninety-nine percent of secretaries, 96 percent of nurses, 91 percent of bank tellers, 89 percent of health aides, and 87 percent of librarians are women. Women managers and administrators earn 60.5 percent of what men earn, women in blue collar jobs 67.1 percent, and women professionals 70.8 percent of what male professionals earn.

☐ While percentages of women in nontraditional jobs have increased, often the increase is in the lower-paying areas. About 17 percent of women work in what the U.S. Census labels "professional and technical jobs"; however, women are employed in only five out of the fifty job titles that compose that area. Of the 55 million women who worked or were looking for work in 1988, 13 million were employed in managerial or professional specialty occupations.

☐ Women make up 40.9 percent of managers and 48.1 percent of professionals, including teachers and registered nurses. In professions, women have made the following gains in the last ten years: women are 15.8 percent of doctors and dentists, up from 9.3 percent; in traditionally male jobs, women are now 2.1 percent of pilots and navigators, up from 1.5 percent, and 1 percent of firefighters, up from .5 percent; since 1976 female full-time workers have increased more than 10 percent in accounting and computer programming.

Tables 5.A through 5.C summarize the continuing discrepancy between the percentages of women and men in selected occupations and the levels of pay between women and men. Table 5.A also illustrates the discrepancy in the percentage of African Americans and Latinos in selected occupations. However, the percentages are changing every year. Notice how the Educational and Related category is 53.4 percent women; in 1982 the figure was closer to 35 percent. Health Administrators are 67.6 percent women; in 1982 the figure was closer to 50 percent. Electrical and Electronics Engineers are 8.5 percent women; in 1982 the figure was only 3.9 percent. Designers are 51.5 percent women, compared with only 29 percent in 1982. In protective service, women represent 10.2 percent of police forces and detectives, compared with 5.7 percent in 1982. We can only conclude that with each passing year there will be a gradual increase in the numbers of women and ethnic minorities in fields previously associated with the traditional white male work force.

Earlier statistics were not conclusive in comparing the job market for Latinos and African Americans between 1982 and 1989. But again, projections for new workers entering the workplace indicate that ethnic minorities will become the majority during the 1990s in most urban centers.

The Aging Population. Ten years ago, there were 20 million people over age 65 in the United States. Today, the figure is 26 million, or 13 percent of the population; by the year 2000, it will be 35 million, or 14 percent; and by 2030, it could go as high as 55 million, or 15 percent. There will be more single people older than 65, particularly women, and more of them will be older. Currently 38 percent of the elderly are over 75, but by 2000, it will be 45 percent.

If trends stay as they are today, the older generation of women will be the poorest in society. Additionally, health care of aging adults will be as common a concern as child care is today. Because of no-fault divorce laws and lack of retirement plans in their traditionally female jobs, many divorced women must continue to work long after men of similar ages have retired.

College Education. In 1900, 1 American out of 60 was a college graduate; now it is closer to 1 out of 5. Over half of all college-educated women work after marriage. Although a technical bachelor's degree is most marketable, a liberal arts degree plus a technically oriented master's degree could equip people for some of the new careers that call for broad general knowledge in economics, financial planning, resource management, and general business management. College graduates will continue to be less likely to be unemployed (though they may be underemployed) and more likely to hold the highest-paying professional and managerial positions.

"High Tech." By 1995, no more than one out of eight jobs will be in a field of high technology. However, it will be necessary to be computer literate even in a nontechnical job. Many jobs will be affected by changes in technology.

Global Competition. In 1900, the Western world accounted for 30 percent of the world population. Currently, the population of the United States accounts for 15 percent. A decade ago the United States was generating 75 percent of the world's technology. Now the United States shares about 50 percent. Even China, with over 20 percent of the world population, expects to be at the leading edge of every technology by the end of the century. Perhaps half of the new scientists and engineers will be in developing countries (and many will obtain their training in the United States).

Temporary Agencies. In the past decade, more employers turned to temporary office help for both clerical and professional workers.

Two-Income Families. In 1973, males 25 years old and older who worked full-time earned an average of $469 weekly in 1980 dollars. By 1984, a decade later, their earnings had declined about 10 percent, to $421 weekly. Logically, one would assume that declining income signals declining standard of living. This has not been the case. Rather, American couples have opted to have the woman work outside the home. As male incomes dropped over the decade, more and more women joined the work force, and society began to accept the concept of "working women."

The Changing Economy. Global competition, two-income families, and older people remaining in the work force have already been mentioned. However, the corporate world is changing its structure. The one-time hierarchy in which young professionals could look forward to "climbing the ladder" at the same company for the rest of their lives is becoming an unstable job market. Middle management is being reduced. Each year, large companies change their organization in order to become more competitive and more productive. Each year, several hundred thousand workers lose their job because of import competition. According to the U.S. Office of Technology Assessment between 1980 and 1990, millions of workers lost jobs due to plant closings and layoffs.

Affirmative Action. These policies have encouraged employers to encourage qualified underrepresented applicants to compete for positions and to recruit them. The effort to consciously reflect diversity in the work force is designed to serve a broader spectrum of community and cultural needs.

Other Cultural Considerations

Other economic, social, and cultural customs present possible obstacles to opportunities. African American and Latina women are more likely to be living without a husband; to have more dependents, a shorter life span, and lower education; and to be unemployed or underemployed. Asian and Asian-Pacific men and women (Philippine, Japanese, Chinese, Vietnamese, Thai, Cambodian, Hawaiian, Samoan) are likely to be part of a family in which tradition is very strong and women are not taught to voice their opinions. It is harder for such women to learn to assert themselves in a society in which some assertiveness is necessary for success.

Cultural biases may limit choices

Additional conditions that limit opportunity include living in a rural area with few job options and a lack of transportation, being a former prisoner, and being a former mental patient. Anyone possessing these identities needs to strengthen their self-confidence and skills and to focus on a specific job target.

Implications

How do all these social and cultural changes affect you? Basically your expectations about your future are shaped by your early socialization. You might look back at Super's theory in Chapter 3. Work and life satisfactions depend on the extent to which you have found or can find adequate opportunities to use and develop your abilities, interests, personality traits, and values. Opportunities can be found through family, childhood play, school experiences, and early work activities. But opportunity is not equally distributed throughout the society. As this chapter has illustrated, job opportunities may be limited by sex stereotyping, by educational requirements, by discrimination, or by the changing economy. However, with changing perceptions about sex stereotyping in occupations, there is more encouragement for both men and women to train for the type of career that best suits their personality.

(1) As longevity increases, more jobs related to serving senior citizens will be available. People who remain healthy and live longer may change careers more than five times during their lifetime. Your most prosperous time may be after age 50. Colonel Sanders started Kentucky Fried Chicken after he was 50; Armand Hammer became an oil czar (Occidental Petroleum) after he was 60. At the same time, the "graying of America" will reduce the market for, say, competitive sports-related merchandise for a while because it's always been younger people who have been involved in such sports. Walking shoes may become more popular than running shoes. Finally, younger people coming into the job market will find more opportunities as members of the older generation begin to retire.

(2) High technology means that new jobs will be created for those who have a math and science background; concomitantly jobs will be improved and enhanced for many who do not possess high-tech skills. Today's printer can complete many more projects using computer graphics than anyone could have imagined twenty years ago. However, technology will in turn render some jobs obsolete. There are already computers that can listen to voices in a courtroom and can print out a transcript of multiple voices immediately. Once such technology becomes less costly, fewer court reporters will be needed. Word processors are being designed specifically for radiologists who must review X rays and make immediate reports. Such technology can produce a precise 150-word summary without misspelling a word (such as "lymphadenopathy") on the basis of a few trigger phrases in a few minutes. Such a system costs only $22,000 now and may reduce the number of medical transcribers required in the future. Remember, however, that high technology will account for less than 10 percent of jobs. Services related to technological jobs will involve, at most, an additional 20 percent of jobs. Meanwhile, as Table 5.F shows, there will continue to be hundreds of thousands of entry-level ("low-tech") jobs in every community. Traditionally, custodians, cashiers, and sales clerks have high turnover.

Because you are reading this book, you are preparing for the career that best fits your personality. Thus, you won't get stuck in just any job that happens to be available. The authors hope you will look at the jobs most available to allow you to maximize your values, interests, and skills and to review currently offered careers with the future in mind.

(3) Global competition can mean possibilities for you with an American firm in Japan, China, or Indonesia. These locations compose the Pacific Rim. Now is the time to learn a foreign language and think about working in the Pacific Rim for a while. As the following newspaper article suggests, global competition may also mean that you may work for a foreign employer in the United States.

> The British are coming. And so are the Swedes, the Japanese, the Italians and retailers from dozens of other countries.
>
> Foreign specialty stores are invading America's malls and fashion avenues in record numbers. At least 89 international retailers have set up shop in the United States—most during the past five years—and 32 have opened or announced store openings in the past 12 months.
>
> Most of the largest chains appear to be flourishing in this country. Laura Ashley, which carries fine lace clothing and home fashions, in April reported annual sales of $279.6 million. At the time, company officials announced plans to operate a store in every U.S. city with a population of 1 million or more.
>
> Benetton, with 4,000 licensed stores in 50 countries—including 700 in the United States—is the most ubiquitous international retailer. Known as the McDonald's of retailing, it racked up more than $1 billion in sales last year (1986–87).
>
> Denise L. Smith, *Orlando Sentinel*

(4) Temporary employment agencies, in addition to providing secretarial and clerical professionals who traditionally have been available on a contract basis, offer work in such areas as accounting, health care, telemarketing, the paralegal field, and computers. Technical service contracting firms, often known as job shops, place a range of engineering and computer professionals as well as technicians and draftsmen. With the new trend in temporary employment, many people will find themselves working for an employee-leasing firm. The firm sets the wages and offers benefits, incentives, and raises even though the employee may work at one or several other companies.

(5) In an attempt to attain and maintain a high standard of living, many Americans are marrying later and having fewer or no children; in addition, both husband and wife are working outside the home.

TRENDS—MOVING INTO THE TWENTY-FIRST CENTURY

It helps to have a picture of tomorrow's opportunities when defining a reasonable job target. For example, experts are suggesting that now is not the time to prepare for a lifelong job in a factory assembling auto parts. Such positions are predicted to be phased out in the next twenty years, with computerized robots taking over such tasks in the future; as a matter of fact, 70 percent of General Motors employees today work at jobs other than assembly.

Tomorrow's opportunities

**The
Information
Society**

The so-called Third Wave, or Information Society, will accelerate faster than other ages. Some observers say that within a decade or two, the sum of all human knowledge will have doubled. By the year 2000, you will have been exposed to more information in one year than your grandparents experienced in a lifetime! In fact, approximately 90 percent of all scientific knowledge has been generated in the last thirty years and 90 percent of all scientists who have ever lived are alive today!

The development of the computer is the greatest indicator of the arrival of the new age. Computers are used for everything from data processing to product design and manufacturing. In an increasingly white-collar work world, computer based recordkeeping, report writing, decision analysis, and communication networks have emerged. Most of the largest corporations have begun to adopt these systems. Furthermore, automated telecommunications (as in telemarketing, teleconferencing, telepolling, and instant tellers) are becoming commonplace.

Getting the right skills and education now will give you an advantage tomorrow. There is great fear among employers that jobs will be impossible to fill until enough workers learn the needed skills. There appears to be no shortage of jobs being created. Twenty-one million new jobs were created in the last decade. Currently, there are an additional 4 million jobs advertised but unfilled.

Growth areas

Over 80 percent of jobs need some postsecondary education. Computer literacy along with strong reading and writing skills will open up job possibilities for people. Meanwhile, the Bureau of Labor Statistics has made some predictions for the 1990s based on projected demands for products and services, advances in technology, and changes in business practices. Service occupations grew the fastest, between 23 percent and 30 percent during the 1980s. These included jobs in food, health, maintenance, personal, and protective services.

Eighty percent of new managerial positions will be in service industries. In actuality, 70 percent of the U.S. work force is employed in the service sector. The following list of occupations is a cross section of some of the growth areas in the United States.

- ☐ *Health services.* Demand will be especially great for primary-care workers such as nurse practitioners, nutrition counselors, gerontological social workers, and health service administrators.
- ☐ *Hotel management and recreation.* This category includes restaurants, resorts, and travel services, as well as opportunities in conference planning.
- ☐ *Food service.* Managers and chefs will be in demand for all those restaurants and hotel kitchens, as well as for food processing plants and labs.
- ☐ *Engineering.* In-demand specialties will be as diverse as robotics, aviation and aerospace, and waste management.
- ☐ *Basic science.* Look at molecular biology, chemistry, and optics.
- ☐ *Computers.* Opportunities will continue strongly in design, engineering, programming, and maintenance.
- ☐ *Business services.* Accounting, statistical analysis, payroll management, and temporary workers.

- ☐ *Human resources or personnel.* This includes job evaluation, hiring and firing, benefit planning, and training.
- ☐ *Financial services.* Financial planning and portfolio management.
- ☐ *Teaching.* Demand is growing in elementary school grades to serve the children of the baby-boom generation, as well as in certain specialties: math, sciences, engineering, computer operations, and foreign languages, such as Russian and Japanese.
- ☐ *Maintenance and repair.* The people who will take care of all the equipment that will keep tomorrow's world running.
- ☐ *Artistic.* Writers, entertainers, party planners, painters, and advertisers will have good prospects but must be entrepreneurial types.

Furthermore, demand for computer service technicians should expand 93–112 percent, for systems analysts 68–80 percent, and for legal assistants 109–139 percent. Other expanding areas not even reported by the Bureau of Labor Statistics include laser technician work and jobs related to medical technology, biochemistry, biogenetics, energy storage, resource exploration, the space shuttle, and artificial intelligence. For specific predictions regarding growing job fields and related salaries, see Tables 5.E through 5.N at the end of this chapter. Since data are presented from several sources, figures may differ from table to table even when dealing with the same profession. Figures are meant to be representative.

Flexibility

More important than knowing what jobs will be open is having the ability to adapt to this changing world of work. Sixty percent of the jobs available by the year 2000 are yet to be created. Furthermore, it is estimated that people will have three to five careers during their lifetime. Thus they will need to seek out new training opportunities a number of times. It has been estimated that up to 80 percent of a worker's development occurs on the job, and only 10 percent comes through formal continuing education courses. A general education is important to provide flexibility, as are computer literacy and competence in mathematics, science, and oral and written communication skills. Since information is accumulating at such a fast pace, it is also useful to be able to know how to retrieve and manage information and see the common threads and patterns in the information.

General education is important

As many avenues for promotion will involve managerial-level openings, information management and interpersonal communication skills will be especially important abilities to possess. However, there will be stiff competition for management positions from the "baby boom" population, which equaled one third of the entire population by 1990. This is the generation that increased the percentages of the college educated among the general population. They are finding that in order to compete for the "best" jobs, they need to commit to lifelong continuing education to bolster job skills or prepare for a change in careers.

Lifelong learning

Engineers, computer scientists, and others in fast-changing technical fields are constantly pressured to update their knowledge. According to one estimate, an engineer's knowledge either becomes obsolete or is incorporated into computers every ten years. Remember, 90 percent of all scientific knowledge has been generated in the last thirty years. This knowledge will again double in the next ten to fifteen years!

Twenty-three million Americans are involved in continuing education programs, and more than two thirds of them take job related courses (*U.S. News & World Report,* March 19, 1984, p. 51).

Although the job market may seem as if it's becoming totally technical and computerized, businesses still need clerical support services, public relations specialists, technical and advertising copywriters, personnel experts, and sales and marketing staff. Some fields have always been difficult to enter, yet some people have managed to get jobs in them. Thus, it isn't absolutely necessary to prepare only for those areas most likely to have openings. In fact, as will be discussed in job search strategy considerations, the best direction to follow might rather be to head toward what you really want to do. The key is *desire*. Desire plus talent and perseverance get people jobs in even the tightest job markets.

The Nontechnical Person

One might ask what kind of jobs are available to people who don't train for the technical job market. The Department of Labor indicates that already more than 60 percent of the work force is composed of computer programmers, teachers, accountants, stockbrokers, secretaries, and technicians. The majority of people who graduate with a liberal arts degree do not find employment in fields related to their major (e.g., history majors do not necessarily become historians). For example, in a survey of 1,072 humanities majors (with a 51 percent return), over 11 percent became attorneys, 10 percent sales representatives and buyers, 9.8 percent administrators or managers, 5.1 percent clerks and tellers, and 4.2 percent retail clerks and waiters; the remaining replies represented a variety of miscellaneous occupations (Trzyna, 1980).

Career opportunities for the liberal arts graduate

In addition, teachers with liberal arts degrees have moved into a variety of alternative careers. Such occupations include administrative assistants, association executives, building managers, business owners, cable TV program coordinators, communication experts, computer sales reps, educational brokers, employment agency staffers, financial planners, fitness program coordinators, insurance agents, parenting workshop leaders, personnel and training coordinators, public relations experts, purchasing agents, relocations managers, researchers (for city planning, developers, government proposals, stockbrokering), technical writers, and wastewater managers. By and large, liberal arts graduates obtain management training positions or other entry-level positions in industry and work their way up. According to *Changing Times* magazine (January 1990), many of the best job prospects of the 1990s require cross-disciplinary training to broaden qualifications. This means that dual majors, interdisciplinary programs, and studying foreign languages can make the difference in the competitive, increasingly global job market.

Furthermore, college is no longer a four-year-degree process. More and more people are working full-time and attending college part-time. Many companies are paying tuition costs for their employees and encouraging them to attend college to learn technical skills. Additionally, many companies have in-house educational programs to help employees master new skills and upgrade old skills. As mentioned previously, most continuing education occurs on the job.

On-the-job training

In case you aren't interested in a job that requires a degree, there will always be a need in society for people selling merchandise, running businesses, maintaining homes, doing the laundry, caring for children, working in restaurants, attending to health and fitness needs, and working in a variety of trades that may or may not require further training beyond high school. In fact, many of these jobs will increase due to a sociological change mentioned previously in this chapter: the increase in the number of two-income households. People don't often regard such jobs as careers but they are.

Careers that do not require a degree

Consider the fact that more jobs are created by small businesses than by large corporations. During the 1970s, 9.6 million jobs were generated by firms with fewer than 20 employees; in contrast, the 1,000 largest firms created only 75,000 jobs. Between 1981 and 1990, small firms created over 20 million new jobs. If you want variety and responsibility, and you are results oriented, a small business might be the place you'll want to work. All of the above jobs can be considered careers if you are using your best talents in them and if you feel energized by the work that you do. The fact of the matter is that every day new small businesses are created to serve such needs.

Opportunities in small business

SUMMARY

This chapter has explored social and cultural considerations, highlighted future trends, indicated where the general population is employed, discussed the value of a liberal arts degree, and indicated that many companies have comprehensive training programs to supplement formal education. In addition, job trends and salary information are in the tables at the end of this chapter.

The Unknown Future—Beware of Accepting
All Predictions as Fact:

More than two decades ago—on Feb. 16, 1964, to be exact—we ran the following item, titled "No Housework": "Twenty years from now, claims the American Home Economics Association, the average U.S. housewife will lead a life without housework. Plastic crockery will be disposed of after each meal. Clothing will be made of disposable paper. Homes will be electronically dusted and deodorized. Madame will do little or no cleaning, will have more time for children, leisure, study and husband."

Parade Magazine, 1988

The future is only partially predictable, but it's a good idea to be prepared!

?? WRITTEN EXERCISES

It is our hope that you will develop your own personal objective, believe in yourself, acknowledge stereotypes in occupations, and develop a strategy to enter the career of your choice. Whether or not you have consciously or directly experienced stereotype barriers to employment, we would like you to use the following written exercises to reflect upon your personal, social, and cultural opinions and biases. Exercise 5.1 helps you to become aware of how you could react to events and people that may be different from those to which you are accustomed. Exercise 5.2 lists fourteen questions about things that tend to be common knowledge to people of different ethnic and age groups. Lack of knowledge about these questions suggests a lack of exposure to a variety of ethnic groups. Exercise 5.3 asks you to list your own ideas about stereotypes. Be spontaneous with your answers; do not censor yourself because you may suspect that your answers are only partially true. Exercise 5.4 asks you to list the advantages and disadvantages of belonging to several distinct groups. Exercise 5.5 helps you to become aware of your amount of association with different groups of people. The more difficult for you to identify names of people, the less likely that you have associated with such people. Stereotypes tend to develop when there is a lack of interaction between groups. Exercise 5.6 asks you to consider how stereotypes about you would affect your ability to get a job.

5.1 FIRST IMPRESSIONS

What are your first impressions about each of the following situations?

1. You are applying for a job. A male receptionist ushers you into an office where you are greeted by a female vice president who will conduct the interview.
2. You are flying to Chicago. A male flight attendant welcomes you aboard the plane; later a female voice says, "This is your captain speaking."
3. You go to enroll your 4-year-old in a nearby nursery school and discover that all three teachers at the school are male.
4. You are introduced to a new couple in the neighborhood and discover that the man stays home all day with two small children while the wife works outside the home.
5. You are African-American and live in a neighborhood that is all Caucasian.
6. You have a conference with your child's teacher, who grew up in Vietnam.
7. You are in a class with other students whose native language is different from yours.
8. You move into an apartment, and your neighbors are homosexual.
9. You are temporarily disabled and must use a wheelchair.
10. You arrive at your new dentist's office and find she has green and orange spiked hair.
11. You are referred to a hospital known for excellence in surgery, and your team of doctors are all Latino.
12. You go to court and find you have an all-African-American jury.
13. You go to a job interview and find yourself faced with a panel of older Caucasian men.
14. You find yourself in a statistics class where all the other students are Asian-American.

5.2 ETHNIC AWARENESS SURVEY

This exercise comprises subjects that represent various ethnic groups. Throughout the next decade you will find yourself working with people from different parts of the United States and the world. How familiar are you with the customs and rituals of other cultures? How many answers do you know? (Answers are on page 94)

1. Nochebuena means (a) dark, sweet sugar (b) Christmas Eve (c) a clear, starry night (d) Goodbye.
2. Mariachi is (a) a musical instrument (b) a hopping beetle (c) the first president of Mexico (d) a musical group.
3. A Koto is (a) an article of clothing (b) one of the movements in karate (c) an endearing term for "grandfather" (d) a musical instrument.
4. The principal ingredient of menudo is (a) tripe (b) chorizo (c) corn (d) chicken.
5. Juneteenth is (a) a mint julip mixed with scotch (b) a black term for Flag Day (c) the day slaves were freed in the United States (d) ghetto slang for the tenth day of June.
6. A Canton or chante refers to (a) a song (b) a home (c) a kind of food (d) a dance.
7. Joseph was the head of which tribe: (a) Hoopa (b) Hopi (c) Clatsop (d) Nez Percé.
8. Which name is out of place? (a) Muhammad Ali (b) Ali Akbar Khan (c) Kareem Abdul-Jabbar (d) Malcolm X.
9. Chop suey originated in (a) Formosa (b) Hong Kong (c) California (d) Tokyo.
10. Mano is a slang term for (a) a pickpocket (b) a close friend (c) "all-man" or masculine (d) tomorrow.
11. Sashimi refers to (a) a traditional dance (b) a kind of fish (c) the ink used in scroll painting (d) a major religious holiday.
12. A mensch is (a) a real human being (b) an exotic fruit (c) a tool (d) a place of residence.
13. A homeboy is (a) one of us (b) comfortable at home (c) a mama's boy (d) couch potato's cousin.
14. Yom Kippur is (a) a fish (b) a young boy (c) a game (d) a holiday.

5.3 SEX ROLES QUESTIONNAIRE

Complete these sentences.

a. Women are happiest in careers when _____

b. Men are happiest in careers when _____

c. The most difficult emotion for a man to display is _____

d. The most difficult emotion for a woman to display is _____

e. Women tend to be better than men at _____

f. Men tend to be better than women at _____

g. Men get depressed about _____

h. Women get depressed about _____

i. Men are most likely to compete over _____

j. Women are most likely to compete over _____

k. Men tend to get angry about _____

l. Women tend to get angry about _____

m. As a man/woman, I was always taught to _____

n. Men feel pressured on the job when _____

o. Women feel pressured on the job when _____

5.4 PROS AND CONS

List advantages and disadvantages of being any of the following.

a. *Female*

Advantage:

Disadvantage:

b. *Male*

Advantage:

Disadvantage:

c. *Caucasian*

Advantage:

Disadvantage:

d. *African American*

Advantage:

Disadvantage:

e. *Latino*

Advantage:

Disadvantage:

f. *Asian American*

Advantage:

Disadvantage:

g. *Native American*

Advantage:

Disadvantage:

5.5 FAMOUS PEOPLE

For each of the groups listed above, name 5 famous people (may be currently living or a historical personage).

5.6 WHAT ABOUT YOU?

How do you think gender, race, or physical disability could affect your ability to get a job? While doing these exercises, did you discover anything about your stereotypes of people? Summarize those feelings.

EXERCISE SUMMARY

Write a brief paragraph answering these questions: What did you learn about yourself? How does this knowledge relate to your career/life planning? How do you feel?

_____
_____
_____
_____
_____
_____
_____
_____
_____
_____
_____

Answers to Exercise 5.2

1. b Mexican—Latino
2. d Mexican—Latino
3. d Japanese
4. a Mexican—Latino
5. c African American

6. b Chinese
7. d Native American
8. b African American
9. c Chinese American
10. b Mexican—Latino

11. b Japanese
12. a Jewish—Yiddish
13. a African American
14. d Jewish

TABLE 5.D
Equity definitions.

Affirmative action: Programs, policies, or procedures that attempt to overcome the effects of past discrimination, bias, and/or stereotyping.

Ageism: Any action or policy that discriminates solely on the basis of age, affecting employment advancement, privileges, or rewards.

Discrimination: Racist or sexist practices, policies, or procedures that are specifically prohibited by law; any action that limits or denies a person or group of persons opportunities, privileges, roles, or rewards on the basis of their sex or race.

Feminist: Any person (male or female) who believes that women should have political, economic, and social rights equal to those of men.

Nontraditional job: A man in an area of work that has typically 80 percent or more female population or a woman in an area of work that has typically 80 percent or more males employed; e.g., nursing has only 5 percent males employed, while construction work has only 1 percent women employed.

Pay inequity: Occupations that employ a majority of male workers and that pay more than occupations that employ a majority of female workers.

Sex bias: An attitude or behavior that reflects adversely upon a person or group because of sex but that may not be covered under present legislation; behavior resulting from the assumption that one sex is superior to the other.

Sex fair: Practices and behaviors that treat males and females similarly; may imply separate but equal.

Sexism: Any attitude, action, or institution that subordinates or assigns roles to a person or group of persons because of their sex. Sexism may be individual, cultural, or institutional; intentional or unintentional; effected by omission or commission.

Sex role: Social behavior that is prescribed and defined by tradition, as contrasted with actual biological differences.

Sex stereotyping: Attributing behaviors, abilities, interests, values, and roles to a person or group of persons on the basis of their sex.

TABLE 5.E
Fastest growing occupations, 1986–2000 (numbers in thousands).

OCCUPATION	EMPLOYMENT		CHANGE IN EMPLOYMENT, 1986–2000		PERCENT OF TOTAL JOB GROWTH
	1986	PROJECTED, 2000	NUMBER	PERCENT	1986–2000
Paralegal personnel	61	125	64	103.7	.3
Medical assistants	132	251	119	90.4	.6
Physical therapists	61	115	53	87.5	.2
Physical and corrective therapy assistants and aides	36	65	29	81.6	.1
Data processing equipment repairers	69	125	56	80.4	.3
Home health aides	138	249	111	80.1	.5
Podiatrists	13	23	10	77.2	0
Computer systems analysts, electronic data processing	331	582	251	75.6	1.2
Medical records technicians	40	70	30	75.0	.1
Employment interviewers, private of public employment service	75	129	54	71.2	.3
Computer programmers	479	813	335	69.9	1.6
Radiologic technologists and technicians	115	190	75	64.7	.3
Dental hygienists	87	141	54	62.6	.3
Dental assistants	155	244	88	57.0	.4
Physician's assistants	26	41	15	56.7	.1
Operations and systems researchers	38	59	21	54.1	.1
Occupational therapists	29	45	15	52.2	.1
Data entry keyers, composing	29	43	15	50.8	.1
Peripheral electronic data processing equipment operators	46	70	24	50.8	.1
Optometrists	37	55	18	49.2	.1

The Bureau of Labor Statistics predicts the labor force will grow at only half the rate experienced in the mid-1970s, while job opportunities will grow by more than a million a year, topping 122 million by 1995. There are now 106.5 million jobs.

Out of the fastest-growing occupations, only six will require a baccalaureate degree for job entry, while most of the other jobs will require some form of postsecondary education. The associate degree is becoming the preferred entry ticket for a whole host of midrange occupations.

TABLE 5.F

Occupations with the largest job growth, 1986–2000 (numbers in thousands).

OCCUPATION	EMPLOYMENT		CHANGE IN EMPLOYMENT, 1986–2000		PERCENT OF TOTAL JOB GROWTH
	1986	PROJECTED, 2000	NUMBER	PERCENT	1986–2000
Salesperson, retail	3,579	4,780	1,201	33.5	5.6
Waiters and waitresses	1,702	2,454	752	44.2	3.5
Registered nurses	1,406	2,018	612	43.6	2.9
Janitors and cleaners, including maids and housekeeping cleaners	2,676	3,280	604	22.6	2.8
General managers and top executives	2,383	2,965	582	24.4	2.7
Cashiers	2,165	2,740	575	26.5	2.7
Truck drivers, light and heavy	2,211	2,736	525	23.8	2.5
General office clerks	2,231	2,824	462	19.6	2.2
Food counter, fountain, and related workers	1,500	1,949	449	29.9	2.1
Nursing aides, orderlies, and attendants	1,224	1,658	433	35.4	2.0
Secretaries	3,234	3,658	424	13.1	2.0
Guards	794	1,777	383	48.3	1.8
Accountants and auditors	945	1,322	376	39.8	1.8
Computer programmers	479	813	335	69.9	1.6
Food preparation workers	949	1,273	324	34.2	1.5
Teachers, kindergarten and elementary school	1,527	1,826	299	19.6	1.4
Receptionists and information clerks	682	964	282	41.4	1.3
Computer systems analysts, electronic data processing	331	582	251	75.6	1.2
Cooks, restaurant	520	759	240	46.2	1.1
Gardeners and groundskeepers, except farm	767	1,005	238	31.1	1.1
Licensed practical nurses	631	869	238	37.7	1.1
Maintenance repairers, general utility	1,039	1,270	232	22.3	1.1
Stock clerks, sales floor	1,087	1,312	225	20.7	1.0
First-line supervisors and managers	956	1,161	205	21.4	1.0
Dining room and cafeteria attendants and barroom helpers	433	631	197	45.6	.9
Electrical and electronics engineers	401	592	192	47.8	.9
Lawyers	527	718	191	36.3	.9

Source: Silvestri and Lukasiewicz (1987); Bureau of Labor Statistics, 1989.

TABLE 5.G
Median weekly earnings of wage and salary workers, by detailed occupation and sex, who usually work full-time (numbers in thousands).

	1989					
	BOTH SEXES		**MEN**		**WOMEN**	
OCCUPATION	**NUMBER OF WORKERS**	**MEDIAN WEEKLY SALARY**	**NUMBER OF WORKERS**	**MEDIAN WEEKLY SALARY**	**NUMBER OF WORKERS**	**MEDIAN WEEKLY SALARY**
Total, 16 years and over	84,553	$ 399	48,949	$ 468	35,605	$ 328
Managerial and Professional Specialty	22,645	583	12,281	693	10,363	486
Executive, administrative, and managerial	11,335	579	6,544	698	4,791	458
Administrators and officials, public administration	484	585	280	650	204	504
Administrators, protective services	58	570	50	623	9	( )
Financial managers	441	667	252	848	189	510
Personnel and labor relations managers	126	668	59	909	66	520
Purchasing managers	111	651	86	772	26	( )
Managers, marketing, advertising, and public relations	495	753	346	862	150	540
Managers, properties and real estate	259	424	127	500	131	368
Management-related occupations	3,326	5,16	1,597	615	1,729	453
Accountants and auditors	1,187	522	591	620	596	463
Underwriters and other financial officers	715	543	351	684	364	465
Management analysts	88	693	54	761	34	( )
Personnel, training, and labor relations specialists	387	553	156	645	231	491
Buyers, wholesale and retail trade, except farm product	153	475	82	542	72	376
Professional Specialty	11,310	586	5,737	688	5,572	506
Engineers, architects, and surveyors	1,797	771	1,639	782	158	630
Architects	107	667	83	756	24	( )
Engineers	1,667	775	1,534	784	133	672
Mathematical and computer scientists	767	695	501	738	267	604
Computer systems analysts and scientists	497	711	342	747	155	620
Operations and systems researchers and analysts	225	662	133	710	92	594
Natural scientists	346	642	253	699	93	544
Chemists, except biochemists	107	633	78	700	29	( )
Biological and life scientists	64	572	43	( )	21	( )
Health-diagnosing occupations	288	786	216	871	72	600
Physicians	242	792	181	887	60	623
Health assessment and treating occupations	1,577	564	266	634	1,311	551
Registered nurses	1,113	569	79	629	1,035	564
Pharmacists	114	748	75	768	38	( )
Dietitians	59	428	4	( )	55	428
Therapists	230	511	64	565	167	496
Physical therapists	55	534	13	( )	42	( )
Therapists, not elsewhere classified	52	457	19	( )	34	( )
Physician's assistants	60	513	44	( )	16	( )
Teachers, college and university	493	711	342	785	152	581

continued

OCCUPATION	1989					
	BOTH SEXES		MEN		WOMEN	
	NUMBER OF WORKERS	MEDIAN WEEKLY SALARY	NUMBER OF WORKERS	MEDIAN WEEKLY SALARY	NUMBER OF WORKERS	MEDIAN WEEKLY SALARY
Teachers, except college and university	3,148	$ 503	926	$ 568	2,222	$ 486
Teachers, prekindergarten and kindergarten	275	373	9	( )	265	374
Teachers, elementary school	1,315	498	214	544	1,102	491
Teachers, secondary school	1,082	545	544	579	538	517
Counselors, educational and vocational	177	598	79	650	97	553
Librarians, archivists, and curators	147	483	26	( )	121	477
Social scientists and urban planners	253	609	141	708	113	522
Economists	115	704	68	809	46	( )
Psychologists	106	523	51	603	55	501
Social, recreation, and religious workers	844	411	448	434	396	392
Recreation workers	75	261	23	( )	52	253
Lawyers and judges	424	993	301	1,021	123	733
Writers, artists, entertainers, and athletes	1,050	488	600	559	450	413
Designers	321	489	194	595	127	345
Photographers	53	349	34	( )	19	( )
Editors and reporters	205	494	112	589	93	442
Public relations specialists	125	576	46	( )	79	493
Technical, Sales, and Administrative Support	25,195	359	9,332	480	15,863	317
Technicians and related support	3,042	475	1,666	538	1,376	403
Health technologists and technicians	972	380	203	467	769	367
Clinical laboratory technologists and technicians	250	423	70	478	179	412
Radiologic technicians	99	435	31	( )	68	410
Licensed practical nurses	306	354	11	( )	295	353
Engineering and related technologists and technicians	848	492	686	506	162	428
Electrical and electronics technicians	295	512	249	521	46	( )
Drafting occupations	272	486	217	499	54	446
Sales Occupations	7,982	384	4,581	487	3,401	278
Supervisors and proprietors	2,354	424	1,507	495	846	329
Sales representatives, finance and business services	1,493	502	812	612	681	408
Insurance sales	333	513	206	603	127	422
Real estate sales	351	505	162	675	189	432
Securities and financial services sales	238	651	162	773	75	484
Sales occupations, other business services	451	455	228	569	223	364
Sales workers, retail and personal services	2,817	235	1,203	304	1,614	208
Administrative Support, Including Clerical	14,171	331	3,085	421	11,085	316
Supervisors	731	490	306	599	425	427
General office	438	465	150	615	288	408
Computer equipment operators	760	356	283	417	477	320
Secretaries, stenographers, and typists	3,659	325	49	( )	3,610	325
Transportation ticket and reservation agents	101	392	33	( )	67	373
Receptionists	522	261	11	( )	510	260
Mail carriers, postal service	298	528	232	540	66	480

continued

OCCUPATION	1989					
	BOTH SEXES		MEN		WOMEN	
	NUMBER OF WORKERS	MEDIAN WEEKLY SALARY	NUMBER OF WORKERS	MEDIAN WEEKLY SALARY	NUMBER OF WORKERS	MEDIAN WEEKLY SALARY
Service Occupations	8,836	$ 253	4,351	$ 306	4,487	$ 218
Private household	325	158	15	( )	310	157
Protective services	1,714	445	1,490	460	224	354
Supervisors	179	622	163	643	16	( )
Firefighting and fire prevention	206	536	199	537	8	( )
Police and detectives	778	497	682	502	96	451
Guards	551	280	446	287	104	248
Service Occupations, Except Private Household and Protective	6,799	234	2,846	262	3,953	219
Health service occupations	1,423	254	170	294	1,254	249
Dental assistants	121	280	—	—	121	280
Health aides, except nursing	282	277	51	308	231	269
Nursing aides, orderlies, and attendants	1,020	244	118	289	902	239
Cleaning and building service occupations	1,967	261	1,279	285	687	224
Personal service occupations	800	226	193	289	607	214
Precision Production, Craft, and Repair	11,175	430	10,249	446	926	302
Mechanics and repairers	3,850	439	3,713	441	137	392
Supervisors	253	589	232	588	21	( )
Mechanics and repairers, except supervisors	3,597	428	3,481	431	116	375
Vehicle and mobile equipment mechanics and repairers	1,446	399	1,433	399	13	( )
Automobile mechanics	657	354	654	354	3	( )
Bus, truck, and stationary engine mechanics	292	408	291	409	1	( )
Aircraft engine mechanics	132	519	126	523	7	( )
Automobile body and related repairers	130	379	129	381	1	( )
Construction trades	3,691	422	3,622	423	69	335
Supervisors	437	551	428	558	9	( )
Construction trades, except supervisors	3,253	407	3,194	408	59	312

Source: *Employment and Earnings,* Bureau of Labor Statistics, U.S. Dept. of Labor, January 1990, pp. 222–231.

TABLE 5.H

1990 salary estimates. (Most of these salaries are averages, not entry level unless otherwise stated.)

ACCOUNTANT/AUDITOR

	Public	*Corporate* (Financial)
Manager, large firm	$ 50,000–$ 62,000*	$ 40,000–$ 52,000*
Entry, large firm	28,000– 33,000*	28,000– 33,000*

* Subtract .5% if not a CPA; add 10% for a graduate degree.
Source: *Robert Half's Salary Survey 1990.* Robert Half International, Inc.

ADVERTISING

Agencies

Chief Executive Officer	$105,300
Account Manager	35,600
Copywriter	41,100
Marketing Manager/Branch Manager	59,800
Advertising Manager	42,600

1989 average salaries. Source: *Adweek* magazine.

ARCHITECT

Entry level with B.A.	$ 20,000
Level IV: 2 yrs at Level III (Licensed)	36,780
Chief Architect	54,000

1989 median salaries. Source: Detrich Associates, Phoenixville, PA.

ATTORNEY

	Salary	*Compensation*
Chief Legal Officer	$164,270	$180,000
Managing Attorney	100,387	112,263
Regular Attorney	66,379	66,750
Legal Administrator	46,989	44,600
Recent graduate working in corporate law	42,020	42,250

1990 median salaries. Source: *Law Department Salary Survey,* Altman & Weil, Inc., Haverford, PA.

BANKER/FINANCIAL OFFICER

	By Bank Assets	
	($100M–$500M)	($500M–$1B)
Head of Lending	$ 65,000–$ 80,000	$ 78,000–$ 90,000
Commercial Lendor	30,000– 40,000	30,000– 40,000
Operations Officer/Branch Manager	25,000– 35,000	30,000– 40,000
Trust Officer	31,500– 40,000	33,000– 42,000

1990 median salaries. Source: *Robert Half's Salary Survey 1990.* Robert Half International, Inc.

BROADCASTING (TV & RADIO)

News Anchor	$ 52,284
Reporter	25,647
Operations Manager	42,988
Program Director	41,326

continued

News Director	51,150		
Sales Account Executive	42,757		

(Median salaries for stations nationwide; salaries at network affiliate and in major markets are much higher.) 1989 average salaries. Source: BFM/NAB 1989 Television Employee Compensation and Fringe Benefits Report. National Association of Broadcasters.

CHEMIST

(9 years after B.S.)	B.S.	M.S.	Ph.D.
Male	40,466	42,253	50,342
Female	37,131	40,859	48,186

Source: American Chemical Society. Copyright 1989.

COLLEGE AND UNIVERSITY STAFF

Administration

Chief Executive Officer, Institutional System	$ 91,400
Chief Executive Officer, Single Institution	87,000
Dean, Medicine	151,410
Dean, Law	109,472
Dean, Arts and Sciences; Dean, Business	66,000
Director, Admissions	41,974

Faculty	*Public*		*Private*	
	Women	Men	Women	Men
Professor	$ 48,490	$ 53,890	$ 51,820	$ 60,650
Associate Professor	38,340	40,920	38,700	42,140
Assistant Professor	31,830	34,620	31,860	35,390

Administration: 1989–90 mean salaries for all institutions. Source: 1989–90 Administrative Compensation Survey, published by the College and University Personnel Association. Faculty: 1989–90 weighted average salaries. Source: Academe, the bulletin of the American Association of University Professors.

COMPUTER SPECIALIST

Nonmanagement	2–3 YRS	4–6 YRS	7+ YRS
Systems Programmer (Software)	$ 33,000	$ 38,000	$ 43,000
Software Engineer	33,000	38,800	46,000
Database-Management Analyst	32,000	38,000	43,000

Management	
Management Information Systems Director/Vice President	$ 65,000
Programming Development Manager	58,000
Technical Services Manager	56,000

1990 median salaries. Source: 1990 Computer Salary Survey. Source EDP.

DENTIST

Oral Surgeon	$157,222
General Practitioner	80,938
Orthodontist	78,889

1989 mean net incomes of unincorporated dentists with solo practices. Source: Dental Management magazine. June 1990.

continued

ENGINEERING

Department Head	$121,537
Chief Engineer	87,038
Senior Engineer	50,882
Fully Competent Engineer	44,076
Engineer or Assistant Engineer	35,674
Junior Engineer	33,145

1990 median salaries. Source: Engineer Income and Salary Survey 1990. National Society of Professional Engineers.

FINANCIAL SERVICES

Institutional Broker	$165,730		
Retail Broker	78,711		
	Junior	*Intermediate*	*Senior*
Research Analyst	$ 39,384	$ 67,469	$111,555
Bonus	10,651	37,394	119,964
Corporate Financial Associate	56,699	63,642	83,165
Bonus	32,012	57,501	115,812
Government Securities Trader	35,451	48,194	81,834
Bonus	33,389	92,286	222,466
Block Trader	39,250	47,206	71,059
Bonus	16,985	24,466	117,255

Mean salaries as of May 1990. Source: Securities Industry Association.

GOVERNMENT

Level	Mean Salary	Includes
GS15	$ 70,316	Attorneys VI, Engineers VIII
GS14	58,363	Personnel Supervisors/Managers IV, Engineers VII, Chemists VII
GS13	49,300	Attorneys IV, Chief Accountants III
GS11	33,812	Personnel Supervisors/Managers
GS9	27,793	Attorneys, Systems Analysts
GS7	23,500	Public Accountants, Registered Nurses
GS5	18,699	Accountants, Auditors, Buyers, Computer Programmers
GS4	16,453	Computer Operators, Secretaries, Medical Machine Operators
GS3	14,284	Engineering Technicians, Personnel Clerks, Purchasing Clerks
GS1	10,947	General Clerks, Nursing Assistants

1990 mean salaries. Source: Pay Structure of the Federal Civil Service. U.S. Office of Personnel Management. March 31, 1990.

INSURANCE

Managing Actuary	$74,000
Manager, Auditing	56,868
Senior Auditor	36,503
Auditor	29,113
Account Manager, Group Pension Sales	55,827

continued

Account Manager, Client Services	45,583
Supervisor, Life Claims	36,578
Supervisor, Group Health Claims	31,974

1990 average salaries. Source: *1990 Management Compensation Survey.* Life Office Management Association.

NURSE

	Small Hospital	*Large Hospital*
Head Nurse (Medical/Surgical)	$29,200	$36,900
Nurse Practitioner	34,400	37,700

1989 average salaries. Source: Wyatt Data Services Company Survey. Copyright 1989.

PERSONNEL (Human Resources Development)—LABOR RELATIONS

Top Corp HRD Management Executive	$131,500
Employment and Recruiting Manager	50,000
Compensation Manager	57,900
Labor Relations Supervisor	54,100

1990 Human Resource Management Corporation Survey. **Source: William Mercer, Inc.**

PHYSICIAN

General Practitioner	$ 86,860
Surgery	105,000
Pediatrics	101,800
Ob/Gyn	102,700
Psychiatry	103,570

1989 average salaries. **Source: ECS, a Wyatt Data Service Company Survey.**

PUBLIC RELATIONS

| Corporate Executive or Senior Vice President (Top Pay) | $ 76,861 |
| Account Executive | 31,083 |

Published in **PR Journal,** June 1990. **Source:** PR Society of American, 1989.

SALES MANAGER

Manufacturing	$ 56,600
Banking/Financial	48,800
Retail, Wholesale Sales	52,700
Utilities	49,900
Service (Employment, business entertainment)	46,800

Source: Administrative Management Society, Trevose, PA

TEACHER

| Elementary/Secondary, starting | $ 20,476 |
| (average after 10 years) | 31,315 |

Survey and Analysis of Salary Trends 1990. Source: American Federation of Teachers.

WRITER

| Hollywood Screenwriter Major Film Studio | $ 40,000 |
| Independent TV Company | 32,000 |

1987 median earnings. Source: *The 1989 Hollywood Writers' Report* commissioned by the Writers' Guild.

All sources were contacted by *Working Woman* magazine for its Annual Salary Survey published January, 1991. Compiled by Richard S. Hollander, Catherine Romano, and Alexandra Siegel.

TABLE 5.I

Estimated average starting salaries. The following reflects how the average starting salaries have climbed during the 1980s, by degree.

Bachelor's Degrees	1980-81	1988-90
Engineering	$20,155	$30,081
Electrical engineering	NA	$36,215
Chemical engineering	NA	$35,039
Computer science	$18,018	$29,778
Physics	$17,169	$28,964
Chemistry	$16,587	$26,704
Accounting	$15,614	$25,051
Mathematics	$16,613	$23,968
Marketing, sales	$15,024	$22,951
Financial administration	$15,162	$22,829
General business administration	$14,672	$22,346
Communications	$13,851	$20,534
Social science	$12,970	$20,496
Hotel, restaurant management	$13,457	$19,751
Education	$12,672	$19,641
Agriculture & natural resources	$14,530	$19,360
Personnel administration	$14,827	$19,176
Liberal arts	$13,447	NA
Human ecology	$13,392	$18,466
Physical therapy	$29,364	NA
Nursing	NA	$28,206
Allied health	NA	$26,943
Marketing	NA	$25,447
Economics/Finance	NA	$25,158
Business Administration	NA	$23,318
Master's Degrees	**1980-81**	**1988-90**
M.B.A. with nontechnical B.A.	$21,672	$39,264
M.B.A. with technical B.S.	$22,632	$36,252
Engineering	$23,136	$35,532
Other technical fields	$20,748	$33,324
Other nontechnical fields	$21,360	$32,376
Accounting	$18,420	$31,284
Doctorates, other advanced degrees	**1980-81**	**1988-90**
M.D.s	$64,400	$96,100
D.D.S.s	$33,250	$60,410
J.D.s, LLB.s	NA	$35,814
Ph.D.s	$22,688	$34,608

NA = Not available.

Note: Figures are 1989 projections except for J.D.s, M.D.s and D.D.S.s, which are actual 1987 averages. Figures for D.D.S. salaries refer to general practitioners under the age of 35, and figures for M.D.s refer to doctors 36 years old and younger.

USN&WR–Basic data: Michigan State University. *Recruiting Trends.* 1980-81. 1988-90: Northwestern University. *Lindquist-Endicott Report* 1990. 1989: National Association for Law Placement, American Dental Association, American Medical Association's Center for Health Policy Research. College Placement Council.

TABLE 5.J
18 best bets.

JOB TITLE	TRAINING NEEDED	TOTAL EMPLOYED	GROWTH BY 1995	SALARY
Accountants/auditors	4 yrs. college	882,000	34.8%	$ 35,000
Computer operators	1-2 yrs. technical training	241,000	50.0	16,000
Computer programmers	varies: 1-2 yrs. technical training; 4 yrs. college	341,000	71.7	24,000
Computer service technicians	1-2 yrs. technical training	55,000	56.0	22,350
Computer systems analysts	4 yrs. college	254,000	68.7	28,500
Cosmetologists	6 mos.-1 yr. cosmetology school	524,000	29.0	16,800
Dietitians	4 yrs. college	48,000	26.0	24,800
Electrical and electronics technicians	2 yrs. technical training	404,000	50.0	23,000
Engineers	4-8 yrs. college	1,331,000	36.0	30,000
Food service and lodging managers	varies: on the job; technical training; 4 yrs. college	657,000	13.6	27,000
Lawyers	7 yrs. college	490,000	35.5	50,000
Medical assistants	1-2 yrs. technical training preferred	100,000	62.0	15,000
Paralegals	2-4 yrs. college	53,000	98.0	23,750
Physical therapists	4 yrs. college	58,000	42.0	23,000
Physicians and surgeons	8-10 yrs. college	476,000	23.0	100,000
Registered nurses	2-4 yrs. college or hospital-based program	1,377,000	32.8	20,000
Secretaries	varies: career or business school; junior college; 4 yrs. college	2,797,000	9.6	19,500
Teachers, kindergarten and elementary school	4 yrs. college	1,381,000	20.3	21,000

Source: *Changing Times*, 1986; *U.S. News & World Report*, September 17, 1990.

TABLE 5.K
Fastest-growing occupations requiring a high school diploma or less.

	PERCENT CHANGE 1984–95
Medical Assistants	62
Correction Officers	35
Cashiers	30
Cooks, Restaurant	30
Numerical Control Machine Tool Operators, Metal and Plastic	30
Plastic Molding Machine Operators	30
Combination Machine Tool Setters, Metal and Plastic	29
Nursing Aides, Orderlies, and Attendants	29
Social Welfare Service Aides	29
Switchboard Operators	29
Bartenders	28
Hosts and Hostesses, Restaurants, Lounges, and Coffee Shops	28
Photographic Processing Machine Operators	27
Photographic Process Workers, Precision	27
Amusement and Recreation Attendants	26

Source: U.S. Bureau of Labor Statistics, 1989.

TABLE 5.L
Fastest-growing occupations requiring a bachelor's degree.

	PERCENT CHANGE 1984–95
Computer Programmers*	72
Computer Systems Analysts*	69
Electrical and Electronics Engineers*	53
Physical Therapists	42
Securities and Financial Services Sales Workers	39
Lawyers	36
Accountants and Auditors	35
Mechanical Engineers	34
Public Relations Specialists	32
Occupational Therapists	31
Aeronautical and Astronautical Engineers	30
Chiropractors	29
Industrial Engineers	29
Architects	27
Optometrists	27

* Each of these top three will generate fewer than 100,000 new jobs between 1984 and 1995. Adding in replacement openings will raise total openings to 500,000–700,000.

Source: U.S. Bureau of Labor Statistics, 1989.

TABLE 5.M

Service workers are projected to have larger job gains than other major occupational groups.

	EMPLOYMENT GROWTH, 1984–95	
	Thousands	**Percent Distribution**
All Occupations	15,919	100.0
Service, Except Private Household	3,328	20.9
Professional	2,773	17.4
Executive, Administrative, and Managerial	2,488	15.6
Sales	2,220	13.9
Administrative Support, Including Clerical	1,783	11.2
Precision Production, Craft, and Repair	1,425	9.0
Operators, Fabricators, and Laborers	1,277	8.0
Technicians and Related Support	913	5.7
Farming, Forestry, and Fishing	–107	–.7
Private Household	–182	–1.1

Source: U.S. Bureau of Labor Statistics, 1989.

TABLE 5.N
Predicted new jobs for the year 2000.

WHAT JOBS SHOULD WE BE TRAINING STUDENTS FOR?

The Monthly Labor Review* projects strong growth in health care, business services, and professional services. Occupations expected to grow at the fastest rate are computer service technician, legal assistant, computer systems analyst, computer programmer, and computer operator. A very different list emerges in terms of numbers of jobs. Just forty occupations are expected to account for about half of all job openings between now and 1995. Leading this list are building custodian, cashier, secretary, general office clerk, and salesclerk. Kindergarten and elementary school teachers appear on the most-growth list for the first time in many years.

In an article entitled "Getting Ready for the Jobs of the Future" in *The Futurist,* June 1983, Melvin Cetron projected that the following new technician jobs would be opening up in the 1990s.

Automotive Fuel Cell (Battery) Technician (250,000 jobs)

Bionic-Medical Technician (200,000 jobs)

Computer-Assisted Design Technician (300,000 jobs)

Computer-Assisted Graphics Technician (15,000 jobs)

Computer-Assisted Manufacturing Specialist (300,000 jobs)

Computerized Axial Tomography, Technologist/Technician (45,000 jobs)

Computerized Vocational Training Technician (300,000 jobs)

Dialysis Technologist (30,000 jobs)

Energy Auditor (180,000 jobs)

Energy Technician (650,000 jobs)

Genetic Engineering Technician (250,000 jobs)

Geriatric Social Worker (700,000 jobs)

Hazardous Waste Management Technician (300,000 jobs)

Holographic Inspection Specialist (200,000 jobs)

Housing Rehabilitation Technician (500,000 jobs)

Industrial Laser Process Technician (600,000 jobs)

Industrial Robot Production Technician (800,000 jobs)

Materials Utilization Technician (400,000 jobs)

Nuclear Medicine Technologist (75,000 jobs)

On-Line Emergency Medical Technician (400,000 jobs)

Positron-Emission Tomography Technologist (165,000 jobs)

**Monthly Labor Review* of the U.S. Bureau of Labor Statistics is available from U.S. Bureau of Labor Statistics regional offices and the U.S. Government Printing Office.

Information Integration 6

You may be on the right track, but if you just sit there you'll get run over.

Will Rogers

LEARNING OBJECTIVES   AT THE END OF THE CHAPTER YOU WILL BE ABLE TO:

Demonstrate how your interests, values, and
skills can be grouped into job clusters

Familiarize yourself with printed sources of
information to use in further clarifying your
career choices

INVESTIGATING YOUR CAREER OPTIONS

By now you probably have one or several career areas in mind. This chapter will
help you get more specific. It will enable you to review, clarify, and integrate the
information that you've collected about your needs, desires, values, interests,
skills, and personal attributes. It is important to put these pieces together to
identify some specific occupational areas that you can begin to research.

This chapter is divided into two sections. The first section, Identifying Job
Clusters and Fields of Interests, illustrates how interests, values and skills can be
grouped into job categories or clusters so that you can begin to select specific
fields of interest to research.

The second section of this chapter, Written Information Sources, will introduce you to the written resources available in libraries and college career centers.
By using these references, you will have the information necessary to further
clarify and confirm your tentative career choices. In Chapter 7, you will be
encouraged to make a tentative career decision to use the remainder of the book
effectively.

In case you get stuck or blocked in listing specific occupations, try using the
guided fantasy (Exercise 6.6). Start by quickly reviewing all the written information that you've recorded (at the end of this chapter). Then close your eyes and
visualize yourself in your perfect career. "Mental visualization" can sometimes

focus your thoughts into areas that suit you perfectly. This technique helps you tap into and integrate the wealth of information, intuition, and wisdom that you already have about yourself. It is only natural to feel hesitant and even fearful about committing yourself to a career decision. These are the feelings that block you from making a decision and getting specific. Mental visualization is a technique to help your mind "wander" into a career choice.

In this chapter, the exercises are integrated into the text in order to help you gather information about your tentative career goal. This tentative goal will be confirmed or changed by additional information you will gather from written resources and information interviews (the latter will be discussed later in this book).

Objectives

After reading and completing Section I, you will:

1. Identify the job clusters and Holland Personality Types that interest you.
2. Match your interests to occupations using the Worker Trait Groups along with any other inventory you may have taken.
3. Identify and compare where your interests fall in the job clusters that are often used in career centers (U.S. Office of Career Education categories).

After reading and completing Section II, you will:

1. Improve your knowledge of written resources.
2. Refine your skills in gathering information about specific occupations and career-related opportunities by using library materials.
3. Confirm or revise your first impressions about your top career choices.

SECTION I—IDENTIFYING JOB CLUSTERS OR FIELDS OF INTEREST

Interest Inventories

Many interest inventories ask if you like or dislike a variety of subjects and then offer you a profile of results. The results group your preferences into fields, such as science, technology, service, arts, communications, or other clusters as found in the *Guide to Occupational Exploration (GOE)* Worker Trait Groups. We have included in the following pages an interest inventory (available from the U.S. Department of Labor) that groups results according to the clusters in the *GOE* Worker Trait Groups. Another commonly used system was developed by Professor John Holland and is used in several interest inventories. Holland's clusters are known as "personality

Holland's "environments"

types" or "environments" and are based on the following assumptions: (1) People express their personality through their vocational choices; (2) people are attracted to occupations that they feel will provide experiences suitable to their personality; (3) people who choose the same vocation have similar personalities, and they react to many situations in similar ways. The clusters are as follows.

REALISTIC (R) types like realistic jobs such as automobile mechanic, aircraft controller, surveyor, farmer, electrician. They like to work outdoors and to work with tools. They prefer to deal with things rather than with people. They are described as:

Doers

Conforming	Materialistic	Practical
Frank	Modest	Shy
Honest	Natural	Stable
Humble	Persistent	Thrifty

INVESTIGATIVE (I) types like investigative jobs such as biologist, chemist, physicist, anthropologist, geologist, medical technologist. They are task oriented and prefer to work alone. They enjoy solving abstract problems and understanding the physical world. They are described as:

Problem solvers

Analytical	Independent	Modest
Cautious	Intellectual	Precise
Critical	Introverted	Rational
Curious	Methodical	Reserved

ARTISTIC (A) types like artistic jobs such as composer, musician, stage director, writer, interior decorator, actor/actress. They like to work in artistic settings that offer opportunities for self-expression. They are described as:

Creators

Complicated	Idealistic	Independent
Disorderly	Imaginative	Intuitive
Emotional	Impractical	Nonconforming
Expressive	Impulsive	Original

SOCIAL (S) types like social jobs such as teacher, clergy, counselor, registered nurse, personnel director, speech therapist. They are sociable, responsible, and concerned with the welfare of others. They have little interest in machinery or physical exertion. They are described as:

Helpers

Convincing	Helpful	Responsible
Cooperative	Idealistic	Sociable
Friendly	Insightful	Tactful
Generous	Kind	Understanding

Persuaders ENTERPRISING (E) types like enterprising jobs such as salesperson, manager, business executive, television producer, sports promoter, buyer. They enjoy leading, speaking, and selling. They are impatient with precise work. They are described as:

Adventurous	Energetic	Self-confident
Ambitious	Impulsive	Sociable
Attention getting	Optimistic	Popular
Domineering	Pleasure seeking	

Organizers CONVENTIONAL (C) types like conventional jobs such as bookkeeper, stenographer, instrument assembler, banker, cost estimator, tax expert. They prefer highly ordered activities, both verbal and numerical, that characterize office work. They have little interest in artistic or physical skills. They are described as:

Careful	Efficient	Persistent
Conforming	Inhibited	Practical
Conscientious	Obedient	Self-controlled
Conservative	Orderly	Unimaginative

If you review Chapter 1, Exercise 1.7, you will notice the Adjective Checklist is based on these six types. Most interest inventories compare how your interests are similar to these six fields or types, and they usually provide a list of jobs that are related to these interests. If you are in a class that uses the Self-Directed Search or the Strong (previously Strong-Campbell) Interest Inventory, your instructor will explain which jobs are related to these six environments.

If you don't have access to separate inventories, the interest inventory developed by the U.S. Department of Labor (Exercise 6.1 below) should give you a general idea about how your interests relate to potential jobs.

6.1 INTEREST CHECKLIST*

It is important to all of us that we like our job; doing so will increase our chances of success.

This Interest Checklist may help you decide what kinds of work you would like to do. It lists activities that are found in a broad range of industries and occupations in the United States today.

Read each of the statements carefully. If you think you would "like" to do this kind of activity, write a check (✓) under the "L"; if you "don't like" the activity, make a check under the "D"; if you are not certain whether you would like the activity or not, make a check under the "?". After you have checked each activity, go back and double-check (✓✓) at least five activities that you think you would like most to do.

You may check an activity even if you do not have training or experience in it, if you think you would enjoy the work. Check the "?" *only* when you cannot decide whether you would like or dislike the activity or when you do not know what the activity is. There are no right or wrong answers. Check each activity according to how *you* feel about it.

*Source: U.S. Dept. of Labor, Employment and Training Administration, U.S. Employment Service 1979.

TABLE 6.A
Interest check list.

Read each of the items below and indicate how you feel about the activity described by placing a check ✓ under

| | L (Like) | | ? (Uncertain) | | | D (Dislike) | | |

		L	?	D			L	?	D
01.01	Write short stories or articles	—	—	—	02.03	Examine teeth and treat dental problems	—	—	—
	Edit work of writers	—	—	—		Diagnose and treat sick animals	—	—	—
	Write review of books or plays	—	—	—		Give medical treatment to people	—	—	—
01.02	Teach classes in oil painting	—	—	—		Prepare medicines according to prescription	—	—	—
	Carve figures of people or animals	—	—	—	02.04	Study blood samples using a microscope	—	—	—
	Design artwork for magazines	—	—	—		Test ore samples for gold or silver content	—	—	—
01.03	Direct plays	—	—	—		Manage a beef or dairy ranch	—	—	—
	Perform magic tricks in a theater	—	—	—	03.01	Operate a commercial fish farm	—	—	—
	Announce radio or television programs	—	—	—		Manage the use and development of forest lands	—	—	—
01.04	Conduct a symphony orchestra	—	—	—		Supervise farm workers	—	—	—
	Compose or arrange music	—	—	—	03.02	Supervise a logging crew	—	—	—
	Play a musical instrument	—	—	—		Supervise a park maintenance crew	—	—	—
01.05	Create routines for professional dancers	—	—	—		Train horses for racing	—	—	—
	Dance in a variety show	—	—	—	03.03	Feed and care for animals in a zoo	—	—	—
	Teach modern dance	—	—	—		Bathe and groom dogs	—	—	—
01.06	Restore damaged works of art	—	—	—		Pick vegetables on a farm	—	—	—
	Carve designs in wooden blocks for printing greeting cards	—	—	—	03.04	Catch fish as a member of a fishing crew	—	—	—
	Design and paint signs	—	—	—		Trim branches and limbs from trees	—	—	—
01.07	Analyze handwriting and appraise personality	—	—	—		Direct police activities	—	—	—
	Introduce acts in a circus	—	—	—	04.01	Issue tickets to speeding motorists	—	—	—
	Guess weight of people at a carnival	—	—	—		Enforce fish and game laws	—	—	—
01.08	Model clothing for customers	—	—	—		Guard inmates in a prison	—	—	—
	Pose for a fashion photographer	—	—	—	04.02	Guard money in an armored car	—	—	—
	Be a stand-in for a television star	—	—	—		Fight fires to protect life and property	—	—	—
	Develop chemical processes to solve technical problems	—	—	—		Plan and design roads and bridges	—	—	—
02.01	Analyze data on weather conditions	—	—	—	05.01	Design electrical equipment	—	—	—
	Develop methods to control air or water pollution	—	—	—		Plan construction of a water treatment plant	—	—	—
	Study causes of animal diseases	—	—	—		Direct operations of a power plant	—	—	—
02.02	Develop methods for growing better crops	—	—	—	05.02	Direct construction of buildings	—	—	—
	Develop new techniques to process foods	—	—	—		Supervise operations of a coal mine	—	—	—

Go on to next page

L (Like)			? (Uncertain)			D (Dislike)		
	L	?	D		L	?	D

05.03
- Survey land to determine boundaries _____ _____ _____
- Make drawings of equipment for technical manuals _____ _____ _____
- Operate a radio transmitter _____ _____ _____
- Design and draft master drawings of automobiles _____ _____ _____
- Direct air traffic from an airport control tower _____ _____ _____
- Conduct water pollution tests _____ _____ _____

05.04
- Pilot a commercial aircraft _____ _____ _____
- Operate a ferry boat _____ _____ _____
- Be captain of an oil tanker _____ _____ _____

05.05
- Build frame houses _____ _____ _____
- Make and repair dentures _____ _____ _____
- Prepare and cook food in a restaurant _____ _____ _____
- Plan, install, and repair electrical wiring _____ _____ _____
- Repair and overhaul automobiles _____ _____ _____
- Set up and operate printing equipment _____ _____ _____

05.06
- Operate generators at an electric plant _____ _____ _____
- Operate boilers to heat a building _____ _____ _____
- Operate water purification equipment _____ _____ _____

05.07
- Inspect fire-fighting equipment _____ _____ _____
- Inspect aircraft for mechanical safety _____ _____ _____
- Grade logs for size and quality _____ _____ _____

05.08
- Drive a tractor-trailer truck _____ _____ _____
- Operate a locomotive _____ _____ _____
- Operate a motorboat to carry passengers _____ _____ _____

05.09
- Prepare items for shipment and keep records _____ _____ _____
- Receive, store, and issue merchandise _____ _____ _____
- Record amount and kind of cargo on ships _____ _____ _____

05.10
- Develop film to produce negatives or prints _____ _____ _____
- Repair small electrical appliances _____ _____ _____
- Paint houses _____ _____ _____

05.11
- Operate a bulldozer to move earth _____ _____ _____
- Operate a crane to move materials _____ _____ _____
- Operate an oil drilling rig _____ _____ _____

05.12
- Recap automobile tires _____ _____ _____
- Operate a duplicating or copying machine _____ _____ _____
- Clean and maintain office buildings _____ _____ _____

06.01
- Set up and operate a lathe to cut and form metal _____ _____ _____
- Drill tiny holes in industrial diamonds _____ _____ _____
- Hand polish optical lenses _____ _____ _____

06.02
- Operate a drill press _____ _____ _____
- Operate a power saw in a woodworking factory _____ _____ _____
- Assemble refrigerators and stoves in a factory _____ _____ _____
- Operate a power sewing machine to make clothing _____ _____ _____
- Operate a dough-mixing machine for making bread _____ _____ _____
- Assemble electronic components _____ _____ _____

06.03
- Inspect bottles for defects _____ _____ _____
- Sort fruit according to size _____ _____ _____
- Test electronic parts before shipment _____ _____ _____

06.04
- Operating a grinding machine in a factory _____ _____ _____
- Work on a factory assembly line _____ _____ _____
- Operate a machine that fills containers _____ _____ _____
- Hand package materials and products _____ _____ _____
- Assemble parts to make venetian blinds _____ _____ _____
- Drive a forklift truck to move materials in a factory _____ _____ _____

07.01
- Take dictation, type, and handle business details _____ _____ _____
- Search records to verify land ownership _____ _____ _____
- Maintain records on real estate sales _____ _____ _____

07.02
- Maintain charge account records _____ _____ _____
- Keep time card records _____ _____ _____
- Compute average weekly production from daily records _____ _____ _____

Go on to next page

L (Like)	? (Uncertain)	D (Dislike)

	L	?	D			L	?	D
07.03 Receive and pay out money in a bank				**09.02** Serve meals and beverages to airline passengers				
Sell tickets at places of entertainment				Give haircuts				
Operate a cash register in a grocery store				Style, dye, and wave hair				
				Give scalp-conditioning treatments				
07.04 Answer questions at an information counter				**09.03** Drive a bus				
Operate a telephone switchboard				Drive a taxicab				
Interview persons wanting to open checking accounts				Teach automobile driving skills				
				09.04 Wait on tables in a restaurant				
07.05 Check typewritten material for errors				Park automobiles				
Compile and maintain employee records				Cash checks and give information to customers				
Deliver mail to homes and businesses				**09.05** Check passenger baggage				
				Help hotel guests get taxicabs				
07.06 Type letters and reports				Operate a carnival ride				
Operate a computer typewriter to send or receive information				**10.01** Plan and carry out religious activities				
Operate a billing machine to prepare customer bills				Work with juveniles on probation				
				Help people with personal or emotional problems				
07.07 File office correspondence				**10.02** Provide nursing care to hospital patients				
Locate and replace library books on shelves				Plan and give physical therapy treatment to patients				
Handstamp return addresses on envelopes				Teach the blind to read Braille				
08.01 Sell telephone and other communications equipment				**10.03** Give hearing tests				
Sell newspaper advertising space				Care for children in an institution				
Select and buy fruits and vegetables for resale				Prepare patients for examination by a physician				
08.02 Sell automobiles				**11.01** Plan and write computer programs to help solve scientific problems				
Demonstrate products at a trade exhibit				Plan collection and analysis of statistical data				
Sell articles at auction to highest bidder				Apply knowledge of statistics to set insurance rates				
08.03 Sell merchandise from door to door				**11.02** Teach courses in high school				
Sell candy and popcorn at sports events				Teach vocational education courses				
Persuade nightclub customers to pose for pictures				Manage the library program for a community				
09.01 Supervise activities of children at vacation camp				**11.03** Do research to develop new teaching methods				
Greet and seat customers in a restaurant				Do research to understand social problems				
				Review and analyze economic data				

Go on to next page

L (Like)			? (Uncertain)			D (Dislike)		
	L	?	D				L	?	D

11.04
Serve as a court judge ____ ____ ____
Advise clients on legal matters ____ ____ ____
Settle wage disputes between
labor and management ____ ____ ____

11.05
Manage a department of a large
company ____ ____ ____
Plan and direct work of a
government office ____ ____ ____
Purchase supplies and
equipment for a large firm ____ ____ ____

11.06
Examine financial records to
determine tax owed ____ ____ ____
Approve or disapprove requests
for bank loans ____ ____ ____
Buy and sell stocks and bonds
for clients ____ ____ ____

11.07
Direct administration of a large
hospital ____ ____ ____
Serve as principal of a school ____ ____ ____
Direct operations of a museum ____ ____ ____

11.08
Write news stories for
publication or broadcast ____ ____ ____
Broadcast news over radio or
television ____ ____ ____
Direct operations of a
newspaper ____ ____ ____

11.09
Plan advertising programs for
an organization ____ ____ ____
Direct fund raising for a
nonprofit organization ____ ____ ____
Lobby for or against proposed
legislation ____ ____ ____

11.10
Direct investigations to enforce
banking laws ____ ____ ____
Inspect work areas to detect
unsafe working conditions ____ ____ ____
Inspect cargo to enforce customs
laws ____ ____ ____

11.11
Manage a hotel or motel ____ ____ ____
Direct activities of a branch
office of an insurance company ____ ____ ____
Manage a grocery, clothing, or
other retail store ____ ____ ____

11.12
Investigate and settle insurance
claims ____ ____ ____
Obtain leases for outdoor
advertising sites ____ ____ ____
Sign entertainers to theater or
concert contracts ____ ____ ____

12.01
Manage a professional baseball
team ____ ____ ____
Referee sporting events ____ ____ ____
Drive in automobile races ____ ____ ____

12.02
Perform as a trapeze artist in a
circus ____ ____ ____
Perform stunts for movie or
television scenes ____ ____ ____
Perform juggling feats ____ ____ ____

NOW GO BACK AND DOUBLE-CHECK (✓ ✓) AT LEAST FIVE ACTIVITIES THAT YOU WOULD MOST LIKE TO DO

WORKER TRAIT GROUPS

The number beside each group of activities in the Interest Checklist refers to a Worker Trait Group. The Worker Trait Groups are broad, general categories of interest. The trait groups describe many of the occupational functions and factors related to these areas of interest: physical requirements, necessary academic skills, specific vocational preparation time and the like. These descriptions then lead to a listing of some possible occupations that fall within the interest categories and Worker Trait Groups. Look at the five activities that you would most like to do (the double checks), and identify them by the number on the side of the inventory. Find the corresponding number in the following list. This gives you some idea of the kinds of occupations that are of greatest interest to you.

More complete and detailed descriptions may be found in the *Guide to Occupational Exploration (GOE)* and McKnight's *Worker Trait Group Guide* (1980), which are found in college career centers. The letters to the side of the trait groups indicate the related Holland Types.

A   01. Artistic

01.01   Literary Arts
01.02   Visual Arts
01.03   Performing Arts: Drama
01.04   Performing Arts:
01.05   Performing Arts: Dance
01.06   Technical Art
01.07   Amusement
01.08   Modeling

I   02. Scientific

02.01   Physical Science
02.02   Life Science
02.03   Medical Science
02.04   Laboratory Technology

R   03. Nature

03.01   Managerial Work: Nature
03.02   General Supervision: Nature
03.03   Animal Training and Care
03.04   Elemental Work: Nature

R   04. Authority

04.01   Safety and Law Enforcement
04.02   Security Services

R   05. Mechanical

05.01   Engineering
05.02   Managerial Work: Mechanical
05.03   Engineering Technology
05.04   Air and Water Vehicle Operation
05.05   Craft Technology
05.06   Systems Operation
05.07   Quality Control

05.08   Land-Vehicle Operation
05.09   Materials Control
05.10   Skilled Hand & Machine Work
05.11   Equipment Operation
05.12   Elemental Work: Mechanical

R   06. Industrial

06.01   Production technology
06.02   Production Work
06.03   Production Control
06.04   Elemental Work: Industrial

C   07. Business Detail

07.01   Administrative Detail
07.02   Mathematical Detail
07.03   Financial Detail
07.04   Information Processing: Speaking
07.05   Information Processing: Records
07.06   Clerical Machine Operation
07.07   Clerical Handling

E   08. Persuasive

08.01   Sales Technology
08.02   General Sales
08.03   Vending

09. Accommodating

09.01   Hospitality Services
09.02   Barbering and Beauty Services
09.03   Passenger Services
09.04   Customer Services
09.05   Attendant Services

continued

S   10. Humanitarian

10.01   Social Services
10.02   Nursing and Therapy Services
10.03   Child and Adult Care

S/E 11. Social-Business

11.01   Mathematics and Statistics
11.02   Educational and Library Services
11.03   Social Research
11.04   Law
11.05   Business Administration
11.06   Finance

11.07   Services Administration
11.08   Communications
11.09   Promotion
11.10   Regulations Enforcement
11.11   Business Management
11.12   Contracts and Claims

R   12. Physical Performing

12.01   Sports
12.02   Physical Feats

Career Clusters

Career centers tend to be organized by the following career clusters (these clusters were originally created by the U.S. Office of Career Education):

☐ Agriculture and Home Economics
☐ Arts and Letters
☐ Business
☐ Education and Welfare
☐ Engineering and Architecture
☐ Government and Law
☐ Health
☐ Industry, Trade, and Service (includes apprenticeships)
☐ Science

If you are attending school and have chosen a major, you might research the cluster in which your major falls. Otherwise, select one area that seems to relate to your interests, values, and skills, and explore it.

The following exercise (6.2) will help you to examine the various clusters and to ensure that the ones you repeatedly select are your definite preferences.

6.2 CONFIRMING OCCUPATIONAL INTEREST AREAS

Circle the areas or words in 1, 2, and 3 that you find most interesting. If you had 2 hours to research careers, which area(s) would you select?

1.   What fields interest you?

   a.   *Social:* Do you like to work with people? Do you help others organize activities? Are you active in social events?

   b.   *Sales-Verbal:* Do you like to sell, convince, persuade, influence, lead? Do you like to talk, write, read?

c. *Mechanical:* Do you like to fix things? Do you use and repair machines, appliances, equipment? Do you like to make or build things?

d. *Scientific:* Are you curious about ideas and abstract processes? Do you like to experiment and solve problems?

e. *Clerical-Computational:* Do you like to keep things orderly? Do you like to keep records, type, be accurate?

f. *Artistic:* Do you like music, dance, art, literature, photography, decorating? Do you like to express yourself creatively?

2.   Occupational categories according to the six Holland Types.

a. *Realistic* (R) occupations include jobs in industry, trade, and service.

b. *Investigative* (I) occupations include jobs in the fields of science and technology.

c. *Artistic* (A) occupations include jobs in the fields of art, music, and literature.

d. *Social* (S) occupations include jobs in the fields of education and welfare.

e. *Enterprising* (E) occupations include jobs in sales and management.

f. *Conventional* (C) occupations include office and clerical jobs.

3.   Occupational fields—Job families or job clusters (letters relate to Holland Types described above).

a.   Agriculture and Home Economics—R&I

b.   Arts and Letters—A

c.   Business—C

d.   Education and Welfare—S

e.   Engineering and Architecture—R&I

f.   Government and Law—E&S

g.   Health—I&S

h.   Industry, Trade, and Service—R&C

i.   Science—I&R

SECTION II—WRITTEN INFORMATION SOURCES

Certain occupations are related to each other and naturally fall into clusters or groupings such as Holland's types, the U.S. Office of Career Education's Career Clusters, or the *GOE* Worker Trait Groups. To improve your skills in gathering job information, we will describe job clusters designed by the American College Testing Program (ACT), which divides job clusters by the educational preparation needed. Additionally, to help you choose your specific career direction, we will explain how to examine career paths and common organizational divisions in business and industry.

Occupational Classification System

Career clusters

The ACT has devised a useful system of organizing jobs into job clusters (Table 6.B). A valuable aspect of the ACT cluster system that differentiates it from the U.S. Office of Career Education's system is its reference to the educational preparation needed by cluster. Table 6.C provides you with a further breakdown of the business, sales, and management cluster, including educational preparation information. At some point you will have to decide how much education you will need to enter the career of your choice. This example allows you to see which jobs require a high school education and which require higher education.

TABLE 6.B
ACT Job Clusters

Business, Sales, and Management
Job Cluster

A. Promotion and Direct Contact Sales

Public relations workers, fashion models, travel agents, sales workers who visit customers (for example, real estate brokers, insurance agents, wholesalers, office supplies sales workers)

B. Management and Planning

Hotel, store, and company managers, bankers, executive secretaries, buyers, purchasing agents, small-business owners

C. Retail Sales and Services

Sales workers in stores and shops, auto salespersons, retail sales workers

Business Operations
Job Cluster

D. Clerical and Secretarial Work

Typists, file clerks, mail clerks, office messengers, receptionists, secretaries

E. Paying, Receiving, and Bookkeeping

Bank tellers, accountants, payroll clerks, grocery check-out clerks, ticket sellers, cashiers, hotel clerks

F. Office Machine Operation

Adding, billing, and bookkeeping machine operators, computer and data processing machine operators, telephone operators

G. Storage, Dispatching, and Delivery

Shipping and receiving clerks, stock clerks, truck and airplane dispatchers, delivery truck drivers, cab drivers, mail carriers

Technologies and Trades
Job Cluster

H. Human Services Crafts

Barbers, hairdressers, tailors, shoemakers, cooks, chefs, butchers, bakers

I. Repairing and Servicing Home and Office Equipment

Repairing and servicing—TV sets, appliances, typewriters, telephones, heating systems, photocopiers

J. Growing and Caring for Plants/Animals

Farmers, foresters, ranchers, gardeners, yard workers, groundskeepers, plant nursery workers, animal caretakers, pet shop attendants

K. Construction and Maintenance

Carpenters, electricians, painters, custodians (janitors), bricklayers, sheet metal workers, construction laborers (buildings, roads, pipelines, etc.)

L. Transport Equipment Operation

Long-haul truck and bus drivers, bulldozer operators, crane operators, forklift operators

continued

TABLE 6.B (continued)

M. Machine Operating, Servicing, and Repairing

Auto mechanics, machinists, printing press operators, sewing machine operators, service station attendants, laborers and machine operators in factories, mines, lumber camps, etc.

N. Engineering and Other Applied Technologies

(For science and medical technicians, see Job Families O and P.) Engineers and engineering technicians, draftsmen and draftswomen, pilots, surveyors, computer programmers

Natural, Social, and Medical Sciences Job Cluster

O. Natural Sciences and Mathematics

Biologists, chemists, lab technicians, physicists, geologists, statisticians, agricultural scientists, ecologists

P. Medicine and Medical Technologies

Dentists, doctors, veterinarians, medical technologists and lab workers, pharmacists, X-ray technicians, optometrists, dental hygienists, dietitians

Q. Social Sciences and Legal Services

Sociologists, lawyers, political scientists, historians, psychologists, home economists

Creative and Applied Arts Job Cluster

R. Creative Arts

Authors, concert singers, musicians, actresses and actors, dancers, artists

S. Applied Arts (Verbal)

Reporters, technical writers, interpreters, newscasters, newswriters, ad copy writers

T. Applied Arts (Visual)

Interior decorators, architects, commercial artists, photographers, fashion designers

U. Popular Entertainment

Nightclub entertainers, popular singers and musicians, disc jockeys, circus performers

Social, Health, and Personal Services Job Cluster

V. Education and Social Services

Teachers,* counselors, social workers, librarians, athletic coaches, recreation workers, clergymen and clergywomen

W. Nursing and Human Care

Child care aides, nurses, dental assistants, physical therapists, hospital attendants

X. Personal and Household Services

Waiters and waitresses, airline stewardesses and stewards, housekeepers, porters, car hops, butlers and maids

Y. Law Enforcement and Protective Services

Police officers; building, food, and postal inspectors; watchmen; plant guards; firefighters

*NOTE—Teachers: Students thinking about high school or college teaching should consider whether their main goal is *teaching students* (mark Job Family V) or *doing work or research in the subject area,* for example—chemistry (mark Job Family O), art (mark R or T), economics (mark Q).

There are more than 21,000 job titles in the world of work. This table illustrates how a sample of jobs can be clustered into related categories.

Source: Reprinted with permission from the American College Testing Program (American College Testing Program 1977).

TABLE 6.C
Business, sales and management cluster.

TYPICAL FORMAL PREPARATION

The left-facing arrow (←) for certain jobs means that workers may also enter that job with the type of preparation shown in the column at the left. The right-facing arrow (→) refers to the type of preparation shown in the column at the right.

	HIGH SCHOOL GRADUATION DESIRABLE	UP TO TWO YEARS OF PREPARATION BEYOND HIGH SCHOOL	THREE OR MORE YEARS OF PREPARATION BEYOND HIGH SCHOOL	RELATED HIGH SCHOOL COURSES
A. Promotion and direct contact sales	House-to-house salesperson Sample distributor Promotion worker Demonstrator Interviewer Survey worker Telephone solicitor Car rental clerk Sound truck operator	Fashion model Travel clerk or agent Radio–TV time salesperson → ← Auctioneer Encyclopedia salesperson → Bridal consultant Wholesale workers → Who visit customers who sell products such as computers, medical supplies, office machines, food products, etc.	Fashion coordinator ← Lobbyist ← Public relations worker ← Advertising worker ← Business agent ← Salesworker who sells services to customers; for example, stocks and bonds salesperson, insurance agent, account executive, real estate agent, investment analyst	General business Speech Bookkeeping General math Economics Distributive education programs such as sales, marketing, product information
B. Management and planning	See note below (*)	Credit manager → Buyer → Import-Export agent → Store or hotel manager → Sales manager → ← Automobile parts manager ← Apartment house manager Postmaster → City planning aide Funeral director ← Manager or owner of → small business such as skating rink, record shop, beauty shop, donut shop, etc.	Bank officer Assessor Controller Treasurer City manager Urban planner ← Purchasing agent Hospital administrator Personnel manager Athletic director	Business law Bookkeeping Speech Economics General business Distributive education programs such as business operation, product information
C. Retail sales and services	Concession attendant Newspaper carrier Will-call clerk Lost-and-found clerk Counter attendants in restaurants, dry cleaners, and snack bars Salesclerks and retail salesworkers → In stores selling products such as shoes, clothing, flowers, garden equipment, books, pets, etc.	← Sales clerks and retail salesworkers in stores selling such products as furniture, drapery, radios, televisions, gas and electric appliances, stereos, automobiles, sporting goods, hearing aids, photographic supplies, jewelry	See note below (*)	Economics General math General business Distributive education programs such as product information, sales, marketing

* Workers with this type of job preparation are sometimes employed in jobs listed in the other columns of this chart. Jobs in another column might have arrows pointing toward this column. Check with your counselor if you want to know about other jobs with this type of preparation. Remember that the jobs on these charts are listed under the type of preparation typical of most, but not all, workers entering the jobs.

Source: Reprinted by permission of American College Testing Program.

Career Paths

Sometimes a greater awareness of the job market can be gained by researching career paths or career ladders in a specific industry (Stair, 1980). Most career centers and libraries have books that outline career paths. Exhibit 6.A illustrates how jobs are related in the insurance field. Once you've assessed where you currently fit in, you can start preparing to move up the ladder. The insurance industry is recognized as a field in which people can obtain entry-level employment with a high school diploma and work their way up the ladder. If you are currently working, your immediate supervisor and the personnel department can provide information about routes for advancement; e.g., in-house workshops, institutes, community college associate degrees, and bachelor's degrees.

Career ladders lean to advancement

Common Organizational Divisions

Although the world of work includes a number of different broad fields, for example, business, education, government including the military, health care, and nonprofit agencies, all of these fields share certain common functional needs and have some common departmental organizations. As an example, all five of the fields mentioned above need the accounting functions of payroll computation and disbursement, budgeting, and servicing of accounts payable and receivable. Administration, finance, human resources, marketing and public relations, management information systems, and research and development are departmental functions common to almost all work fields. The following list explains the general functions of these and other departments in typical business-area operations; however, you will find identical or very similar departments performing very similar functions in the fields of education, government, nonprofit agencies, or health care.

If you have been concentrating on specific industries in your search for job possibilities, you can gain a fresh perspective by selecting functions that may be interesting to you and then researching jobs in those departments but within different industries.

- □ **Administration**   An organization's top executive officers and other managers; secretarial and word processing personnel are also included in this function.
- □ **Corporate Relations**   Responsible for advertising, public relations, community relations.
- □ **Distribution**   Sometimes called transportation department; oversees warehousing and shipping of the company's products.
- □ **Engineering**   Product design and modification; often oversees manufacturing of product (process engineers).
- □ **Finance**   Accounting functions, including payroll, budgets, accounts payable and receivable.

EXHIBIT 6.A
Sample career paths, using the insurance industry as an example.

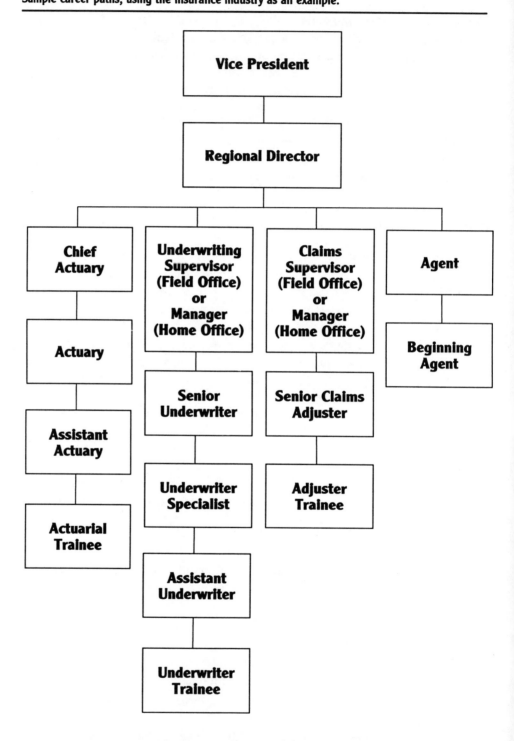

Organization charts listing career paths are sometimes found in personnel office files.

☐ **Human Resources Development** Sometimes called personnel or industrial relations; in charge of hiring, firing, training employees, administering equal employment law.

☐ **Management Information Systems** All tasks involving handling information, including computer operations and recordkeeping.

☐ **Marketing** Responsible for sales of a product or service and possibly market research.

☐ **Operations** The line workers who assemble the product; salesclerks; nurses in hospitals.

☐ **Production Management** Responsible for securing parts, supplies, inventory; also called purchasing or buying.

☐ **Quality Assurance** Responsible for maintaining a certain quality standard for the product manufactured.

☐ **Research and Development** Designs and develops new products.

☐ **Strategic Planning** Looks at long-range economic forecasts, plans strategies for company's advancement.

Written Information Sources for Researching Specific Jobs

Now that you have a clearer idea of the jobs that best suit your personality, it is necessary to research the actual requirements of the job. There are several ways to obtain job information. Basically you can either search through written materials in the library or contact people who already work in your area of interest. This section focuses on books and written materials, whereas Chapter 10 focuses on people and contacts. Your local library or college career development and placement center should be able to provide you with some or all of the following resources.

Federal Government Offices and Publications

Government
listings offer
opportunities

You may obtain employment with the federal government by applying for a position announcement. Printed job information is available at your Federal Job Information Center. Table 6.D lists the positions.

Did you know that the federal government hires some 1,500 people each day? No one in the federal government knows all the positions vacant on a particular day, week, or month, and you must contact the personnel office of each agency for a complete listing of vacancies in that agency. An alternative to going in person to each agency is using a private publication. The Federal Research Service, Inc. (a private firm), publishes announcements of 2,500 vacancies every two weeks in its *Federal Yellow Pages,* which also outlines the organization of all executive agencies and gives the names, addresses, and phone numbers of key officials. The *Congressional Yellow Book* is a similar volume on congressional agencies as well as personal and committee staff in the House and Senate. Two new resources for developing federal career plans are *The Federal Career Directory* and *Career Opportunities for the College Graduate in the Federal Government.* Both are available from the Government Printing Office order desk at (202) 783-3238 or at your nearest Office of Personnel Management.

Federal Job Information Centers may also have access to a national computerized job bank. This would be especially useful for people who want to know about job opportunities located some distance away.

U.S. Department of Labor Publications

The *Dictionary of Occupational Titles (DOT)* lists over 35,000 job titles and over 20,000 different occupations. This resource has been mentioned in previous chapters and will be referred to in Chapter 9 as a tool to use in writing a resume. It is especially useful because it lists specific tasks to be done on a job, e.g., COPY WRITER:

> *COPY WRITER*
>
> *Writes advertising copy for use by publication or broadcast media to promote sale of goods and services: Consults with sales media and marketing representatives to obtain information on product or service and discuss style and length of advertising copy. Obtains additional background and current development information through research and interview. Reviews advertising trends, consumer surveys, and other data regarding marketing of specific and related goods and services to formulate presentation approach. Writes preliminary draft of copy and sends to supervisor for approval. Corrects and revises copy as necessary. May write articles, bulletins, sales letters, speeches, and other related informative and promotional material.*

The *Occupational Outlook Handbook (OOH)* includes information on job descriptions, places of employment, training, educational requirements, and salary ranges. It is updated every other year and represents a national survey of occupations. Salary information should be compared with local salaries and local cost-of-living factors. For example, Los Angeles tends to pay $1000-$2000 more per year than many of the generalized estimates shown in the *OOH*.

TABLE 6.D
Federal employment.

Executive Departments	Federal Employment Positions Covered by Announcements	
Agriculture	Accountant	Manual Arts Therapist
Commerce	Aerospace Technologist	Mathematician
Defense	Air Traffic Controller	Medical Record Librarian
Education	Animal Husbandry	Metallurgist
Energy	Architect	Meteorologist
Health and Human Services	Astronomer	Microbiologist
Housing and Urban Development	Attorney	Nurse
Interior	Bacteriologist	Occupational Therapist
Justice	Biologist	Oceanographer
Labor	Cartographer	Patent Examiner
State	Chemist	Pest Controller
Transportation	Dietitian	Pharmacist
Treasury	Education Officer	Physicist
Veteran Affairs	Engineer	Plant Scientist
	Entomologist	Prison Administrator
	Equipment Specialist	Range Conservationist
	Estate Tax Examiner	Refuge Manager
	Forester	Social Worker
	Geodesist	Soil Conservationist
	Geophysicist	Special Agent
	Hospital Administrator	Speech Pathologist
	Hydrologist	Teacher
	Illustrator	Therapist
	Internal Revenue Agent	Urban Planner
	Landscape Architect	Veterinarian
	Librarian	

Major Independent Agencies

Environmental Protection Agency

Equal Employment Opportunity Commission

Federal Deposit Insurance Corporation

Federal Emergency Management Agency

General Services Administration

National Aeronautics and Space Administration

National Archives and Records Administration

Nuclear Regulatory Commission

Office of Personnel Management

Panama Canal Commission

Small Business Administration

Smithsonian Institution

Tennessee Valley Authority

U.S. Information Agency

U.S. International Development Cooperative Agency

U.S. Postal Service

Between editions of the *OOH*, the *Occupational Outlook Quarterly* provides updates of occupational projections as well as compensation ranges and cost-of-living comparisons throughout the United States.

The *Guide to Occupational Exploration (GOE)* provides detailed information about the interests, aptitudes, skills, and job activities of various occupational groups. The data in this publication are organized into 12 interest areas, 66 Worker Trait Groups, and 348 subgroupings. The Worker Trait Groups are listed after the Interest Inventory.

State and Local Government

**Local government
is a large
employer**

State and local governments hire the majority of people in public work. Local government alone hires over 50 percent of all public employees. Table 6.E lists the types of positions generally available. State personnel offices have applications, tests, job descriptions, and occupational outlook data for their state. For example, in California there is a *Guide to the Use of Labor Market Publications*. It is important to consider that it takes six to nine months to complete the application, test, interview, and hire process. This is not a resource for someone who needs immediate employment. Many college students start the application and test process during their senior year in college; this enables them to interview for jobs before they graduate.

Directories

**Let your fingers
do the
researching**

Information about a variety of enterprises, from foundations to corporations, can be found in directories. Directories list an employer's name and address, product, and geographic location, as well as other information, including size in terms of volume of sales, number of employees, and names of top-level executives. Don't forget to use your local telephone directory. The white pages list government agencies and departments, and the yellow pages list other places of employment. A phone call will get you specific information.

☐ *California Manufacturers Directory:* Lists companies by location and product with an additional section on companies that have import/export business.

☐ *Dun and Bradstreet Middle Market Directory:* Lists companies with assets between $500,000 and $1-million.

☐ *Dun and Bradstreet Million Dollar Directory:* Lists names and addresses of thousands of companies earning more than $1-million annually.

☐ *Encyclopedia of Associations:* Lists names of 15,000 associations in every field with names of officers, telephone numbers, and brief descriptions of orientations and activities.

☐ *Encyclopedia of Business Information Services:* Lists source materials on businesses.

☐ *Geographical Index:* Lists companies by cities and towns.

☐ *Guide to American Directories:* Describes 3,300 directories subdivided into 400 topical areas.

☐ *Poor's Register of Corporations, Directors, and Executives* Gives names and addresses of 260,000 leading executives by company and product.

☐ *Regional and community magazines:* Most large cities and metropolitan areas have community magazines that focus on business, industry, education, the arts, and politics; states and regions also have their own magazines.

☐ *Standard Directory of Advertisers:* Lists fifty major industries with names, addresses, and telephone numbers.

☐ *Standard Periodical Directory:* Describes 50,000 periodicals and directories.

☐ *Standard Rate and Data Business Publications Directory:* Lists names and addresses of thousands of trade publications.

☐ *State Directories:* Each state has a directory of trade and industry. If one is not in your library, contact the local or state chamber of commerce, or write to U.S. Chamber of Commerce, 1615 H Street, NW, Washington, DC 20006.

☐ *Thomas' Register of American Manufacturers:* Lists 100,000 manufacturers by location and product.

☐ *Who's Who in Commerce and Industry:* Gives names and biographical sketches of top executives.

☐ *World Trade Academy Press:* Lists U.S. firms in eighty-five countries. (The U.S. Embassy and U.S. Chamber of Commerce also list U.S. companies overseas.)

TABLE 6.E
State and local government departments and independent government organizations.

STATE	INDEPENDENT GOVERNMENT ORGANIZATIONS	LOCAL GOVERNMENT
Conservation	Board of Governors of the Federal Reserve System	Courts
Criminal Justice	Central Intelligence Agency	Elections
Education Programs	Energy Research and Development Administration	Financial Services
Elections	Federal Bureau of Investigation	Fire Protection
Employment Services	Foreign Service of the United States	Health
Financial Operations	International Monetary Fund	Law Enforcement

Newspapers

Check out all the newspapers in the geographical area in which you would be interested in working. Read the help-wanted section for openings as well as local wage and fringe benefit information. There may be a separate business section that advertises professional jobs. Read everything in terms of your own job target.

Want ads = Only 15% of job openings

Keep a file. Beware that only 15 percent of job openings are listed in want ads. Therefore, note other parts of the paper, such as articles that announce business expansion, personnel changes, and new ideas. Planning commission announcements usually mention new industrial plazas and the expected number of employees to be located in the plaza. Marriage announcements usually list the bride's and groom's occupations and may give you the name of an important executive of a firm that interests you. "Living Sections" may profile leaders in the community; gossip columns may suggest where to find trend setters.

Trade Journals

Almost every trade and profession has at least one regularly published journal. The business section of your library should have references. The following three resources are useful in tracking down particular trade journals: *Ulrich's International Periodical Directory*, the *Encyclopedia of Business Information Sources*, and the *Encyclopedia of Associations*. Use these trade journals to locate job ads and to familiarize yourself with the people, products, current trends, and specific vocabulary of a field.

Magazines

The *Reader's Guide to Periodicals,* available at any library, can be used both to locate names of magazines and to find out informative and useful titles of articles about any field you wish to research. Do you want to learn the latest in word processing careers, the outlook for engineers in the western United States, opportunities for liberal arts graduates? It's been covered in some magazine recently! Business magazines also provide profiles of both businesses and their executive officers, which is information you might use in comparing companies.

Useful Magazines for Business Information

Business Week
Entrepreneur
Executive Female
Forbes
Fortune
Inc.
Kiplinger's
Success
Wall Street Journal
Working Woman

Specialized Magazines for College Graduates

Black Collegian (Black Collegian Service Inc., New Orleans, LA)
Business World, a career magazine for college students (University Publications Inc., P.O. Box 1234, Rahway, NJ 07065)
College Placement Annual; check with college placement office (P.O. Box 2263, Bethlehem, PA 18001)
Business Week's Guide to Careers
Hispanic Times Magazine, P.O. Box 6368, Westlake Village, CA 91359
Women's Careers (Equal Opportunity Inc., Chicago, IL)

In-House Bulletins and Announcements

Personnel offices in virtually every business, agency, school, and hospital post jobs as they become available. Job posting best serves the people already employed at such places; however, some of the jobs may be open to anyone.

Computer Information Sources

Probably the largest resource on occupational information is the Career Information Service (C.I.S.; also known as EUREKA in California). This service has occupational information specific to the state in which it is located. Occupational information; job descriptions; locations for training, such as vocational schools and colleges; and financial aid information are included in the software. Another component of C.I.S., called QUEST, helps users identify the work characteristics that are common to certain occupations. A second program, S.I.G.I. (System of Interactive Guidance and Information), is designed to clarify your values and to match your values with occupations. A third program, GIS (Guidance Information System), acts as a source of national occupational information.

In many colleges, computers located in counselors' offices or in the career center use software to help students explore occupations related to their college major. Three thousand college majors can be scanned by a computer in 3–5 seconds to locate the ones that match a student's interests. Often this software includes a file with information on all two- and four-year colleges in the United States. This assists students in choosing a college, preparing for admission, and planning a course schedule.

The computer resources available will vary from location to location. Check with your local library, college career center, college adviser, and computer store to explore how computers can help you obtain information that will aid you in your career planning.

?? WRITTEN EXERCISES

The following written exercises serve to help you digest the contents of Section II. They can be completed by using the local library or college career center to explore some of the resources mentioned in this chapter. Exercise 6.3 requires that you investigate written resources utilizing the local library, college library, and local newspaper. Exercise 6.4 asks that you learn what your college career center and local state employment office or other employment offices might have available. Exercise 6.5 gives you the format by which you can gather the facts about your three top choices. Exercise 6.6 is a guided fantasy.

6.3 LIBRARY RESEARCH

a. What directories are most helpful to you now, and what do you need to know? Where are directories found? _____

_____

b. What are the names of three trade journals related to your field of interest? Where are they found?

1. _____

2. _____

3. _____

c. What are some of the current trends reflected in these journals?

_____

_____

_____

d. Name one professional association related to your field. Also list where and when local meetings are held. (What about the national conference: Can you attend or join as a student?) For example:

American Society of Women Accountants (ASWA)   Your field: _____
Local Contact: Joan Smith—phone 805-555-1213   Association: _____
Meeting time & location: 3rd Thursday of each month   Contact: _____
7 p.m. (dinner)   Meeting: _____
Colonial House Restaurant, Oxnard, Calif.   _____

e. Study the newspaper for three weeks, and make a scrapbook of articles that relate to your field. (Include want ads as well as feature articles or names of executives in your field whose names appeared anywhere in the paper.)

6.4 LOCAL RESOURCES

a. Investigate local career and placement centers. Ask whether they place people in your field or whether they can give you referrals.

b. Visit the state employment office as well as private employment agencies to find out how they place people and how long it might take to get a job.

6.5 GATHERING THE FACTS

Using the following outline in this exercise, select three jobs to research in a library or career center. You may select either three different jobs (e.g., teacher, social worker, personnel manager), three jobs that are related (e.g., lawyer, paralegal, legal secretary), or three that represent the same field but vary in degree of education or experience (e.g., marketing executive, graphic artist, display assistant).

Once you identify some interesting job titles, you need to gather the following information from a library or college career center.

1. Title of career

2. Salary

3. Hours

4. Benefits

5. Outlook (Will there be jobs in the future?)

6. Educational requirements
   Minimum training necessary:
   If college is necessary, what types of classes are available in the local area?

7. Schools or colleges offering the training

8. Personal requirements

9. Physical demands

10. Work description

11. Working conditions

12. Location

13. Opportunities for advancement

14. Related occupations
    No additional training needed:
    Some college needed:
    B.A. or B.S. degree needed:
    Other training (e.g., master's degree or special license):

15. Sources (may include written resources in the career center or names of local people working in this field):

16. After researching the specifics, are you still interested? How does this mesh with your vision of a life-style?

If after reading about three different careers you are still confused about how to choose one to pursue, work with exercise 6.6, a guided fantasy. Try to visualize yourself in each career. Which one feels most comfortable, most consistent with who you are?

Chapter 7 will help you narrow your focus and help you decide between different careers.

6.6 GUIDED FANTASY

Close your eyes, take a few deep breaths, and relax. Remove all feelings of tension from your body, and erase all previous thoughts and worries from your mind. . . .

Imagine that you are getting up on a typical workday about five years from now. You're sitting on the side of your bed trying to decide what kind of clothes you are going to wear. Take a moment and look over your wardrobe. . . . What type of clothing do you finally decide to wear? . . .

Imagine yourself getting ready for work Any thoughts about the day to come while you're getting ready? . . . What kind of feelings do you have as you look forward to your workday? . . . Do you feel excited? Bored? Apprehensive? . . . What gives you these feelings? . . .

It's time for breakfast now. Will you be sharing breakfast with someone, or will you be eating alone? . . .

You've completed your breakfast now and are headed out the door. Stop for a moment and look around your neighborhood What does it look like? . . . What does your home look like? . . . What thoughts and feelings do you experience as you look around? . . .

Fantasize now that you're heading toward work. How are you getting there?. . . How far is it? . . . What new feelings or thoughts are you experiencing? . . .

You're entering your work situation now. Pause for a bit and try to get a mental picture of it. Think about where it is and what it looks like. Will you be spending most of your time indoors or outdoors? . . . How many people will you be working with? . . .

You are going to your specific job now. Who is the first person you encounter? . . . What does he or she look like? . . . What is he or she wearing? . . . What do you say to him or her? . . .

Try to form an image of the particular tasks you perform on your job. Don't think about it as a specific job with a title such as nurse or accountant. Instead, think about what you are actually doing, such as working with your hands, adding figures, typing, talking to people, drawing, thinking, etc.

In your job, do you work primarily by yourself or mostly with others? . . . In your work with others, what do you do with them? . . . How old are the other people? . . . What do they look like?. . . How do you feel toward them? . . .

Where will you be going for lunch? . . . Will you be going with someone else? Whom? What will you talk about?. . .

How do the afternoon's activities differ from those of the morning?. . . How are you feeling as the day progresses?. . . Tired?. . . Alert?. . . Bored?. . . Excited?. . .

Your workday is coming to an end now. Has it been a satisfying day? . . . If so, what made it satisfying? . . . What about the day are you less happy about? . . . Will you be taking some of your work home with you? . . .

Part I

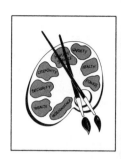

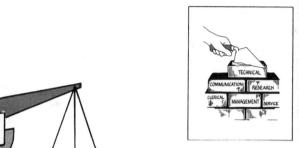

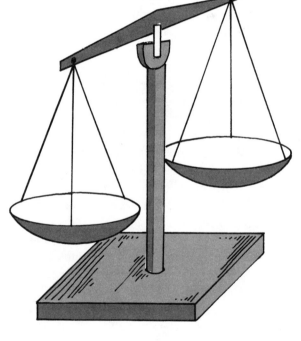

Part II

Sizing Up Your Options 7

LEARNING OBJECTIVES   AT THE END OF THE CHAPTER YOU WILL BE ABLE TO:

Identify and explore the decision-making process

Apply the principles of decision making to your career search

Identify psychological barriers to decision making and develop alternative strategies for success

Summarize insights gained from past chapters and identify potential occupations

Make tentative career/education/training choices

DECISION MAKING

Career decisions are the Olympic trials of your career fitness program. They give you an opportunity to integrate and test out all the components of your career fitness program—your attitudes, values, skills, interests, and biases. For most of us it is safe to assume that whatever decisions we make are the best we can make given the information, circumstances, and feelings of the moment. However, we can all improve our decision-making performance by examining some of the assumptions and strategies that other people have used in the decision-making process.

This chapter will review decision-making strategies that are potentially limiting and those that are potentially empowering and success oriented. The primary focus of this chapter is devoted to explaining a decision-making model that involves setting realistic goals. To bring about change, you must set specific goals with specific time frames. These must be realistic for you, and you must maintain an attitude that you are deserving and capable of reaching these goals.

In most of the previous chapters, exercises have been placed at the end of the chapter. This was done to help you solidify and integrate what you had read in the entire chapter. In this chapter on decision making, you will find some of the exercises included in the text as well as at the end. This is done so that you can turn immediately to the exercise and begin to test your aptitude for using various aspects of the decision-making model directly after they are presented in the chapter.

Overcoming Barriers to Decision Making

Attitude affects decisions

Because you are reading this book, you probably want to improve your life and increase your career options. Attitude has already been identified as an important internal factor in making decisions. Essentially, your ability to use your skills and potential is controlled by your attitude. Our attitudes are "gut level" feelings that indicate what we expect of ourselves. We must be aware of our attitudes and habits in order to enhance our daily effectiveness. A decision is accepted only if it is compatible with our current attitudes and self-concepts. Again, if we believe we can, we can!

Much of human behavior is based on attitudes that are limiting. People often make decisions that involve limited conscious involvement or personal responsibility, sometimes in an effort to simplify or accelerate the decision-making process. The following list suggests some of the ways people go about making decisions.

 ## Decision-Making Strategies

- □ *Planning:* "Weighing the facts." Consideration of values, objectives, necessary information, alternatives, and consequences. A rational approach with a balance between thinking and feeling.
- □ *Impulsive:* "Don't look before you leap." Little thought or examination; taking the first alternative.
- □ *Intuitive:* "It feels right." Automatic, preconscious choice based on "inner harmony."

☐ *Compliant:* "Anything you say, sir." Nonassertive; let someone else decide; follow someone else's plans.

☐ *Delaying:* "Cross that bridge later." Procrastination, avoidance, hoping someone or something will happen so that you won't have to make a decision. Taking a moratorium; postponing thought and action.

☐ *Fatalistic:* "It's all in the cards." What will be will be. Letting the environment decide; leaving it up to fate.

☐ *Agonizing:* "What if? I don't know what to do." Worrying that a decision will be the wrong one. Getting lost in all the data; getting overwhelmed by analyzing alternatives.

☐ *Paralytic:* "Can't face up to it." One step further from "what if"—complete indecision and fear. Accepting responsibility but being unable to approach it.

Read the following story to determine what decision-making strategies Art used.

An example of decision making

At the age of 21, Art decided to leave Southern California and go to Alaska to work on the pipeline. He left his friends and his easygoing sun-and-surf life-style behind to make his fortune. After two years in the fields, Art was promoted to lead supervisor and was earning close to $100,000 a year. He met and married a young woman who was earning $60,000 as an apprentice heavy-equipment operator. Although the climate was severe and the life-style pressures (intense work, intense alcohol, and drug parties) were not to their liking, they adjusted well, saved, invested, and made the best of the circumstances. After two successful years together, Art, along with many others, was laid off. The couple decided that he would go back to California to pursue his educational goals and she would stay on to finish her apprenticeship. Initially they were able to maintain their relationship through letters, phone calls, and frequent visits. After several months, she began to succumb to the "heavy party scene" that was part of the life-style in the labor camps, which were hundreds of miles from civilization. Despite all of Art's attempts to support and reinforce his wife to maintain her values and her commitment to him, Art felt his wife slipping away. They are currently involved in divorce proceedings.

Were Art's decisions appropriate to his circumstances? What would you have decided given similar circumstances? (Answer Exercise 7.1 at the end of this chapter.)

Choosing a career is a life development process. At different points of the process, different issues must be decided. Thus, planning (the first of the strategies listed above) is the key to reaching your goals. It implies gaining control of your life. You might glance back at the life line you completed in Chapter 1. Analyze which strategy you used most often. Then note the other strategies used. Planning and intuitive strategies are the only two positive strategies listed. The others contain a hint of fear: fear of failure, fear of imperfection, fear of rejection, fear of ridicule.

Getting unstuck, gaining control

When you feel "stuck" or unable to make a decision, try asking yourself the following questions.

1. What are my assumptions (attitudes)?

2. What are my feelings?

3. Why am I clinging to this behavior? (What are the rewards or payoffs?)

There is no "right" decision

1. *What are my assumptions?* Many of us assume that if we could only make the one right decision about the matter at hand, everything else would fall into place and we'd be happy. In fact, most decisions do not have such power over our lives. Decisions are not typically black and white in terms of their consequences. Decisions simply move you in one direction rather than another. Decisions open up some options and close off others. If you assume that most decisions can be changed or altered, that most decisions do not, in fact, signify life or death, then you will not be as hesitant to make a decision, act on it, assess the implications as they occur, and make adjustments (or new decisions) as necessary.

Avoid "either/or" ultimatums

2. *What are my feelings?* Some people create unnecessary stress about making decisions because they give themselves an "either/or" ultimatum. Neither option really feels right, but they panic and impulsively choose one just to ease the anxiety, or they become paralyzed and don't make any choice, allowing circumstances to decide for them. When you are feeling impulsive or paralyzed about making a decision, stop, take several deep breaths, and begin to generate some additional alternatives. A friend, counselor, or skilled listener can often help with this process. As you gain more information about your options, you will realize which decision is best for you.

Other people cry over spilled milk; in other words, they think back over past decisions and lament not having decided differently. This psychological stance wastes time and energy and can be destructive to self-image. When you begin to feel self-doubt or regret about past decisions, remind yourself that you made the best decision you could, given the time, circumstances, and information available.

Old habits can limit you

3. *Why am I clinging to this behavior?* If you acknowledge that you are causing this indecisiveness, it may generate a different point of view. For example, sometimes people cling to old, nonproductive behaviors because they are the safe ways to act; they don't have to deal with the unknown or the possibility of making mistakes (also known as taking risks). However, without risk there is no challenge and no growth.

Visualize yourself at your best

We find that it is difficult to change habits because such habits usually give us some form of positive payoff or reward. A person who enjoyed the status and praise gained by being an excellent and achieving student might find that equal achievement in a work environment alienates others on the job. You must recognize when the old, comfortable ways of doing things no longer give you the payoffs you once received.

Whether you consider yourself a risk taker or not, it is important to remember that we have all taken risks. What has been your greatest risk? What risk have you taken in the last two weeks? In its most basic sense, risk taking means moving from the safe and familiar to the unknown and scary. Most of us are fairly safe risk takers in that we want the odds to be at least 50-50 before we jump in. Yet millions of people play the lottery, start businesses, and get married even when the odds are clearly not in their favor. Why? Because along with the probability of success (the odds), people take risks based on the desirability of the anticipated outcome. As with the lottery, the probability is a million to one against winning; yet people continue to gamble because of the high desirability of the outcome— winning. You are in the best position to take a calculated risk when you assess both the probability and desirability of an outcome and weigh it against the other possible outcomes. Failure to consider outcomes in this fashion is the most common cause of unsuccessful risk taking. For example, most people are afraid to take the risk of changing careers or even changing jobs. They immediately think of the worst possible outcome: "I'll fail" or "I will never find another job if I quit this one." They don't ask themselves how probable is this to happen, how desirable is this outcome. The probability of their worries actually materializing is very low, and the likelihood of a negative outcome is very low. Many people paralyze themselves with this "worst possible consequence" thinking, they decide not to risk it, and they feel trapped. What they haven't done is generate other possible outcomes that are more probable and more desirable. What are some of these? A new job that is more energizing and financially rewarding, a new career with an opportunity to grow and develop, a chance to get retraining. The probability and desirability are, in fact, much higher, and therefore the decision is less risky. Yet many people miss opportunities because they fail to generate and assess all possible outcomes. This process often takes the assistance of another person who can help identify negative or limiting thinking as well as some realistic and positive outcomes.

Generate other possible outcomes

Decision-Making Model

Exhibit 7.A, "Choice, Not Chance: Decisions Are in Our Power," summarizes a suggested model for making informed decisions. The five steps necessary to make an informed decision are the following: defining your goal; knowing your alternatives; gathering information; considering the consequences (both probable and desirable); and defining your plan of action or the steps needed to achieve your goal.

Rational/Linear Decision Making

"Planning" is also known as the rational, or linear, approach to decision making. Decisions involve prediction. Prediction involves uncertainty. And uncertainty makes most people uncomfortable. Planning is one approach that decreases the amount of uncertainty and discomfort and increases your chances of achieving your designated goals.

Rational decision making uses the talents of the "left brain," which is analytical and logical and deals with deductive thinking. It ideally follows the sequential step-by-step procedure described in Exhibit 7.A.

- ☐ Define a goal.
- ☐ Assess alternatives.
- ☐ Research and gather information about each alternative.
- ☐ Predict or estimate the outcome and the chances of success with each alternative, and assess its desirability (the ideal that matches your values).
- ☐ Select the best choice and make a time line (plan of action) so that you will know when you've achieved your goal.

Intuitive Decision Making

Personality/temperament studies have estimated that up to 75 percent of the population prefer and use the "rational" decision-making approach. Studies also suggest, therefore, that 25 percent of the population prefers to use the strategy known as "intuitive." People who prefer the intuitive approach tend to be more creative and artistic. Intuitive decision makers look for the direction that "feels right." They use their "right brain," which thrives on imagination, creativity, and adapting to change spontaneously. They feel confined when asked to write out a step-by-step process.

When faced with career planning and job search, such individuals tend to research to the point at which they have several alternatives that they believe would satisfy them equally. They like to get a feel for the overall, global picture and then to decide where they fit in. So once they have researched several options, talked to people in the field, and walked around the work environment, they tend to know if it's right for them. Call it an "intuitive hunch," but it is based on the cumulative insight that fits their personality. Intuitive decision makers are most apt to say they were "lucky" in finding the right job, the right major, or the right college. However, their luck is actually "preparation meeting opportunity." Intuitive decision makers are most adept at finding opportunities. Thus, it is very important that such people be truly familiar with their values, interests, skills, and passions as they explore careers.

*Luck =
Preparation
meeting
opportunity*

Sometimes, the best approach for the intuitive decision maker is to fantasize and describe an ideal occupation or to be given examples of people who have an appealing career. Intuitives tend to be able to fantasize, daydream, and create verbal or written pictures of what they think is appealing. Thus, a "collage" of images depicting a career plan may be as useful as the written action plan created by a rational decision maker. True intuitive decision making may work for some people, but for the majority of us, a logical, step-by-step approach will yield better results.

EXHIBIT 7.A
Choice, not chance: Decisions are in our power.

1. **Define goal or objective**

   Can you change part of the problem into a definite goal?
   What do you want to accomplish by what date?
   Can you state your objective early?

2. **Assess alternatives**

   What are your alternatives or options?
   Are your alternative choices consistent with your important values?
   Can you summarize your important values in writing?
   What is a reasonable amount of time in which to accomplish your alternatives?

3. **Gather information**

   What do you know about your alternatives?
   What more do you need to know about your alternatives?
   What sources will help you gather more information about your alternatives?
   What sources will help you discover further alternatives?

4. **Assess outcomes or consequences**

   Probability:
      What is the probability of the success of each alternative?
      Are your highest values part of each alternative?
   Desirability:
      Can you eliminate the least desirable alternatives first?
      When you consider the best possible alternative, how much do you want it?
      What are you willing to give up in order to get what you want?

5. **Establish a plan of action**

   Weighing everything you now know about your decision, what is your plan
      of action?
   What dates will you start and complete your plan of action?
   Does your plan of action state a clear objective?
   Does your plan of action specify the steps necessary to achieve its objective?
   Does your plan of action specify the conditions necessary to achieve its
      objective?

Until you start your plan of action, you haven't really made a decision. So start now.
Make systematic decision making an adventure!

Goal Setting

Your goals and objectives are the vehicles that lead you to what you want to attain in your life. A goal must be distinguished from an objective.

Goals are broad statements of purpose. They are general and long range. They refer to an ongoing process, a challenge that's meant to stretch our limits. If you have trouble defining your goal, try listing the dissatisfactions and problems in your life that are bothering you. Now ask yourself what you can do about them. You have just defined a goal. Thus, if you have been analyzing yourself while reading each chapter, you may now recognize that your problem is that you are not working in a field that utilizes your values, interests, attitudes, and skills. The goal would be to find a career that best allows you to utilize your talents. (At this point, answer the questions in Exercises 7.2 and 7.3. Exercise 7.2 will help you identify and rank some long-term goals that have importance for you. Exercise 7.3 will help you assess how ready you are to begin working on your goals.)

Long-range career goal

Short-term career goal

A career that meshes with your values, interests, attitudes, and skills but requires five or more years of training could be considered a long-range career goal. The entry-level jobs that can prepare you for this career could be considered your short-term career goal. Thus, becoming a manager or executive would be the long-range career goal, whereas working toward a bachelor's degree in business management and/or becoming an assistant manager would be the short-term goal.

Objectives are the specific and practical steps used to accomplish goals. Objectives are short-term "baby steps." They are visible and measurable signposts that indicate where we are relative to reaching our goal.

The more specific our objectives are, the higher the probability that we will accomplish them. A specific objective has some indication of the action, conditions, and amount of time it will take to achieve it. Most of us have said, "I'm going to lose weight." That's an example of an unspecific objective. We know what the action is but we don't know how, when, and to what extent it will be accomplished. We rarely follow through with an unclear objective. Occasionally you will hear someone say, "I'm going to lose one pound this week by cutting out all bread, butter, and sweets from my diet." Now, that's an example of a specific objective with the action, losing weight, made specific by information on how much, when, and how it will be accomplished.

What will you give up to get what you want?

Four points should be remembered in setting goals. First, *consider what you are willing to give up* to get what you want. When most people make career changes, life in general changes for them. You may need to give up free time to take special courses. You may need to take a cut in pay (temporarily or permanently) to obtain better fringe benefits, security, and a potential chance for growth in another field, or you may need to give up being the old-timer and become the new kid on the block (and need to prove to others again that you are a competent worker).

Develop a time line

Second, *give yourself a realistic time line* to reach your goal. If you've incorporated baby steps (objectives) into your time line, you are more likely to achieve your goals. A time line is just a way of listing in chronological order all the objectives needed to accomplish your goal. For example:

Goal: To explore alternative careers to teaching by August of this year.
Objectives:

1. By February, I will start reading *The Career Fitness Program* and will finish it by June 1.
2. Each week I will complete the reading and respond to the exercises in one chapter.
3. I will allow myself three or four separate weeks to goof off.
4. By May, I will have identified the strategies needed to identify three jobs that utilize my talents.
5. By June, I will have attended one job search workshop conducted at the college.
6. By July, I will have researched three jobs by reading about them in a career center or local library and identifying three or more local people working in those jobs.
7. By August, I will have visited three people at their job.

Once you've written a time line, it's a good idea to show it to a close friend or counselor and to sign and date it as if it were a contract. In actuality, this can be considered a contract with yourself. At best, you will achieve your goals; at worst, you will need to revise them and alter the time line. At this point, complete Exercise 7.17 to reinforce your ability to formulate clear objectives.

Third, set your goals high. Of course, the goal still must be realistic enough to be achievable. You must believe you are deserving and capable. If your initial steps are specific, clear, and small enough, you will achieve them. The example stated earlier seeks to illustrate that each objective must have importance in itself and must help lead to the overall (larger) goal. **Set your goals high**

Finally, the fourth point about setting goals is quite simple indeed: Be sure to reward yourself after completing each objective and after reaching each goal. Some say that the mere accomplishment of the goal should be reward enough. However, most of us tend to be more motivated toward success when we have both internal and external reward systems. The internal reward is the feeling of success; the external reward is something outside of ourselves, e.g., crossing off the objective on the checklist, a grade on a paper, recognition from a group of friends, dinner at a special place, or a new outfit. How do you reward yourself when you attain an objective or reach a goal? **Reward yourself**

One way that you can reward yourself is by learning to manage your time so that you can create the best possibilities for success. Alan Lakein, a time management expert, gives some practical tips on how to set and rank goals and how to make the best use of your time. These remarks on rational decision making incorporate his suggestions. People who are successful in reaching their goals know how to manage their time. Try using the following tips from Lakein (Lakein, 1973). **Manage your time**

1. I build on successes.
2. I don't waste time regretting my failures.
3. I don't waste my time feeling guilty about what I don't do.
4. I remind myself that there is always enough time for the important things; if it is important, I'll make the time to do it.
5. I skim books quickly looking for ideas.
6. I've given up forever all "waiting time." If I have to wait, I consider it a "gift of time" to relax, plan, or do something I would not otherwise have done.
7. I keep my watch three minutes fast, to get a head start on the day.
8. I always plan and set priorities for the day first thing in the morning.
9. I keep a list of specific items to be done each day, arrange them in priority order, and then do my best to get the important things done as soon as possible.
10. I have confidence in my judgment of priorities, and I stick to them.
11. If I seem to procrastinate, I ask myself, "What am I avoiding?"
12. I concentrate on one thing at a time.
13. I set deadlines.
14. I try to listen actively in every discussion.
15. I make use of specialists to help me with special problems.
16. I recognize that inevitably some of my time will be spent on activities outside my control, and I don't fret about it.
17. I'M CONTINUALLY ASKING MYSELF, "WHAT IS THE BEST USE OF MY TIME RIGHT NOW?"

Moving Toward a Decision

At this point you should be focusing your thoughts regarding your values, interests, and skills toward either a college major or a few occupations that will express your career goals.

Deciding on a major   If you are thinking about a major, you will need to gather information about how jobs are related to college majors. The last chapter explained how to gather written information about careers; however, most libraries and career centers have books with titles such as *What to Do with a Major in. . . .* Whenever you meet people who have interesting jobs do your own research by asking them if they have a degree and in what major. Since most people have majored in subjects seemingly unrelated to their jobs, your big choice will be to decide whether you should choose a major closely related to an interesting area of work, for example, a business major to become a manager, or if you should select a major that seems most interesting to you at this time in your life, for example, communications or psychology. The fact of the matter is that either major can lead you to a successful business career.

If all of your personal assessment does not suggest a specific major, you may need to sample some introductory classes to see if they appeal to you; for example, you might want to take such a course as an introduction to interior design, an introduction to management, or an introduction to engineering. It is better to sample several majors during one or two semesters than to prematurely choose one only to find out after several semesters that you don't really like that line of study.

Remember, many occupations do not have a strong relationship to a specific college major. Employers are looking primarily for candidates who are well-rounded individuals and who have done well at college no matter what their major. Therefore, identify a major that interests you and in which you can excel and enjoy the learning experience.

Deciding on Training

If you are not interested in attending college but want to select a job that can best fulfill your career goals as soon as possible, then you have at least two issues to address: (1) job information and (2) training requirements. If the job information you have collected indicates that you are ready to enter the field, then you are also ready to read the chapter on job search strategy. If the job you want requires that you obtain further training, you will need to find out where to obtain it. Such information is listed in the written resources section of Chapter 6. Using personal contacts or the yellow pages, you can call people working in the field of your interest, who can direct you to credible training centers. Usually people who work in a field know which schools have the best reputation. Public community colleges, technical junior colleges, and adult schools also offer a variety of training programs. Be sure to compare the courses that you will be required to take with the preparation and skills necessary to perform the job. Making informed decisions is dependent upon acquiring accurate information.

SUMMARY

Successful career planning involves two processes related to goals: (1) defining your goals and (2) knowing how to reach them. The more completely you plan out your objectives, the more likely you will be to achieve your goals. The key to the process is overcoming the hurdle of negative thinking. You must temporarily block out the tendency to be critical. You must dare to put aside your anticipation of failure, your fears and excuses, and your past habits. You must create goals that energize you and take you beyond your past efforts.

Define your goals and know how to reach them

The following exercises are designed to help you become aware of steps in the decision-making process and to encourage you to set some career and life goals. For example, you will be asked to decide what you want to do by the end of the current year and then one year from now. This can mean acquiring new skills or improving current skills, moving toward career advancement or career change, or staying where you are. Don't forget, try to picture in your mind what you want in your work life (e.g., type of work, responsibility, surroundings, salary, management relationship), and then focus on the exact steps necessary to help you reach your goals. If you can't picture the necessary steps, you need to gather more information in order to make attainable career decisions (e.g., from people who have been in similar positions or from written materials about the field). Following the outline from the decision-making model, you need to choose from alternatives, select the one that has the best possibility of success for you, create a plan of action, set specific objectives, and take action. As you attain objectives that move you toward your goal, reassess your decisions. Constantly take in and process information about how you feel in moving toward this goal. Be honest with yourself. If you do not feel successful, enlist the help of a career guidance professional to assist you in formulating a goal that you can successfully attain.

?? WRITTEN EXERCISES

The written exercises that follow serve to increase your awareness about how you make decisions. Exercise 7.1 asks that you rank yourself on two dimensions of decision-making style. There are no right or wrong answers. This is a chance to become aware of your personal style of decision making. Exercises 7.2 and 7.3 review goal setting. Exercises 7.4–7.7 assess whether you actually do what you say is important to you. Exercises 7.8–7.15 should clarify other factors that can affect your decisions. Exercise 7.16 asks you to think about some alternatives to your current life choices. Exercise 7.17 indicates your ability to recognize and state clear objectives (there are right and wrong answers). Exercise 7.18 checks your ability to solve a problem creatively. Exercise 7.19 asks that you list your time savers. Exercise 7.20 asks you to choose a long-term goal along with clear short-term activities that will start you toward the long-term goal now. With Exercise 7.21 you will have an opportunity to summarize the insights you gained in working through the previous chapters by filling in exercise summaries for each of the previous six chapters. Exercises 7.22 and 7.23 help you integrate all of this information and set a career goal.

7.1 RANKING YOURSELF

On a scale of 1 to 10, rank yourself as a decision maker. Circle one number for each line.

cautious	1 2 3 4 5 6 7 8 9 10	risk taking
intuitive	1 2 3 4 5 6 7 8 9 10	logical
dependent	1 2 3 4 5 6 7 8 9 10	independent
influenced by others	1 2 3 4 5 6 7 8 9 10	self-motivated
feeling/emotional	1 2 3 4 5 6 7 8 9 10	rational
passive	1 2 3 4 5 6 7 8 9 10	active
quiet	1 2 3 4 5 6 7 8 9 10	assertive

7.2 REVIEWING GOAL SETTING

In Chapter 2, we discussed long-term goals. Now, let's try to become much more specific. List three specific long-term goals. Use additional paper if you have more than three.

1. _____

2. _____

3. _____

Let's assume you knew that you would not survive an earthquake six months from now. Would your short-term goals be any different? List at least three goals that relate to how you would live the next six months.

1. _____

2. _____

3. _____

Now you have a list of long-term and short-term goals. Deciding which ones are most important to you is the next step. This is called *setting priorities*. To do this, mark with the letter A those goals that are of most importance or value to you. Those of medium importance, mark with a B, and those of low importance, with a C. Let's look at the A's first. With more than one A goal, you will want to rank the A's, for example, A_1, A_2, A_3, with the A_1 goal being the most important to you at this time. Do the same for B- and C-marked goals. Now rank your long- and short-term A, B, and C goals.

Activities are those things we do to accomplish our objectives, which in turn get us closer to accomplishing our long-term goals. Take a separate sheet of paper for each of your three long-term goals, and list as many activities as you can think of to get you close to each goal. Don't question or judge the activities that come to mind. Just list whatever they are. After you've listed these activities, ask yourself this question: Am I willing to commit 5 minutes in the next week to working on this activity? If your answer is no, then draw a line through the activity. It's okay if you don't want to spend the time on the activity. You don't have to make excuses. Your decision to choose the activities you're willing to commit 5 minutes to will enable you to choose the high-priority tasks. Now rank (A_1, A_2, A_3, etc.) those activities you will do in the next week. Your activities are now organized. You're on your way toward meeting your goals. Make it an adventure and enjoy your accomplishments along the way.

7.3 WRITE A GOAL STATEMENT

Write a goal statement, describing either a short-term or a long-term goal.

_____

_____

Can you answer yes to the following questions about this goal?

a. Did I choose it personally?

b. Am I ready to make a written commitment to this goal?

c. Am I setting a deadline?

d. Is it within my control?

e. Have I thought through the consequences?

f. Is the goal based on my values?

g. Can I visualize it in considerable detail? (Is this goal specific?)

h. Will I work toward it?

i. Am I taking responsibility for this goal?

j. Is this goal measurable?

7.4 TASK IDENTIFICATION

In 5 minutes, on a separate piece of paper, write all the tasks that you need to do in the next week.

7.5 ONE YEAR TO LIVE

If you had only one year to live, which of the tasks listed would still be important to you?

7.6 MEETING YOUR NEEDS

How much of a week's work is spent reaching your own personal goals versus meeting others' needs?

7.7 YOUR ENERGIZERS

What percentage of your daily activities gives you energy? List your energizing activities.

7.8 RECENT DECISIONS

What are some decisions you have made recently?

7.9 PRIORITIES

Were some of these decisions more important than others? Why?

7.10   IRREVOCABLE DECISIONS

Give an example of a decision you made or might have to make that could be really difficult to change.

7.11   HARMFUL DECISIONS

Give an example of a decision that might be harmful to you or someone you care about in some way.

7.12   LIMITING DECISIONS

Give an example of a decision you could make that might keep you from doing something you want to do.

7.13   CONTINGENT DECISIONS

Give an example of a decision that would have an effect on other decisions.

7.14   VALUES

What value or values were important to you in making those decisions?

7.15   FACTORS ADVERSELY AFFECTING DECISIONS

The purpose of this exercise is both to investigate factors that may unfavorably influence decision making and to determine whether any patterns are evident. First, state on the lines provided below, three decisions you have made. Then, using the chart that follows, indicate which of the factors influenced you (and to what extent) in making each decision. To do this, use a " ✓ " to represent decision 1, an "X" for decision 2, and an "O" for decision 3. (Some sections of the chart may contain two or three symbols when you are done.)

Decision 1 (✓) _____

Decision 2 (X) _____

Decision 3 (O) _____

EXTERNAL FACTORS	SLIGHTLY PRESENT	MODERATELY PRESENT	VERY PRESENT
1. Family expectations			
2. Family responsibilities			
3. Cultural stereotypes			
4. Male/female stereotypes			
5. Other (specify)			
6. Other (specify)			

INTERNAL FACTORS	SLIGHTLY PRESENT	MODERATELY PRESENT	VERY PRESENT
1. Lack of self-confidence			
2. Fear of change			
3. Fear of making a wrong decision			
4. Fear of failure			
5. Fear of ridicule			
6. Other (specify)			

After filling in the chart, look for patterns that may appear:

a. Do you experience more internal or external factors as obstacles to making satisfying decisions?

b. If a particular factor is Very Present only once, but another factor is Slightly Present in two or possibly all three of your decisions, which of the two factors do you think is more significant in affecting your decision making?

7.16 WHAT IF . . .

If you are currently in college, suppose you lost all sources of support and had to leave school. List three things you could do.

a. _____

b. _____

c. _____

How satisfying would these alternatives be to you?

Suppose you had one year to remain in college before losing the support. With one year to prepare, what would you do?

a. What alternatives might you choose?

b. What information would you need about your chosen alternatives?

c. What action would you take?

d. How satisfying would your one-year plan be?

7.17 SPECIFIC/NONSPECIFIC OBJECTIVES

The following statements are objectives. Read each objective and decide, in your own judgment, if the objective is specific or nonspecific. These are statements anyone may make; they don't necessarily apply to you. Suppose someone's standing in front of you in a line making each of these statements. With that in mind, please mark each objective as "S" (specific) or "N" (nonspecific) to the left of the statement.

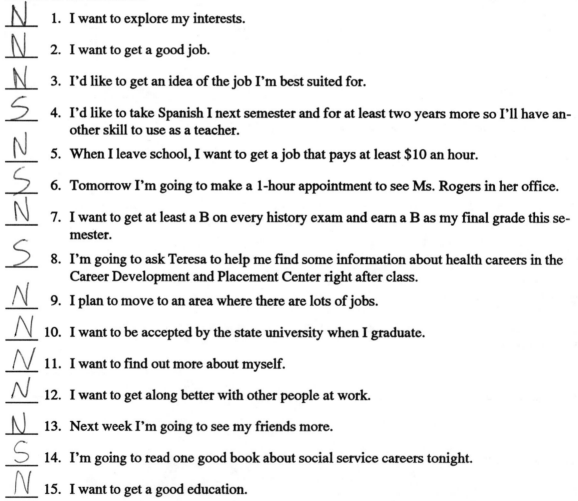

N   1. I want to explore my interests.

N   2. I want to get a good job.

N   3. I'd like to get an idea of the job I'm best suited for.

S   4. I'd like to take Spanish I next semester and for at least two years more so I'll have another skill to use as a teacher.

N   5. When I leave school, I want to get a job that pays at least $10 an hour.

S   6. Tomorrow I'm going to make a 1-hour appointment to see Ms. Rogers in her office.

N   7. I want to get at least a B on every history exam and earn a B as my final grade this semester.

S   8. I'm going to ask Teresa to help me find some information about health careers in the Career Development and Placement Center right after class.

N   9. I plan to move to an area where there are lots of jobs.

N   10. I want to be accepted by the state university when I graduate.

N   11. I want to find out more about myself.

N   12. I want to get along better with other people at work.

N   13. Next week I'm going to see my friends more.

S   14. I'm going to read one good book about social service careers tonight.

N   15. I want to get a good education.

(See page 168 for answers.)

If you are still confused about which career to focus on, start with the one that is most easily attainable, and work through your job search strategy in Part II of this book, using that easily attainable career as your focal point. Once you understand the job search process, you can use it to explore additional career goals.

Congratulations! You are now in the process of exercising your options. You have identified a possible career goal and are about to begin Part II of this book, Job Search Strategy. This will help you further clarify your goals and move you toward the career of your choice. Remember that the clarification process is ongoing throughout your career search. Every new contact and piece of information open new possibilities and options.

Answers to exercise 7.17:

1. N	6. S	11. N
2. N	7. N	12. N
3. N	8. S	13. N
4. S	9. N	14. S
5. N	10. N	15. N

Answers to exercise 7.18

a.

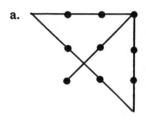

(The directions did not indicate that the lines needed to stay *inside* the dots outline.)

b.   SIX

(The directions did not mandate a "straight line.")

PART TWO

Job Search Strategy— Maintaining Momentum

Part I

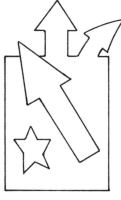

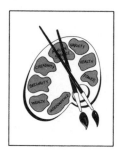

Part II

Focusing in on Your Target **8**

A wise man will make more opportunities than he finds.
Sir Francis Bacon

LEARNING OBJECTIVES AT THE END OF THE CHAPTER YOU WILL BE ABLE TO:

Identify the components of a successful job search

Differentiate between the traditional and nontraditional approaches to the job search

Begin the process of searching for a job

Congratulations! You have just completed the qualifying trials for the Olympics! In other words, you have finished the personal assessment portion of your career fitness program. You have reviewed and analyzed your potentials, your interests, and your values, and you have tentatively selected some career choices. They are tentative because you may find reason to alter your initial decisions as you continue to gather further information. Just as adjustments occur in a physical fitness program based on your body's responses, so must adjustments occur in your career fitness program based on your "gut-level" responses.

The next step is to begin to design your job search strategy, which composes the second part of the career-planning process. Job search strategy involves the long-term process of acquiring the training, background, and experience needed to be competitive in the job market. Simultaneously, you need to begin to identify potential employers for your skills and to develop a resume that reflects your background and your particular career goal. Finally, you need to learn how to present yourself in the best light in job interviews.

The winning edge

173

Your job search must be conducted consistently over a period of time. The U.S. Department of Labor has estimated that it can take nine months of searching to obtain the job that's best suited to your desires. Regardless of how certain or tentative you are currently feeling about your career alternatives, you must have a specific occupation in mind in order to benefit from the remainder of this book. The goal is to choose one of the occupations you have been considering by the end of this chapter, and keep it in mind as you read and work through the following chapters.

A job search requires focus

The rest of this chapter will provide you with the information and skills to enable you to gain control over a competitive job market. In other words, you will learn many techniques to put yourself in the right place at the right time and to present yourself as the best candidate for your desired job. The underlying and most important concept, however, is focusing on what you want. Without this concentration you run the risk of being swayed into random opportunities and jobs that don't live up to your expectations. *Focusing* means that all new information should be evaluated and compared with your needs, values, interests, and skills. Remember, the first job you are seeking should not be considered an end in itself. It is one job on the way to several more that will compose your total career. As the dictionary defines *career,* it is a "pursuit of consecutive progressive achievement in public, professional, or business life." Additionally, career experts predict that the average worker can expect to make three or four career changes in a lifetime.

This approach assumes that you have identified a job objective for which you feel *100 percent enthusiasm,* that you will go after it with *100 percent determination,* and that you will interview for it with *100 percent of your heart.* This approach charges you with the responsibility to make things happen!

DESIGNING A COMPREHENSIVE JOB SEARCH STRATEGY

A comprehensive job search strategy involves much more than just researching to decide what your ideal job is or simply discovering areas of employment where you could expect to find such jobs. It encourages you, once having made these basic decisions, to assertively locate and actually become employed in your ideal job. A comprehensive job search strategy stimulates you to consider a variety of aspects associated with attaining your ideal job goal, such as whether you are likely to find your job in the geographical area where you live or want to live and what sorts of activities and experiences will better qualify you for your career objectives. Equally important, job search strategy helps you to select and become involved in volunteer and entry-level activities that are the vital first steps toward your ultimate job or career goal. You can't always start right out in your ideal job, but, guided by job search strategy, you can almost always start out in jobs and activities that will lead to your goals. Assuming that you have adequate skills and background and that you have identified a job for which you are 100 percent enthusiastic, the following approach is for you.

The assertive approach

1. Be 100 percent committed to your job objective.
2. Compare the tasks and responsibilities required in your chosen job at different companies and organizations.
3. Get involved in voluntary and entry-level jobs related to your ultimate goal.
4. Identify the hidden job market through personal contacts.
5. Utilize both traditional and nontraditional search resources.
6. Utilize professional assistance, if necessary.
7. Conduct information interviews with people who are in a position to hire you. Approach all contacts with enthusiasm and sincerity and send thank-you letters to all contacts.
8. Network: Let everyone know you are looking for a job (friends, neighbors, dentists, etc.).
9. Identify the needs of the organization. If the exact position you would like is not available, your task is to define a problem within the organization that you can help to solve with your own unique skills.
10. Convince an employer that you have the skills the employer needs.

First you must commit yourself, make a contract with yourself, that you will complete all the tasks necessary to get the job. Next, you must become totally informed about the tasks and responsibilities of the job you are seeking. Much of this information can be gained from the written materials previously cited. Additionally, you will need to amplify the written information by making personal contacts with insiders.

Once you have identified your ideal job situation, an important part of your job search strategy is to investigate associated activities that may be indispensable first steps toward your goal. Such activities may be temporary or volunteer or entry-level jobs in your chosen field. They can be very important in adding to your experience and making you a better candidate for your preferred job. For example, a teacher who wanted to move into the advertising business took a job as a secretary in the executive suite of an advertising agency in New York. Of course, he had brushed up on his typing and office skills to get this entry-level job, but he didn't plan to remain at that level for long. Being male, he had high visibility as a secretary. But even more important, he kept his eyes and ears open for ways that he could contribute to the efficiency of the business. Within six months he had learned enough about the advertising business to interview at a competing firm and become assistant to the president.

One final suggestion before you conduct further research. You may find that your ideal job is years of education and experience away from you or that you don't have the dedication or talent to make it in your ideal field. If so, possibly you can be just as happy if you work in some job *related* to the career of your dreams. For example, behind every president of the United States there are advisers, speech writers, guards, secretaries, chefs, press representatives, and chauffeurs. Behind every rock musician there are disc jockeys, public relations representatives, recording technicians, piano tuners, album cover designers, sound editors, cutting designers, concert coordinators, costume and makeup artists, and background musicians.

There is some merit to the idea that if you stay around the field, constantly adding to your experience, you may be at the right place at the right time and get the job of your dreams. Every understudy in a play or musical has the chance to become a star some day!

The Traditional Job Search

To increase your chances of getting the job of your choice, consider using traditional job search strategy as well as the nontraditional strategy described thus far. There are three prime sources in the traditional search strategy: (1) want ads, (2) direct mail, and (3) employment agencies.

Want Ads

Want ads are found in local newspapers, newspapers from your desired geographical area, trade journals, a supplement from the *Wall Street Journal,* and association magazines. Some newspapers have business sections with separate "Help Wanted" sections. You should become familiar with the specialized meanings of words and phrases used in these ads. Other job listings are also to be found in the state employment department, county and city personnel offices, placement centers, private employment offices, and the personnel office of each individual organization.

Understanding Want-Ad Headings

Much important information is given in these headings. Here are a few hints to help you understand the terminology.

- ☐ HELP WANTED—Employment Agencies
  You, the job seeker, will usually pay the agency fee.
- ☐ HELP WANTED—Fee-Paid Jobs
  The employer pays the fee.
- ☐ HELP WANTED—Canvassers–Solicitors
  May be salary or commission (no sales, no pay!).
- ☐ HELP WANTED—Commissions, Bonus, etc.
  Some jobs listed here pay a salary.
  Some jobs may require an investment by you.
  "Draw" is an advance against future commission earnings.
  "Guarantee" generally means you will receive a certain amount of money from the company even though you may make no sales.
- ☐ DOMESTIC HELP WANTED—Work to be done in the employer's home.
  Compensation may be salary or room and board only.

Answering ads promptly and efficiently

☐ CLERK TYPIST

Type 40 wpm, familiar with office practices, telephone procedures, high school graduate. Apply at Personnel Dept. HOME STORES, Ventura.

Apply in person. No phone number in the ad.

☐ GROCERY STORE

In Oxnard—In need of box boy experienced in store pricing and display methods. $5.50 per hour. Call Sunday 9:00 am to noon or Monday 9:00 am to 4:00 pm, 555-4215.

Call (at time indicated) for an appointment.

☐ PET STORE ASSISTANT

Neat, ambitious young man or woman to assist in pet care, sales, and store cleanup. 2000 S. Victor Rd., Moorpark. 555-2152

A good idea to call first for an appointment. NEVER inquire about salary over the phone!

☐ OFFICE TRAINEE

Young and aggressive high school graduate to learn financial firm office procedures. Must type and be capable of using standard office calculating machines and copying equipment. Send resume to Box 24 W, Blade Tribune.

This is a blind ad, since you don't know who placed it. Send your letter and resume to the box number, in care of the newspaper. Use "Dear Sir/Madam" or "To whom it may concern" as a salutation. It is not advisable to use "Dear Sir" only because those reviewing the resume may be female.

It has been found that, in larger cities, regularly reviewing the want ads over several months can lead you to meaningful employment leads. Although it has been estimated that only 15 percent of jobs are found through want ads, there are thousands of ads in large newspapers. You can increase your chances of obtaining a job by applying for different job titles in the want ads. People with accounting degrees may be eligible for Junior Accountant, Management Trainee, Accounts Payable, and Stock Broker, in addition to Accountant.

Another way to increase your chances of finding a good job involves mixing the traditional search in the want ads with your active accumulation of information about companies. When you see in the paper a job opening at a firm that you've already visited, you should have a contact in that company to call and ask for more information about the opening. You may find that the want ad is written with absolute qualifications but that the specific department will accept alternative experiences in lieu of some of the specific qualifications. Only people who have personal contacts would know such information.

Only 15–20% of all available jobs appear in the want ads

Direct Mail

If you fail to find your ideal job in the want ads, you may try two kinds of direct mailings: (1) to all companies in a desired geographical area or (2) to specific organizations or companies most likely to need your qualifications.

Direct mailing can be expensive, depending on how many companies you include in your search. The prime objective is to find job openings. Once the opening is found, you should follow up with a telephone call to arrange for an interview. Since the return rate is very low, it is a good idea to enclose a stamped, self-addressed postcard. The postcard can include check-off statements such as "sorry, no openings"; "opening possible within one month"; "opening available, please contact: _____," as well as blank spaces for the name, address, and telephone number of the organization.

Although this approach sounds sophisticated, you may get fewer than 10 replies per 100 mailed. Traditionally, people have gotten only 15 replies out of 1,000 mailings! You are more likely to get more replies if you have targeted an audience. In order to target the audience, either you need to have read about the company or organization (in any of the resources previously mentioned) to discover that the company is expanding in your specialty area, or you need to have heard through a contact that the company needs your expertise. Annual reports available through the company, a stockbroker, or your local library are excellent sources for identifying companies with potential openings. For example, recently Bank of America indicated in its annual report that it would be expanding its human resources development function at its headquarters in San Francisco. Upon seeing that information, an interested job seeker called the headquarters Staff Development Department, sent her resume to the person identified by the switchboard as the head of the department, and got an interview!

Employment Agencies

Before you register with an agency, check carefully its fees, the types of positions it handles, and its reputation. There is some controversy over the merits of a system that makes a profit by simply placing you on a job with limited concern for your satisfaction. However, there are good agencies that are very concerned about matching people with a job that suits them.

Employment Agencies—Temporary

These provide excellent ways to get back into the work force or to test the climate in a variety of companies. The jobs available are primarily clerical or entry-level computer jobs unless the temporary employment agency specializes in a field like accounting or nursing. Some agencies place people part-time; some place people for short-term assignments. The only drawback is that you are under contract to the temporary agency and cannot be hired by the employer using you, for a specified period of time.

The Nontraditional Job Search

The nontraditional approach to job hunting involves putting yourself in the right place at the right time. It involves strategies that assist you to find openings in your target area before the openings are publicly announced. In situations when you do not appear to be the ideal candidate, the nontraditional approach will assist you in getting noticed and getting an interview.

Many times it is best to try this approach while you are still employed, because potential employers tend to defer unemployed inquirers to the personnel office. This approach requires you to have a specific field and job objective in mind. Let's say you selected real estate development, having majored in business administration specializing in finance and real estate. An important decision would concern whether you want to work for a commercial bank, private developer, government appraisal office or government bureau of land development, or a related association that employs people to interact with the government. Following is an example:

Susan was an assistant to a county supervisor and just happened to find many of her assignments related to land development. While finishing work toward her bachelor's degree in business (attending college after work hours), she increasingly represented her supervisor when land developers appealed to the Board of Supervisors for zoning and code changes. When her supervisor did not run for reelection, Susan was hired as a director for the business-industry association to lobby the county for the industrialization of farmland. Within a few years, Susan became a consultant to land developers and interacted with her present boss, who hired her into his prospering real estate development firm as vice president of government relations.

Even while working in an entry-level job, Susan met people working in the field of her interest, real estate. As an assistant to the county supervisor, she met people in government, associations, and private industry. Susan maintained high visibility by speaking at community events, representing the supervisor when the supervisor was absent, and joining related organizations and community clubs. When she wanted to make a job change, she had already identified and made contact with the types of places and people with whom she wanted to work. She had contacts who were insiders and could recommend her for jobs even before such jobs were announced. But even more important, she had discovered the "hidden job market." She knew the needs of the business-industry association and could tell its people how her skills and contacts could benefit them. She was able to sell herself. She knew she had skills and contacts with government that could enhance her present employer's expansive plans. She was hired because she was able to describe the job she wanted to do in the firm and because her ideal job meshed with the vision of the president of the company. She actually created her current position.

High visibility helps

Networking opens up the hidden job market

Volunteering

Xiao-ying found she was tired of going to college. She was beginning work in a master's degree program in anthropology when she realized that studying native tribes in the wilds of Africa would not enable her to make the personal contribution to other people's lives that she felt necessary for her own job satisfaction. With the help of a career counselor at the local YWCA and by talking with people working in her ideal setting, she became aware that working in a family-planning clinic would best suit her personal needs. So she volunteered for one year in such a clinic and, in addition, conducted some studies on pregnancy and childbirth. Within the next year she had a full-time job in the Education Department of Planned Parenthood.

The importance of getting job-related experience cannot be overestimated. As can be seen in Xiao-ying's story she got volunteer experience to supplement her previous training. Many people have negative images of volunteering. They think volunteering means doing paperwork or "go-fer" work. However, you can create meaningful volunteer positions for yourself rather than taking whatever is available. To optimize your chances for obtaining such useful experience, go through a community voluntary action center, a college volunteer services office (sometimes part of the college placement office), or a college cooperative education office. There may even be some opportunities at your local college, called *internships*. Internships are usually restricted to students who have studied in the subject area of the internship. For example, a history major or a political science major may be most eligible for an internship in local or state government; a graphic arts, public relations, English, or communications major may be most eligible for an internship in an advertising agency. Internship students are generally closely supervised by college professors to ensure that they gain educational learning experiences as well as provide free labor for employers.

Apprenticeships and internships create opportunities

An even more intense volunteer experience for those who have the time and resources may be through the Peace Corps, VISTA, or the UN Volunteers. Such volunteer work requires a commitment of one to three years and provides room, board, benefits (including government service experience), and a living allowance. A good resource for identifying volunteer programs is *Invest Yourself* (obtainable from Susan Angus, P.O. Box 117, New York, NY 10019, $3), which lists names of most of the volunteer organizations in the United States.

Volunteering adds visibility and experience to your job search. However, volunteering does not relate only to jobs. Think about becoming a student member of a professional association. Student membership usually offers all the same benefits of regular membership but costs half as much. Once in an organization, *volunteer* for committees and leadership positions, and gain visibility and recognition. The people in these organizations will soon be your peers. This is also an excellent method of make contacts for both jobs and letters of recommendation.

As a graduate student in counseling, Felipe wanted to focus on human resources development and training in industry. So he joined the American Soci-

ety for Training and Development (ASTD). He volunteered to chair the student recruitment subcommittee and joined the Career Development Special Interest Group. Two years later, when interviewing for a job as assistant to a director of training, he found he knew people who had worked with the director, was able to learn about the firm from former employees who were ASTD members, and made an excellent impression in his interview.

Starting Your Own Business

One final way to get a job, of course, is to start your own business. Career centers and libraries have useful information on starting a business. The Small Business Administration provides seminars and low-cost materials for local communities. A group called SCORE (Service Corps of Retired Executives) is composed of local retired businesspeople who lead low-cost workshops and offer free technical advice. Contact your local chamber of commerce for information about these resources. Also, a local community college or the extension/continuing education division of a local university may offer courses in small-business administration or marketing. If colleges offer such courses, they may also have students available who get college credit by giving free technical assistance to new small businesses.

Become your own boss

Many people find that owning their own business feels more secure than working for another person. Often people don't take the chance until they have been forced out of an old job. Stories abound in the *Wall Street Journal* of ex-factory supervisors who started their own sales or repair or remodeling business. Then there are others who wait until retirement and use their savings to launch a new business.

Ely Callaway invested in land and planted a vineyard three years prior to retirement from Burlington Industries. He now has a flourishing winery. Mr. Callaway also has expanded into several other small business operations, which serve to satisfy him during his "retirement years."

Job Search While Unemployed

Although experts say that it is best to look for a job while you are still employed, not everyone will be in that position. If you are unemployed and currently seeking employment, it is necessary to discipline yourself by sticking to a daily job search schedule. Otherwise, your best intentions may be thwarted by procrastination. Procrastination can then turn into the paralysis described in Chapter 7 concerning poor decision-making strategies.

Discipline helps to avoid procrastination

If you are unemployed, a disciplined job search must be created to replace the work schedule that is suddenly missing in your life. When unemployed, you will be more productive if you begin the day as if you were going to work. Get dressed, have breakfast, and begin the day with a few hours of phone calls. Identify employers who can use your skills. Be aware that sheer numbers of phone calls must be made. The greater the number of calls made, the greater the chances of getting an interview.

Since you can expect that many calls will result in responses such as "No one can speak to you today" or "Sorry, we have no openings," your daily routine must include predictably positive activities. For instance, plan a portion of your day to be spent at the library researching job information, a portion looking for leads, and a portion filling out job applications. Another important part of the day should include being with supportive people, for example, attending networking and association meetings (local newspapers have business sections that announce weekly association meetings), joining friends for lunch, and enjoying recreation. Keeping active will reenergize you and keep you visible to those who might be able to refer you to a job. Somewhere in your present circle of friends, coworkers, and acquaintances is someone who can link you with your next job. This process is further discussed under the topic of networking.

The final part of your day should be saved to return phone calls, redraft letters, revise your resume and cover letter, and/or write specific thank-you letters to people you have met. Planning and preparation can make the critical difference in turning telephone calls into interviews and interviews into job offers. (See Chapter 10 for interviewing techniques.)

Many unemployed people use the services of their state employment agency. (The unemployment office usually requires you to contact a minimum number of employers each week or month in order to remain eligible to collect unemployment insurance.) However, the state employment agency also offers workshops on job search strategy, assistance in writing a resume, and a computerized job bank. Some offices also conduct targeted group meetings for workers in designated fields, for example, aerospace, automotive, banking, executive, manufacturing, and the like. Support groups may meet on a regular basis to offer both encouragement and leads.

College Seniors

Those readers who will be or are seniors in college or who have recently graduated from a college should be in regular contact with their school's career planning and placement office. Obtain the schedule of employers who will be recruiting on campus, and sign up for interviews. If the career planning and placement office offers job search workshops covering resume writing, interviewing techniques, or videotaped interview practice, sign up for these services as well. Find out what services are available, and take advantage of all of these resources.

Action Plan and Organization

Lastly, effective job search strategy requires that you master the skill of goal setting and action planning. This means that you set objectives such as those indicated in the following suggestions and designate specific times to complete each one.

1. Schedule planning time.
2. Maintain a list of activities to get done; for example, write up a weekly calendar and enter each item per day or hour. A pocket calendar may be sufficient for one person whereas a notebook may work better for another. (See Exhibit 8.B.)
3. Start a notebook with one section for contacts' names, addresses, and phone numbers and another section for notes about different companies.
4. Review your progress by checking off completed activities.

Effective job search requires clerical and organizational skills. Every week you will need to update specific names, obtain more exact titles, and confirm addresses. This information can be kept in a file box or in your home computer. (See Exhibit 8.B.) Being able to retrieve at a moment's notice the information you have been collecting can make the difference between getting your resume in the mail today or tomorrow (which may be a day too late). The fastest way to update a resume is to have it stored in your own home computer or on a floppy disk for use in a personal computer at school, at a local copy center, or at a friend's home.

It is advisable to have a designated area in your home for all of your career information. Keeping careful records of all contacts made, applications submitted, resumes sent, interviews held, and correspondence will make your job search much more effective and logistically far easier.

Information Interviewing and Networking

Survey after survey on job hunting confirms a basic fact about job search strategy, namely, that the one best way to find out about a job and to get a job is through people. Now that you have reviewed the written sources of information on jobs, you are ready to begin conducting information interviews. These interviews help you to develop contacts. Your contacts become a source of knowledgeable and experienced people in a field. Your contacts form your network of people who will keep you informed and connected to possible job openings. Once you gain some experience through information interviewing and networking, you will be ready to master the techniques involved in interviewing for a job.

Cultivating contacts

Information Interviewing—The Purpose

Information interviewing involves learning to identify people who are doing what you want to be doing and asking them questions related to their current job. Information interviewing serves several purposes. It helps you further refine your knowledge and understanding of the field you are exploring. It enables you to develop social skills related to your feeling comfortable and knowledgeable while you are being interviewed. Information interviewing creates the setting to develop contacts. These contacts are often helpful to your specific job search. The people you interview may themselves be in a position to hire someone like you for a job or they may simply hear about a job opening and pass the information on to you. Remember that your specific purpose in information interviewing is *not* to look for a job but to confirm your information about the field and to develop contacts that may be helpful in the future. When doing an *information interview, you are asking* the questions. When doing a *job interview, you are being asked* the questions.

Information interviewing is based on the premise that you have already read much of the written information related to a specific type of job and now need confirmation from people who are already doing that job. You want them to tell you basically what the field is really like before you commit your time, effort, and finances to the pursuit of a new field. Or, if you are already in the field, you want to know if one employer's environment would be more appealing to you than another's. Other information you can gain from such an interview involves much more than simply confirming the skills needed and the salary range. On one hand, you can find out if you like the people, if the atmosphere feels comfortable, if the people are friendly and helpful. On the other hand, you may find that no one has time to talk to you, or they keep you waiting, or they let the telephone constantly interrupt your interview, or they work in noisy cubicles. This information is available only through an on-site visit. Thus the overt goal of information interviewing is to collect information, but the covert goal is to make contacts and determine whether you have made an appropriate match between your personal needs and your career goal.

Information Interviewing—The Process

Identify people who are doing what you would like to do

The first step in the process of information interviewing is to identify people who are working in the fields that you've decided are interesting to you. It's especially helpful if you know a relative, friend, or neighbor involved in the field or at least someone who can refer you to a potential contact; it's always easier to talk to someone whose name is familiar. The hardest step is making the first phone call to a stranger or, even worse, a strange firm and asking for the name of a person doing that interesting job! Strangers will be receptive to talking to you if you demonstrate the following characteristics.

1. Indicate that you are seeking personalized information about their field before you decide to enter it.
2. Confirm the person's job title by asking.
3. Sound enthusiastic and delighted to have reached this person.
4. Refer to the research you've already reviewed about this field or company.

5. Ask if you can have a specific amount of time to interview this person (e.g., 15–30 minutes).

6. Try to arrange the interview at the person's work site, so you can determine firsthand how it might feel to work there.

7. Keep to your agreed-upon time frame.

8. Thank your interviewee, and follow up with a thank-you note.

As we noted, it's tough making that first phone call. Here are some specific examples of telephone "lead-ins" to help you get started. Remember to identify yourself, state your purpose, and ask for an appointment with the appropriate person. This straightforward approach is generally effective.
Example:

> *Hello, Mr. Jones, I am Diane Smith from Moorpark College. I'm doing some research in the field of houseplant maintenance service, and I'd like to stop by at your convenience to ask you a few questions. When may I stop by? Is Thursday at 2 p.m. all right?*

or:

> *Hello, this is . . . and the other day in a conversation with . . . your name was mentioned and . . . suggested that I should meet you. So I am calling to find out when you might have a few minutes to see me. Would it be more convenient for me to come by in the morning or afternoon?*

or:

> *Hello . . . this is . . . This morning I talked to . . . about the opportunities in . . . and he spoke very highly of you. I'm calling to find out when you might have a few minutes to see me. Would it be convenient to meet with you in the morning or afternoon?*

Information Interviewing Outline

Now that you have located your contacts and made definite appointments to interview them, you need to consider in specific detail the most efficient ways and the best questions to ask to gain the maximum useful information as quickly and pleasantly as possible. Remember, you will be talking to busy people with many demands on their time; they will expect you to be, and it's to your advantage to be, as businesslike as possible. Finally, having made the telephone contact and set the date to meet, you should send a note confirming the information interview appointment.

Here is a framework to help you design your interview for an information field survey. You may think you already have answers to some of the questions, but personal interviews should help to fill out details and possibly fill in some blanks in your information that you don't realize are there. Try to choose your questions from the general categories of type of business, position classifications, position descriptions, work environment, benefits, and entrance requirements, as follows:

☐ **Type of Business**

What are the services, products, or functions of the organization?

Who utilizes the organization's services or products?

Who are the competitors in this field?

What sets the company apart or distinguishes it from others in the same industry?

What are the projections for future development or new directions?

☐ **Position Classifications**

In each major corporate division, what types of positions are available?

What are the qualifications for entry-level and experienced positions? (Consider education, skills, abilities, etc.)

☐ **Position Descriptions**

What duties and responsibilities are performed in the area in which you are interested?

What are some examples of projects currently under way and problems currently being solved?

What is a typical day like?

What contacts would there be (personal, data, machine, other) with other organizations?

☐ **Work Environment**

What type of physical localities are involved: outdoors, indoors, travel? Is there pressure? Routine? Variety? How much supervision is there? Do flexible work schedules exist? Is overtime typical or atypical?

☐ **Benefits**

How does compensation compare to education and ability level?

What are the opportunities for advancement, promotions, or lateral mobility?

What opportunities are available for advanced training, on-the-job training, or academic course work? Is there a tuition reimbursement plan?

What other benefits are available? Possible benefits might include:

Medical/Dental insurance	Profit sharing
Life, disability insurance	Retirement
Vacations, holidays	Preretirement planning
Expenses for moving, travel	Employee assistance programs (counseling for work-related problems)
Outplacement	
Recreation, personal health services	Job placement assistance (for a spouse)
Child care facilities	

☐ **Entrance Requirements**

What suggestions do you have for an individual wishing to enter this field of employment?

What other companies might employ individuals to perform this type of work? Could you refer me to someone else for more information about opportunities in this field?

Moving from a general categorical framework to more specific detail, here is a sample list of typical questions you might ask in your information interviews.

Be prepared for questions

1. What do you like most about your job and why?
2. What do you like least about your job and why?
3. How did you decide to get into this field, and what steps did you take to enter the field?
4. What training would you recommend for someone who wanted to enter this field now?
5. What is the salary range for a person in this field? Entry-level to top salary?
6. What personal qualities do you feel are most important in your work and why?
7. What are the tasks you do in a typical workday? Would you describe them?
8. What types of stress do you experience on the job?
9. What types of people survive and do well in this field?
10. What are the opportunities for promotion?
11. Is this field expanding? Taking any new directions?
12. What related occupations might I investigate?
13. Can you give me the names of three other people who share your enthusiasm for this kind of work? How can I contact them?

Exhibit 8.A presents an outline/guide/review format that lists all the points we have discussed about information interviewing. You should use this form as a guide in preparing for each interview you attend.

If you approach professionals in your field of interest from a research point of view and *not* as if you want a job, they will often be happy to talk with you. Even the busiest executives will often find time for you. If one person doesn't have time, ask to be referred to another professional in the field. It is the secretary's job to protect the boss from distractions. When a secretary asks, "What is this call regarding?" you might respond, "This is a personal call," or "Mrs. Smith is expecting my call," or "May I talk to Jane," or "I was referred to Jane by her associate Don Reid." Whatever you do, sound confident and friendly. It's best to call on a Tuesday, Wednesday, or Thursday between eight and eleven o'clock in the morning. If the person isn't in and you must leave a message, just leave your name, phone number, and the message "personal."

Once you start interviewing people who work in a field that interests you, the information gained should confirm or revise your views. But even better, you will make contacts who may be able to help you actually find a job in the future. These contacts can suggest groups or associations to join, colleges to attend, and classes to take, as well as the current status of employment activity in their field. If you use this information wisely, you too can become visible in these inner circles. It's never too early to start.

EXHIBIT 8.A
Review guide on information interviewing.

1. FIND SOMEONE WITH WHOM TO START THE INTERVIEW PRO-
   CESS. MAKE SURE YOU GET THE PERSON'S NAME. CALL THE
   PERSON DIRECTLY, BY NAME.

   What is the name of the person you're going to call? _____

2. MAKE A SPECIFIC APPOINTMENT, FOR A SPECIFIC LENGTH OF
   TIME.

   When is your appointment, and for how long? _____

   _____

3. MAKE A LIST OF SPECIFIC QUESTIONS, THINGS YOU WANT TO
   KNOW ABOUT THE JOB.

   Your questions for this interview. (See list in this section.) _____

   _____

   _____

   _____

4. EXPLAIN WHY YOU'RE CALLING FOR THE INTERVIEW. SOME
   EXPLANATIONS:
   a. You want to know more about this kind of work before you decide that
      you're interested, or before you decide you should choose it as a career.
   b. You are getting ready for a job interview and would like to get some
      advice from someone in the field before the interview.
   c. You are interested in the field but haven't found much information on it
      and would appreciate someone filling you in on it.
   d. You are doing some research for a career class and would like some
      specific information in this field.

   Which explanation will you give when you call? _____

   _____

   _____

   (Make up your own if you wish.)

5. TELL THE EMPLOYER WHO IT WAS THAT RECOMMENDED THAT
   YOU CALL. (A REFERENCE HELPS.)

   Who is your reference for this interview? _____

6. AFTER THE INTERVIEW, SEND A NOTE THANKING THE PERSON
   FOR THE TIME AND HELP.

Practice Information Interviews

Some people find it easier to practice information interviews until they become confident in approaching people about their career. If you need to practice, you might try one of the following approaches. Either you can interview someone you already know about a hobby that sounds interesting or you can try to consistently ask people about their hobbies and careers at any informal gathering you attend. These informal activities tend to build your self-confidence in asking questions. Once you get started, you might find you enjoy searching for leads through other people.

Information interviewing leads to contacts and careers

Two interesting success stories may help you get started. Thomas Shanks, assistant professor of communications in a California college, tells how one of his students moved from California to New York. For three months, he sent his resume everywhere and knocked on the door of every friend, relative, and remote acquaintance that he could find. He even found out which after-hours spots the television crowd preferred, and he frequented those places. He eventually got offers from all three networks. Another student, a freshman at Moorpark College, was a business major with an interest in art. In November, the vice president of industrial relations at an engineering firm gave a talk in her leadership class. After class she asked him about summer jobs with his firm (notice how early she did so). By January, he had arranged for her to interview in the graphic arts department of his firm. She got the summer job, a job many art graduates would have coveted.

Last, if you are a student or have access to a college campus, teachers often make fine resources. Many faculty members have had interesting summer jobs and temporary positions prior to becoming a teacher. They have valuable contacts. In turn, if you are a teacher interested in a career change, you might find a lead through a student. Many times a teacher can design a lesson plan to find out the occupations of parents and then invite parents to speak in their class about their career. These parents can become future contacts for both students and teachers!

Networking

Networking refers to the process of developing contacts. While conducting information interviews, you will meet many people. Besides gathering information, you are making contacts. Contacts, if cultivated and used wisely, can lead to or become potential employers. In a tight and competitive job market, contacts often make the difference between your being selected or being passed by. This

Networking provides the edge

is true for several reasons. Often jobs need to be filled before there is time to advertise. Additionally, as has been mentioned, the majority of new jobs that are available each year come from business leads that start off with relatives and neighbors. Most people hear about jobs by word of mouth. You need to let people know that you are looking.

One state employment agency in San Diego experimented in attempting to place some of its "hard-core unemployed" applicants. First, the staff taught the applicants to be positive and confident about their ability to get a job and trained them in using the telephone to make contacts. Then, for one week, using the yellow pages, the applicants called prospective employers from 8 a.m. to 5 p.m. At the end of seven days, 80 percent of the applicants had at least three interviews each! So there *were* jobs out there!

How do you find those hidden jobs if you don't plan to make 56 hours' worth of phone calls? You meet people face-to-face and let them know you are available before a job may be available. On the next page, Exercise 8.A suggests some likely people to contact.

If you really want to get your preferred position, you need to make it your business to let everyone know you are looking (except maybe your current employers, if they aren't expecting to be losing you!). This approach works even better if you have six months to two years in which to make a change. Contacting people may give a prospective employer the idea to create a job for you, but job creation within a company also takes time.

Networking and practice interviewing give you not only contacts but also personal experience with people working in your desired job environment. Additionally, however, they allow you to hear the answers professionals in your chosen field give to the sort of questions that you may be asked in a job interview. While conducting information interviews or discussing people's careers at a conference, try asking people what kinds of questions they were asked in interviews; ask what they considered to be the most difficult questions in their interviews.

SUMMARY

This chapter has discussed traditional and nontraditional job search. It is important that you confirm your impressions about your ideal job. When you first start an exercise program, you are unsure about the correct movements and the results of your labors. After several months of workouts, you learn to know how each workout affects your body. Similarly, you won't know the accuracy of your researched information until you volunteer in the field, do part-time work in the field, or find a job that will put you around the people doing the type of job you really desire. Only then will you know how you feel about the real job environment. It also takes practice to remember to ask everyone about their job. The more jobs you learn about, the more alternative choices you will have.

There is a hidden job market out there. The people you meet through the process of information interviewing may inform you about potential jobs before they are advertised.

?? WRITTEN
.. EXERCISES

The written exercises that follow serve to increase your ability to network effectively. Exercise 8.1 asks you to identify specific people who are part of your network. Exercise 8.2 suggests that you conduct information interviews. Exercise 8.3 helps you expand information about your job target by using practice information gathering, expert information gathering, and interviewing for employment strategies.

8.1 SUPPORT NETWORK CHECKLIST

a. Fill in the names of people who might help you (use checklist below).

b. Specifically ask yourself: What am I going to ask this person to do for me? (Provide information, introduce me to someone, offer advice, write a reference, etc.)

Former employers: _____

Former coworkers: _____

Present employer: _____

Friends: _____

Relatives: _____

Civic group members: _____

Professional association members: _____

Alumni group members: _____

Religious group members: _____

Clients: _____

Counselors: _____

Teachers: _____

Clergy: _____

Neighbors: _____

Classmates: _____

Bankers: _____

Accountants: _____

Financial planners: _____

Insurance agents: _____

Real estate agent: _____

Stockbrokers: _____

Salespeople: _____

Retail store owners: _____

Medical professionals: _____

Other: _____

8.2 INFORMATION INTERVIEWS

Select three individuals who work in fields that are interesting to you, and conduct brief information interviews using the list of sample information interview questions given earlier as your guide. Write up a brief report of each.

8.3 PERSONAL CONTACT LOG

Prepare a log of personal contacts (at least five) using the approaches described in this chapter under Information Interviewing and Practice Information Interviews. Use your own job target and see how much information and how many new contacts you acquire. Use the following outline format.

Name _____ Job Target _____

Using the approaches described under Information Interviewing and Practice Information Interviews, name your own job target and see how much information and how many new contacts you can acquire.

Practice Information Gathering

Hobby or interest _____

Contact _____

Information gathered as a result of the interview _____

_____

_____

Other possible contacts _____

Expert Information Gathering

Occupational interest _____

Contact (who, where employed, how you found this person) _____

_____

Information gathered _____

_____

New contacts _____

_____

Any contradictions _____

_____

Conclusions _____

_____

Interviewing for Employment, Apprenticeship, Volunteer Experience

Choice of possible work site _____

_____

What do you want (job, apprenticeship, volunteer experience) _____

_____

Who is in a position of hire you _____

Your approach (telephone, letter, in person) _____

Outcomes and follow-up _____

_____

EXERCISE SUMMARY

Write a Brief Paragraph Answering These Questions

What did you learn about yourself? How does this knowledge relate to your career/life planning? How do you feel?

_____

_____

_____

_____

_____

_____

_____

_____

_____

_____

_____

_____

_____

_____

_____

EXHIBIT 8.B
Sample contact file format.

1. Company:	Phone No.:	Contact Person & Title:	Type of Contact & Date:
			Letter _____
	Referred by:		Phone _____
			Resume _____
Address:			Application _____
	Job Target:		Interview _____
Follow-up:		Conclusions:	

2. Company:	Phone No.:	Contact Person & Title:	Type of Contact & Date:
			Letter _____
	Referred by:		Phone _____
			Resume _____
Address:			Application _____
	Job Target:		Interview _____
Follow-up:		Conclusions:	

3. Company:	Phone No.:	Contact Person & Title:	Type of Contact & Date:
			Letter _____
	Referred by:		Phone _____
			Resume _____
Address:			Application _____
	Job Target:		Interview _____
Follow-up:		Conclusions:	

4. Company:	Phone No.:	Contact Person & Title:	Type of Contact & Date:
			Letter _____
	Referred by:		Phone _____
			Resume _____
Address:			Application _____
	Job Target:		Interview _____
Follow-up:		Conclusions:	

5. Company:	Phone No.:	Contact Person & Title:	Type of Contact & Date:
			Letter _____
	Referred by:		Phone _____
			Resume _____
Address:			Application _____
	Job Target:		Interview _____
Follow-up:		Conclusions:	

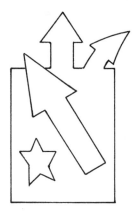

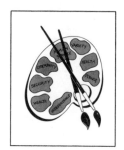

Part I

Part II

Preparing Your Resume 9

Life is a mirror and gives back to us
the reflection of our own self.
Joseph Batten, Expectations and Possibilities

LEARNING OBJECTIVES   AT THE END OF THE CHAPTER YOU WILL BE ABLE TO:

Understand the advantages of developing a resume

Identify guidelines for resume preparation.

Write a resume and cover letter

RESUMES

Every good fitness program includes a chart that indicates visually where you started, where you are currently, and where you are going. In a career fitness program, this chart is called a resume (pronounced "res-u-may"). Eventually, in the course of job hunting, you will be asked to present a resume to a prospective employer. Some career counselors feel that the resume isn't going to get you an interview unless you already have a good contact inside the company; others suggest that a good resume can help you get your "foot in the door." In either case, a resume can be a useful tool. A resume is:

1. A systematic assessment of your skills in terms of a specific job objective.
2. A memory jogger useful in an interview in answering the following questions commonly brought up by interviewers.
   a. Tell me about yourself.
   b. Why should I hire you?
   c. What skills do you bring to this job?
3. An aid in filling out application forms.

This chapter will give you guidelines for writing a resume and will present you with three sample formats: functional, chronological, and a creative combination. Additionally, the importance of cover letters and application forms will be addressed. Once you have finished this chapter you should be able to compile your own resume.

Purpose

The purpose of the resume is to get an interview. Like an advertisement, the resume should attract attention, create interest, describe accomplishments, and provoke action. Brevity is essential: one page is best; two are the limit. The resume tells the prospective employer what you can do and have done, who you are, and what you know. It also indicates the kind of job that you seek. The resume must provide enough information for the employer to evaluate your qualifications, and it must interest the employer enough to invite you for an interview.

An effective resume can get you an interview

Writing a well-constructed resume requires that your research be completed before compiling the resume. You need to keep in mind the type of employer and position as well as the general job requirements in order to tailor your resume to the specific requirements and personality of the employer. To be most effective, your resume should be designed to emphasize your background as it relates to the job being sought. It should also look neat, clean, and organized. This means typed and then photocopied or laser-printed on good-quality paper with no errors.

By now you should have completed all the necessary research. Utilize the information gathered in Chapter 6, "Information Integration," and Chapter 8, "Focusing in on Your Target." Integrate your answers with the categories listed on the following Resume Review.

Resume Review

Review this information mentally. It will help you to write a complete resume.

A. PERSONAL DATA
  1. Name
  2. Address
  3. Phone
B. CURRENT JOB OBJECTIVE
C. EDUCATION
  1. High school and college
      a. Favorite subjects
      b. Best grades
      c. Extracurricular interest
      d. Offices held
      e. Athletic achievements

  f. Other significant facts (e.g., honors, awards)

 2. Other (military, volunteer, correspondence, summer, languages, technical skills, licenses, and/or credentials.)

D. HOBBIES

E. WORK EXPERIENCE

Refer to your experiography or your skills analysis.

 a. Employer

 b. Length of employment

 c. Position

 d. Skills and accomplishments

F. PUBLICATIONS

G. ASSOCIATIONS AND COMMUNITY INVOLVEMENT

Preparation for Composing Your Resume

Although stating an objective is considered optional by some experts (because it can be stated in your cover letter), it is to your advantage to include it on the resume. In actuality, one resume should be designed for each job objective. Remember, there are no jobs titled "Anything."

The job objective is a concise and precise statement about the position you are seeking. This may include the type of firm in which you hope to work (e.g., a fast-growing small company). A clear objective gives focus to your job search and indicates to an employer that you've given serious thought to your career goals. In a limited number of cases, when time does not allow you to develop a resume for several different jobs that interest you, the job objective may be emphasized in the cover letter (which will be discussed at the end of this chapter) and deleted in the resume.

A job objective is sometimes referred to as "Goal," "Professional Objective," "Position Desired," or simply "Objective." It can be as specific as "Community Worker," "Personnel Assistant," or "Junior Programmer" or as general as "Management position utilizing administrative communications and research skills" or "To work as an administrative assistant in a creative atmosphere and have the opportunity to use my abilities." Generally speaking, the more specific the objective statement, the better, because a clear objective enables you to focus your resume more directly on the objective. The effect is pointed, dramatic, and convincing.

As you can see, a resume summarizes your particular background as it relates to a specific job. It summarizes your career objectives, education, work experience, special skills, and interests. Visualize a pyramid or triangle with the job objective at the top, with everything beneath it supporting that objective.

In writing the rough draft of your resume, create 5″ x 8″ index cards for each job you've held (Exhibit 9.A). The index card should contain the following information:

Front of card

1. Name, address, phone number of employer, and immediate supervisor at work site.
2. Dates employed (month/year to month/year).
3. Job title.
4. Special skills utilized.

Back of card

Duties divided into functional areas.

Guidelines for the Resume

Resume appearance counts

The appearance of this document is important. To be acceptable, the resume must be typed clearly, spaced well, and attractive visually. Remember that many employers skim only the first page of a resume. Thus it is crucial that your material be strategically placed so that what is most likely to be read is most relevant to the job desired. Employers have been known to receive hundreds of resumes each day, giving them only minutes to review each one. Therefore, even if you must use two pages, the first is more crucial. Experts advise against using a "resume service." An employer can usually spot a "canned" resume and might assume that the applicant lacks initiative or self-confidence. The time you spend writing your resume will be time well spent. It will give you the opportunity to summarize what you have to offer to an employer.

Put the most relevant information first

In choosing information to include in your resume, avoid anything that may not be considered in a positive light or that has no relationship to your ability to do the job (e.g., marital status, number of children, political or religious affiliation, age, photos). When in doubt, leave it out. One clue: In the next chapter you will be given information about illegal questions in an interview. If it's illegal in an interview, then it's unnecessary in a resume.

Personal computers and resume writing or word processing software can help to turn an average-looking resume into a class act. If possible, store your resume and cover letter on a floppy disk or in hard-drive storage for easy retrieval and updating. Many duplicating shops have personal computers available for an hourly fee.

Although offset printing was once the preferred method of producing resumes, quick copies made at professional copy centers are now acceptable if they are reproduced on high-quality equipment and are clean and free of smudges. Use an attractive bond paper for these copies of your resume; usually a neutral color such as ivory or white is best. Quick-copy centers typically have a wide selection of stationery available. It is often useful to have a career counselor, a potential employer, a family member, or a friend review a draft of your resume before duplicating your final copy. Ask for a careful check for content, format, grammar, spelling, and appearance.

EXHIBIT 9.A
Front and back of resume index card.

Joe's Bar 'n' Grill
555 Stevens Circle   April 1988–December 1992
Simi, Calif. 93065
(805) 555-1211

Supervisor: *Duties:*
Joe Smith   Bookkeeping & waitressing

Special Skills Utilized:
Related well with continuous flow of people. Attentive to detail; organized; energetic.

Functions:

Management   —Coordinated service with customer needs, calculated wages,
                          scheduled employees.

Communications   —Welcomed guests. Directed busboys in performing courteous and
                          rapid service. Responded to complaints.

Bookkeeping   —Maintained records of financial transactions. Balanced books.
                          Compiled reports to show statistics.

Action Words

Remember that your writing style communicates the work activity with which you have been involved. Use phrases and document experiences that both involve the reader and make your resume outstanding and active. Following are basic guidelines for selecting your "power" words.

Select "power" words

☐ Choose short, clear phrases.
☐ If you use sentences throughout, keep them concise and direct.
☐ Utilize the acceptable jargon of the work for which you are applying. Remember: You want your prospective employer to READ your resume.

☐ Avoid general comments such as "My duties were . . . " or "I worked for
. . ." Begin with action words that concisely describe what your tasks were,
e.g.:

Organized new filing system

Developed more effective interviewing procedure

Evaluated training program for new employees

☐ List the results of your activities, e.g.:

Time for completing office filing was reduced 25 percent.

A concise interview evaluation summary form was developed.

A training class was begun.

☐ Don't dilute your action words with too many extraneous activities. Be
SELECTIVE and sell your BEST experiences.

☐ Target your words around the employer's needs.

Here are some examples of action verbs that could be used in your resume.

accomplished	evaluated	negotiated
achieved	expanded	organized
analyzed	facilitated	oriented
arranged	guided	planned
built	implemented	processed
controlled	improved	produced
created	increased	proved
demonstrated	initiated	raised profits
designed	inspired	reduced costs
developed	interpreted	researched
directed	invented	sold
effected	led	supervised
encouraged	managed	supported
established	motivated	wrote

For additional action verbs, see the skills analysis section, Chapter 4, Table 4.A.

References

The expression "References available upon request" is usually sufficient on a
resume. This is typically placed at the end of the resume. Although you don't
have to list specific individual names on the resume, you should have at least
three people in mind who can talk about your work habits, your skills, and your
accomplishments. When you are job hunting, ask these people in advance if you
may use them as references, informing them of your job objective so that they
will be prepared if a prospective employer calls. Many college placement centers
act as a clearing house for the collection of resumes and references. You establish
a file and the center sends your resume and references when you make a request.

EXHIBIT 9.B
Sample resume guidelines.

NAME
ADDRESS
PHONE NUMBER

Job Objective

State and describe as specifically as possible. Refer to the *Dictionary of Occupational Titles* for appropriate descriptive vocabulary.

Education

Depending on your job objective and the amount of education you have had, you may want to place this category directly after Job Objective. Most recent education should be listed first. Include relevant credentials and licenses.

Example: As employers, educational institutions are usually more concerned with appropriate degrees than other employers. Include special workshops, noncredit courses, and self-taught skills when they are appropriate to your job objective.

Experience

Describe *functionally* (by activities performed) your experience relevant to the particular job for which you are applying; start with the most relevant and go to the less relevant. Include without distinction actual job experience, volunteer experience, your work on class projects, and school and class offices held. Alternatively, show your experience *chronologically,* listing your most recent professional experience first.

There is no need to stress dates unless they indicate that you have been continuously advancing toward this job objective.

Use action verbs (see below); do not use full sentences, unless you decide to write your resume as a narrative.

Use the *Dictionary of Occupational Titles* to help you describe accurately what you have done, always keeping in mind how your experiences relate to your job objective.

Special Skills

Put this optional category directly after Job Objective if you feel that your professional experience does not adequately reflect the talents you have that best support this job objective.

Examples: Facility with numbers, manual dexterity, patience, workshops you have led, writing ability, self-taught skills, language fluency.

References

Available on request.
(Use references only if you have space and if the names are well-known to potential employers.)

The placement center often makes this service available for alumni, and it may have reciprocal agreements with other colleges across the country.

TYPES OF RESUMES

To reiterate, there are three general types of resume: functional, chronological, and combination. Comparing the following two sample work experience entries (taken from Exhibits 9.D and 9.H) will give you some idea of the basic difference between functional and chronological resumes, which we referred to in Exhibit 9.B, Sample Resume Guidelines. The next part of this chapter will discuss all three types in detail. The combination resume, as the name implies, is a combination of functional and chronological.

Sample functional entry under professional experience:
- □ *Budgeting/Financial*

   Analyzed and coordinated payroll recordkeeping, budgeted expenditures, requisitioned supplies, prepared attendance accounting reports, and initiated budget system for $10,000 of instructional monies.

Sample chronological entry under professional experience:
- □ *1983 Cashier*

   Builders Emporium
   Wadsworth, Texas 76199
   (214) 555-3933

   Operated cash register and made change. Worked well with public, motivated fellow employees, encouraged customers to buy products.

The Functional Resume

A functional resume presents your experience and job history in terms of the functions you have actually performed rather than as a simple chronological listing of the titles of jobs you have held. Like any resume, it should be tailored to fit the main tasks and competencies required by the job you are seeking. Essentially, you redefine your past experiences according to the functions in the job for which you are applying. You should select and emphasize those activities from previous employment that relate to the specific job sought and deemphasize or omit irrelevant background.

For example, an administrative assistant might perform some administration, communication, and clerical functions. A secretary for an elementary school rewrote her resume to highlight these categories. In order to better define the skills used in her secretarial job, she researched the job description of executive secretary and office manager in her school personnel manual and located the description of administrative assistant in the *Dictionary of Occupational Titles.* (See "Suggestions for Job Descriptions" below.) She then compiled her resume to show how her executive secretarial responsibilities related to the administrative assistant position desired. (See Functional Resume, Exhibit 9.D, at the end of this chapter.) Review the organizational divisions described in Chapter 8, to assess how your past work or life experience can be described in such categories as marketing, human resources, finance, community services, or research and development.

Suggestions for Job Descriptions

Descriptions in the *Dictionary of Occupational Titles* and in some personnel manuals provide a source of helpful phrases and statements to use in writing up your own job history and experience. The following three descriptions, for example, would be especially useful in composing a functional resume for a job in business. However, you would use only relevant sentences, adapting them to your personal background.

Examples:

OFFICE MANAGER

Coordinates activities of clerical personnel in the organization. Analyzes and organizes office operations and procedures such as typing, bookkeeping, preparation of payrolls, flow of correspondence, filing, requisitioning of supplies, and other clerical services. Evaluates office production, revises procedures, or devises new forms to improve efficiency of work flow. Establishes uniform correspondence procedures and style practices. Formulates procedures for systematic retention, protection, retrieval, transfer, and disposal of records. Plans office layouts and initiates cost reduction programs. Reviews clerical and personnel records to ensure completeness, accuracy, and timeliness. Prepares activity reports for guidance of management. Prepares employee ratings and conducts employee benefit and insurance programs. Coordinates activities of various clerical departments or workers within department.

ADMINISTRATIVE ASSISTANT

Aids executive in staff capacity by coordinating office services such as personnel, budget preparation and control, housekeeping, records control, and special management studies. Studies management methods in order to improve work flow, simplify reporting procedures, or implement cost reductions. Analyzes unit operating practices, such as recordkeeping systems, forms control, office layout, suggestion systems, personnel and budgetary requirements, and performance standards to create new systems or revise established procedures. Analyzes jobs to delineate position responsibilities for use in wage and salary adjustments, promotions, and evaluation of work flow. Studies methods of improving work measurements or performance standards.

EXECUTIVE SECRETARY

Coordinates collection and preparation of operating reports, such as time and attendance records, terminations, new hires, transfers, budget expendi-

tures, and statistical records of performance data. Prepares reports including conclusions and recommendations for solution of administrative problems. Issues and interprets operating policy. Reviews and answers correspondence. May assist in preparation of budget needs and annual reports of organization. May interview job applicants, conduct orientation of new employees, and plan training programs. May direct services such as maintenance, repair, supplies, mail, and files.

Creative Functional Resume

Married women who have had no paid experience often find it particularly hard to make their activities sound transferable to the world of work. All they see is domesticity, which they mistakenly think differs markedly from work in business. However, they have usually been performing business functions without realizing it. People without paid work experience and people returning to the job market after taking time out to be homemakers can persuade employers to recognize their ability and practical experience if they describe their life in categories such as these.

Management
- ☐ Coordinated the multiple activities of five people of different ages and varying interests, keeping within tight schedules and continuous deadlines.
- ☐ Established priorities for the allocation of available time, resources, and funds.

Office Procedures
- ☐ Kept lists of daily appointments, reminders, items to be purchased, people to be called, tasks to be accomplished.
- ☐ Handled all business and personal correspondence—answered and issued invitations, wrote stores about defective merchandise, made hotel reservations.

Personnel
- ☐ Recruited, hired, trained household staff; negotiated wages.
- ☐ Motivated children to assume responsibilities and helped them develop self-confidence.
- ☐ Resolved problems caused by low morale and lack of cooperation.

Finances
- ☐ Established annual household budget, and monitored costs to stay within expenses.
- ☐ Balanced the checkbook and reconciled monthly bank statements.
- ☐ Calculated take-home pay of household staff, made quarterly reports to the government on social security taxes withheld.

Purchasing
- ☐ Undertook comparison shopping for food, clothing, furniture, and equipment, and purchased at various stores at different times, depending upon best value.

☐ Planned meals according to specials at different food stores.

☐ Shopped for insurance and found lower premiums than current coverage, resulting in substantial savings.

Pros and Cons

The functional resume is especially useful if you have limited work experience or breaks in your employment record or if you are changing fields. You need not include dates or distinguish paid activities from nonpaid volunteer activities. By deleting previous employers' names, you avoid any stereotyped assumptions that a prospective employer may make about previous employers (McDonald's, the PTA, a school district, etc.). Similarly, omitting job titles helps direct the future employer to the fact that you are someone with specific skills that may be useful in the present job opening. This format also can emphasize your growth and development.

One disadvantage to using this format is that you must identify and write about your achievements. This sometimes requires the assistance of an expert resume writer. Additionally, some employers are not familiar with this format and may prefer dates and job titles.

Exhibits 9.D, 9.E, and 9.F (at the end of this chapter) are examples of functional resumes for various positions.

The Chronological Resume

The chronological resume is considered the traditional and most often used resume style. Basically, it lists your work history in reverse chronological order, meaning the most recent position or occupation is listed first. The work history should include dates employed, job title, job duties, employer's name, address, and telephone number.

Pros and Cons

The chronological resume is most useful for people with no breaks in their employment record and for whom each new position indicates continuous advancement or growth. Recent high school and college graduates also find this approach simpler than creating a functional resume.

As dates tend to dominate the presentation, any breaks or undocumented years of work are glaring. If your present position is not related to the job you desire, you may be eliminated from the competition by employers who feel that current experience is the most important consideration in reviewing resumes.

Exhibits 9.G, 9.H, 9.I, and 9.J (at the end of this chapter) are examples of chronological resumes tailored for various positions.

The Combination Resume

If you have major skills important for success in your desired job in addition to an impressive record of continuous job experience with reputable employers, you can best highlight this double advantage with a *combination* of the functional and chronological styles of resume. This combination style usually lists functions followed by years employed with a list of employers. The combination style also satisfies the employer who wants to see the dates that you were actually employed. See Exhibits 9.K and 9.L.

COVER LETTER GUIDELINES

Want to turn off a prospective employer? Send a resume with no cover letter. Or send a form letter addressed to "Personnel Manager."

An original, personalized cover letter, accompanying every resume you send, should explain why you are writing and why your qualifications would be of interest. It's your best opportunity to communicate on a personal level with an employer you're asking to hire you. The employer is more than a position title, just as you, certainly, are more than a resume. Use your cover letter to spark added interest in you as an individual. Challenge the employer to read your resume before reading the other forty-nine that arrived with yours in the morning mail.

Cover letters get attention

How to do it? For one, address your letter to a specific person. Spell his or her name correctly and use the proper title. These details count. Your opening paragraph should contain the "hook." Arouse some work-related interest. Explain (very briefly) why you are writing. How did you become interested in that company? Summarize what you have to offer. Details of your background can show why you should be considered as a job candidate. The self-appraisal that went into preparation of your resume tells what you can do and like to do, where your strengths and interests lie. Your research on your prospective employer should have uncovered the qualifications needed. If your letter promises a good match—meaning your abilities matched with the company's needs—you've attracted attention.

Keep your letter short and to the point. Refer to your resume, highlighting relevant experiences and accomplishments that match the firm's stated needs. Ask for an interview. Indicate when you will be calling to confirm a convenient time for the interview. Let your letter express your individuality but within the context of the employment situation.

The cover letter should be individually typed for each job desired in contrast to the resume, which can be printed (mass produced). Always review both cover letter and resume for good margins, clarity, correct spelling, and accurate typing. Appearance does count! Review the sample cover letters in Exhibits 9.N through 9.S.

APPLICATION FORMS

A final type of form, accepted sometimes as a substitute for a resume, is an *application form.* The employment application is a form used by most companies to gain necessary information and to register applicants for work. This information becomes a guide to determine a person's suitability for both the company and the job that needs filling. You should observe carefully the following guidelines.

You will probably be asked to fill out an employment application form, usually before the interview takes place. Therefore, it is good practice to arrive at the employment office a little ahead of the time of your interview. Bring along a pen and your resume or personal data sheet. You will be asked to list your name, address, training or education, experience, special abilities, hobbies, and preferences. Practically all application forms request that you state the job you are seeking and the salary you have received in the past. Most firms require an applicant to complete an application form.

Many times the employer wants to make certain rapid comparisons and needs only to review the completed company employment application forms on file. For example, Ms. Ford needed a stenographer who could type fast. She examined several application forms filled out by people who had applied for stenographic jobs. *By referring to the same section each time,* she quickly thumbed through dozens of applications, eliminating all candidates who had only average speed. Thus, there was no need for her to examine resumes or read dozens of letters to find out exactly how fast each candidate could type.

Neatness Counts

The way in which an application form has been filled out indicates the applicant's level of neatness, thoroughness, and accuracy. If two applicants seem to have equal qualifications, but one form is carelessly filled out, the application itself might tilt the balance in favor of the other applicant. Unless your handwriting is especially clear, print or type all answers.

Sometimes you may apply for a job by mail, and a form will be sent to you. The application form should be carefully, completely, and accurately filled out. You should then return it to the company. You may also attach a copy of your resume. When you have completed the application, go over it again. Have you given the information asked? When an item asked for is not applicable, have you written in "N/A"?

Filling Out Application Forms

1. Fill out the application form in ink—or use a typewriter.
2. Answer every question that applies to you. If a question does not apply or is illegal (see Chapter 10) you may write "N/A," meaning "not applicable," or draw a line through the space to show that you did not overlook the question.
3. Give your complete address, including zip code.
4. The question on marital status simply asks whether you are single, married, divorced, separated, or widowed.
5. Spell correctly. If you aren't sure how to spell a word, use the dictionary or try to use another word with the same meaning.
6. The question on place of birth means the city and state in which you were born—not the name of the hospital.
7. A question on job preference or "job for which you are applying" should be answered with a specific job title or type of work. Do not write "anything." Employers expect you to state clearly what kind of work you can do.
8. Have a prepared list of schools attended and previous employers. Include addresses and dates of your attendance or employment.
9. Be prepared to list several good references. It is advisable to ask permission of those you plan to list. Good references include:
   a. A recognized community leader.
   b. A former employer or teacher who knows you well.
   c. Friends who are established in business.
10. When you write or sign your name on the application, use your formal name—not a nickname. Your first name, middle initial, and last name are usually preferred.
11. Be as neat as possible. Employers expect that your application will be an example of your best work.

SUMMARY

This chapter has provided diverse examples of resumes, cover letters, letters of introduction, and application form reminders. Putting the resume together is now your job. Use the forms and ideas in the following written exercises as well as the samples throughout the chapter to assist you in getting your resume into shape.

?? WRITTEN EXERCISES

The written exercises that follow will enable you to prepare a resume as well as critique it. Exercises 9.1 and 9.2 help you to organize pertinent information about yourself. Exercise 9.3 asks you to draft a resume and Exercises 9.4 and 9.5 provide guidelines for critiquing your own resume and obtaining valuable feedback from others about your resume.

9.1 RESUME REVIEW SHEET

Fill in the following blanks. The answers will help you write a complete resume.

A. **PERSONAL DATA**

   1. **Name** _____

   2. **Address** _____

   3. **Phone** _____

B. **CURRENT JOB OBJECTIVE** _____

C. **EDUCATION**

   1. **High school and college** _____

      a. **Favorite subjects** _____

      b. **Best grades** _____

      c. **Extracurricular interest** _____

      d. **Offices held** _____

      e. **Athletic achievements** _____

      f. **Other significant facts (e.g., honors, awards)** _____

         _____

   2. **Other (military, volunteer, correspondence, summer, languages, technical skills, licenses and/or credentials)** _____

D. **HOBBIES**

   _____

   _____

E. **WORK EXPERIENCE**

   Refer to your experiography or your skills analysis.

   a. **Employer** _____

   b. **Length of employment** _____

   c. **Position** _____

    d.   **Skills and accomplishments** _____

    a.   **Employer** _____

    b.   **Length of employment** _____

    c.   **Position** _____

    d.   **Skills and accomplishments** _____

    a.   **Employer** _____

    b.   **Length of employment** _____

    c.   **Position** _____

    d.   **Skills and accomplishments** _____

    a.   **Employer** _____

    b.   **Length of employment** _____

    c.   **Position** _____

    d.   **Skills and accomplishments** _____

F. PUBLICATIONS _____

G. ASSOCIATIONS AND COMMUNITY INVOLVEMENT _____

_____

9.2 CREATE A CARD FILE

Create a card file describing your work experiences, using Exhibit 9.A as a guide. This gives you a chance to write your job tasks in functional terms.

9.3 WRITE YOUR RESUME

Choose the format desired and write your own resume. Refer to the formats and suggestions in the chapter and the samples that follow this chapter.

9.4 CRITIQUE YOUR RESUME

Use the Resume Checklist and Critique Form to evaluate your resume (Exhibit 9.C).

9.5 HAVE OTHERS CRITIQUE YOUR RESUME

Have other people give you feedback about your resume (e.g., career counselors, people who have been receptive to you during informational interviews, teachers, friends, etc.)

EXHIBIT 9.C
Resume checklist and critique form.

	STRONG	AVERAGE	WEAK	PLANS FOR IMPROVEMENT
1. **Resume format.** Does it say "READ ME"?				
2. **Appearance.** Is it brief? Did you use an interesting layout? Type clearly? Use a correct layout format?				
3. **Length.** Are the key points concise?				
4. **Significance.** Did you select your finest experiences?				
5. **Communication.** Do your words give the "visual" impression you want? Is the job objective clearly stated?				
6. **Conciseness.** Does your information focus on the experiences that qualify you for the position?				
7. **Completeness.** Did you include all important information? Have you made a connection between the job desired and your experience?				
8. **Reality.** Does the resume represent you well enough to get you an interview?				

EXERCISE SUMMARY

Write a Brief Paragraph Answering These Questions

What did you learn about yourself? How does this knowledge relate to your career/life planning? How do you feel?

_____

_____

_____

_____

_____

_____

_____

EXHIBIT 9.D
Functional resume for administrative assistant position.

Samuel Gildar
P.O. Box 1111   (805) 555-1212
Simi Valley, California 93065   (805) 555-1111

GOALS

To work as an administrative assistant in a creative
atmosphere and have the opportunity to use my abilities.

SUMMARY OF EXPERIENCE

Ten years of increasing responsibility in the area of office management involving organization,
problem solving, finances, and public relations.

MANAGEMENT

Initiated and organized procedures used in the office, coordinated activities of clerical personnel, and
formulated procedures for systematic retention, protection, transfer, and disposal of records.
Coordinated preparation of operating reports, such as time and attendance records, of performance
data. Reviewed, composed, and answered correspondence. Directed services, such as maintenance,
repair, supplies, mail, and files. Aided executive in staff capacity by coordinating office services, such
as personnel, budget preparation and control, housekeeping, records control, and special
management studies.

PUBLIC RELATIONS

Interfaced with state, county, and district officials as well as district and local employees, student
body, staff members, and parents in our community. Planned and coordinated social functions for
school, staff, and two social clubs. Promoted sales of jewelry, gourmet foods, and liquors in
sales-related jobs.

PROBLEM SOLVING

Made decisions according to district policy in the absence of the principal. Worked under constant
pressure and interruption while attending to student problems regarding their health and welfare.
Liaison between school and community, resolving as many problems as possible before referring
them to superior.

BUDGETING/FINANCIAL

Analyzed and coordinated payroll recordkeeping, budgeted expenditures, requisitioned supplies,
prepared attendance accounting reports, and initiated budget system for $10,000 of instructional
monies allocated to the school.

CREATIVE

Created newscopy using IBM PageMaker, composed on headliner, and assisted in copy paste-up.
Designed flyers, posters, calendars, and bulletins sent home from school to parents. Personal hobbies
include ceramics, oil painting, sculpting, and interior design.

EMPLOYERS

Simi Valley Unified School District   Southern California Blue Cross
1115 Old School Road   5900 Erwin Road
Simi Valley, California 93065   Woodland Hills, California 91360
(805) 555-2345   (213) 622-1212

EXHIBIT 9.E
Functional resume for management position.

OLIVIA MARTINEZ
2406 Adams Avenue
Los Angeles, CA 90025
213-555-0862

PROFESSIONAL OBJECTIVE:

Management position utilizing administrative, communications, and research skills.

SUMMARY OF SKILLS:

Administrative

Designed and implemented disbursement and evaluation program for compensatory education project.

Coauthored grant proposal.

Maintained liaison between volunteers and university administration.

Directed registration program and coordinated staff at registration desk, Western Psychological Association Annual Convention, 1991.

As student senator, initiated Earth Day activities and helped establish faculty evaluation program.

Communication

Planned discussion sections, provided office hours, cowrote and graded examinations for undergraduate courses in developmental psychology and statistics.

Prepared tutorials in science and study methods and offered educational guidance to economically disadvantaged high school students.

Participated in human growth seminar led by clinical psychologist, trained in therapy methods, and helped devise therapy program for young people.

Research

Designed and conducted study investigating memory in 4-year-olds.

Studied mathematical structure underlying Piagetian developmental theory.

Implemented computer simulation model of certain cognitive behaviors in children. Analyzed and categorized data for cognitive anthropologist and psychologist.

EDUCATION:

M.A., August 1991 Developmental Psychology, University of California, Los Angeles, California. California State Graduate Fellow, National Science Foundation Honorable Mention.

B.A., 1989 Psychology, University of California, Irvine. Summa Cum Laude, Outstanding Scholar, Honor Scholar.

EXPERIENCE:

Teaching Assistant and Reader. Psychology Department, University of California, Los Angeles, January 1989–91.

Administrative Assistant. Psychology Department, California State University, Fullerton, February-June, 1989.

Business Manager, Education Motivation. Community Projects Office, University of California, Irvine, August 1986–January 1989.

Research Assistant. Departments of German and Russian, University of California, Irvine, October 1985– June 1986.

REFERENCES WILL BE FURNISHED UPON REQUEST

EXHIBIT 9.F
Functional resume for teacher changing careers.

STACY L. MOLLARD

1001 Gainsborough Street
Chicago, IL 60664

312-555-3581 (home)
312-555-4343 (work)

POSITION OBJECTIVE:

Employee Training Specialist

QUALIFICATIONS IN BRIEF:

B.A. in English, Mundelein College, Chicago, 1987.

Six years' elementary teaching with experience in communications, human relations, instruction, and supervision.

Bilingual.

EXPERIENCE SUMMARY:

COMMUNICATIONS:

Conducted staff development workshops. Presented new curriculum plans to parent groups, sent periodic progress reports to parents, and developed class newsletter. Presented workshops in parent effectiveness training at state and local conferences.

HUMAN RELATIONS:

Directed effective problem solving/conflict resolution between individual students and student groups; initiated program of student self-governance; acted as liaison between families of diverse cultural, ethnic, and economic backgrounds and school personnel/services; and conducted individual and group conferences to establish rapport with parents and discuss student progress.

INSTRUCTION:

Developed instructional modules to solve specific learning problems; developed instructional audiovisual material; used audiovisual equipment such as overhead, opaque, and movie projectors and audio cassettes and video cassettes; did extensive research in various curricula; member of curriculum development committee; introduced new motivational techniques for students.

CURRENTLY EMPLOYED:

Austin Elementary School, Chicago, Illinois

COMMUNITY INVOLVEMENT:

Board member, Chicago Community Services Center

Allocations Committee, Chicago United Way

REFERENCES:

Available upon request

EXHIBIT 9.G
Chronological resume for public relations position.

THUY NGUYEN

532 Casstilian Court   805-555-0109 (Home)
Westlake, CA 91360   805-555-2912 (Work)

OCCUPATIONAL OBJECTIVE:

A position in sales or public relations leading to advanced responsibilities.

SUMMARY OF QUALIFICATIONS:

Three years of increasingly responsible experience in different positions.

BOOKKEEPER   Hungry Hunter and El Torito Restaurants
                                       Thousand Oaks, CA 1990–present

Kept records of financial transactions, entering them in account and cash journals. Balanced books and compiled reports to show statistics, such as cash receipts and expenditures, accounts payable and receivable, and other items pertinent to operation of business. Calculated employee wages from time cards and operated calculating, bookkeeping, and adding machines.

RESTAURANT GREETER   Hungry Hunter Restaurant
                                              Thousand Oaks, CA 1988–89

Welcomed guests, seated them in dining area, maintained quality of facilities. Directed others in performing courteous and rapid service; also assisted in settling complaints. Related well with the continuous flow of people, coordinating the service with the customers' needs.

SPECIAL ACCOMPLISHMENTS:

National Forensic League, vice president (third place, statewide oratory competition); Women's Athletic Association (gymnastic team); Honor Roll and Dean's List; Alpha Gamma Sigma; Who's Who Among American High School Students, 1989–90.

EDUCATION:

Moorpark College, Moorpark, CA

Majoring in Business Administration

GPA: 3.5 on a 4.0 scale

REFERENCES:

Available upon request

EXHIBIT 9.H
Chronological resume for bank teller position.

ELEANOR RUTLEDGE
3388 North Dallas
Wadsworth, Texas 77065
909-555-0026

JOB OBJECTIVE: A position as a bank teller that offers opportunities to learn and
progress.

EDUCATION: 1991—Glencoe College, Dallas, Texas
Courses included:

| Typing 1 | Sociology 1 |
| Calculating Machines | English 1A |

1986-1990—Wadsworth High School,
Wadsworth, Texas.
Courses included:

Typing 1	Algebra 1
English 1 & 2	Geometry 1
Public Speaking	

SPECIAL SKILLS: Facility with numbers, manual
dexterity, patience, excellence
in telephone communications,
organization of fund-raisers for
church group.

EXPERIENCE: 1989-1991—Builders Emporium,
Wadsworth, Texas. Operated cash register and made change, worked well
with public, motivated fellow employees, encouraged customers to
buy products.

1984-1987—Miscellaneous Employment:
Babysitting for local families;
assumed full responsibility while
parents were away, helped children
with their homework.

REFERENCES: Available upon request

EXHIBIT 9.I
Chronological resume for high school graduates with limited experience.

John Jones
(805) 555-1221

1050 Baez Street
Simi Valley, CA 93063

OBJECTIVE: An entry-level position as a *(list one or two related job titles)* that affords opportunities to learn and progress.

SUMMARY: Three years of part-time and summer employment related to sales, public contact, and accounting while attending high school.

EDUCATION: *(List your most recent education first.)*
1990 Valley Vista High School, Zenith, California
Graduated with double major in mathematics and business. Courses included:

Typing 1 & 2	Algebra 1 & 2
Bookkeeping 1 & 2	Trigonometry 1 & 2
Business Machines	Geometry 1
English 1, 2, 3	Business Math 1
Journalism 1 & 2	

EXPERIENCE: *(List most recent experience first.)*
1989–1990 Moorpark General Store. Moorpark, California
Salesperson. Sold ready-to-wear in ladies', men's, and children's departments.

1988–1989 Taco Bell, Simi Valley, California
Counterperson. Assembled customers' orders and packaged orders to go. Operated cash register and made change.

1984–1988 Miscellaneous employment: Babysitting for four local families with up to four children each. Stayed with children weekends and while parents were on vacation, assuming full responsibility for normal household routines.

HONORS: *(If you had a high grade point average, list it. List offices held in a student or community organization. List publications. If none of these apply, omit this section from your resume.)*

ACTIVITIES: Future Business Managers, Association Journalism Club, Student Tutoring Association, Young Republicans Club

EXHIBIT 9.J
Chronological resume for community worker position.

SARITA SANDHA
980 Victory Blvd.
Simi Valley, California 90063
805/555-4150

JOB OBJECTIVE:	**Public Representative or Community Service Worker**
SUMMARY OF QUALIFICATIONS:	Three years' experience in public relations, media work, and writing press releases and newsletters. Organized concerts, rallies, walk-a-thons, and volunteer-a-thons. Basic qualifications in office procedures: phone networking, word processing, mailing, leafletting, outreach, and public speaking.
EDUCATION:	**Moorpark College, currently attending, 1990–present** Sociology major. Additional specialized institute training at Loyola Marymount University in Social Organizing.
	Alemany High School, graduated 1985 Two years as teacher's aide in Los Angeles City School System. Interrelated with a variety of cultural groups.
EXPERIENCE:	**1990–1992 Community service organizations in Los Angeles** Organized, educated, convinced, created social change, and performed security work.
	1988–1990 Self-employed Cleaned and maintained family residence.
	1987–1988 Receptionist and secretary Interviewed applicants for positions in sales and maintained records.
SPECIAL SKILLS:	Interact easily with diverse people while under pressure. Knowledge of fund-raising practices. Self-motivated. Experienced in analyzing and working with issues and strategies underlying a particular campaign.
REFERENCES:	Available upon request

EXHIBIT 9.K
Combination resume for sales executive position.

JOHN BENNETT	(415) 555-3692 (w)
304 Amen Street	(415) 555-1126 (h)
San Francisco, California 94102	

OBJECTIVE

MARKETING DIRECTOR

SALES PROMOTION

Designed and supervised sales promotion projects for large business firms and manufacturers, mostly in the electronics field. Originated newspaper, radio, and television advertising. Coordinated sales promotion with public relations and sales management. Analyzed market potentials and developed new techniques to increase sales effectiveness and reduce sales costs. Created sales training manuals.

As sales executive and promotion consultant, handled a great variety of accounts. Sales potentials in these firms varied from $100,000 to $5 million per annum. Raised the volume of sales in many of these firms 25 percent within the first year.

SALES MANAGEMENT

Hired and supervised sales staff on local, area, and national bases. Established branch offices throughout the United States. Developed uniform systems of processing orders and maintaining sales records. Promoted new products as well as improving sales of old ones. Developed sales training program. Devised a catalog system involving inventory control to facilitate movement of scarce stock between branches.

MARKET RESEARCH

Originated and supervised market research projects to determine sales potentials, as well as need for advertising. Wrote detailed reports and recommendations describing each step in distribution, areas for development, and plans for sales improvement.

SALES

Retail and wholesale. Direct sales to consumer, jobber, and manufacturer. Hard goods, small metals, and electrical appliances.

EMPLOYERS

1987–Present	B. B. Bowen Sales Development Co., San Francisco, California	Sales Executive
1985–1987	James Bresher Commercial and Industrial Sales Research Corp., Oakland, California	Senior Sales Promotion Manager
1984–1985	Dunnock Brothers Electronics Co., San Francisco, California	Order Clerk, Salesworker, Sales Manager

EDUCATION

University of California, Berkeley, B.S., 1984; Major: Business Administration

REFERENCES AVAILABLE UPON REQUEST

EXHIBIT 9.L
Combination resume for programmer trainee position.

ALBERT CHAN
111 East Maple
Moorpark, CA 93021
(805) 555-1122

JOB OBJECTIVE:	Applications programmer trainee
QUALIFICATION BY EXPERIENCE:	Flowcharted, coded, tested, and debugged interactive COBOL and BASIC program for the HP3000. Created a system of five COBOL programs from a system problem statement and flowchart. Built a KSAM file for use by the system. Wrote JCL for the five-program job stream. Designed system flowcharts and wrote other documentation for improved payroll system for previous employer, as Systems Analysis course project.
	Tutored students in BASIC and COBOL, working with Hispanics, Vietnamese, and reentering adults, as well as with other students.
	Currently searching a bibliographic database as a volunteer at Simi Valley Public Library.
EDUCATION:	1988 Associate in Science in Computer Science, Moorpark College.
	3.6 GPA in computer science classes.
	1992 B.A. in English, Florida Southern College.
	Graduate work in research methods.
	Supported self through college by security work at various firms. Gained Secret clearance while at IBM Federal System Division.
SPECIAL SKILLS:	Attentive to detail, organized, work well with little supervision, enterprising, enjoy problem solving and interacting with others to plan projects, work well under pressure, able to see relationships between abstract ideas, good at communication, concise.
COMMUNITY SERVICE EXPERIENCE:	Organized CROP Walks (fund-raisers for Church World Service), which resulted in raising $6,000 in 1986 and $10,000 in 1987.
	Chaired the Planning Committee, recruited members, mapped walk route.
	Obtained parade permits and business tax exemptions.
	Wrote press releases and walkers' instruction sheets.
REFERENCES:	Available upon request

EXHIBIT 9.M
A poorly constructed resume.

PERSONAL:
Age: 24
Marital Status: Single
Height: 5'9"

Henry O'Neil
617 Barclay Street
Carbondale, Illinois

Job Objective:

I am looking for any position dealing with the design and manufacture of furniture. Would prefer a position in the Midwestern United States.

Education:

Carbondale High School—graduate 1985—academic courses

Lehigh University—Bethlehem, Pennsylvania—BS Industrial Engineering, 1989, finished top half of class.

Experience:

1985:	Traveled extensively in Europe.
1989 to present:	White Shoe Company, 1783 Fairlawn Drive, Cicero, Illinois. I started there as time and motion study consultant on assembly line operations, reporting to the cheif Industrial Engineer. I was promoted to Equipment Analysis and purchasing section after one year. In this position I handled several new equipment installations and start-ups, and including a 140,000 PPH boiler and solvent recovery system.
	In 1990 was promoted to Product Supervisor for a special new line of cork-soled deck shoes which were sucessfully marketed in U.S. and foreign markets. In this position I was in charge of several junior engineers and a large production staff.
Miscellaneous:	Have won several awards for furniture design. Finished first in Lake Michigan Class E Sailboat races. Fluent in French and Italian.
Hobbies:	Furniture design and repair. sailing music
REFERENCES:	On request

EXHIBIT 9.N
Resume cover letter guidelines.

Address
City, State Zip
Date

Name of Person
Company Name
Street Address or P.O. Box
City, State Zip

Salutation: (Dear M... ....: or Greetings:)

THE FIRST PARAGRAPH SHOULD INDICATE WHAT JOB YOU ARE INTERESTED IN
AND HOW YOU HEARD ABOUT IT. USE THE NAMES OF CONTACT PERSONS
HERE, IF YOU HAVE ANY.

SAMPLE
ENTRY

Your employment advertisement in Tuesday's News Chronicle indicating an opening
for an administrative assistant is of special interest to me. Mary Smith, who currently is
employed at your firm, suggested I write to you. I have heard that Rohn Electronics is
a growing company and wants dynamic employees who also want to learn and contribute to the firm.

THE SECOND PARAGRAPH SHOULD RELATE YOUR EXPERIENCE, SKILLS, AND
BACKGROUND FOR THE PARTICULAR POSITION. REFER TO YOUR ENCLOSED
RESUME FOR DETAILS AND HIGHLIGHT THE SPECIFIC SKILLS AND COMPETEN-
CIES THAT COULD BE USEFUL TO THE COMPANY.

SAMPLE
ENTRY

During the last five years, I worked as an office manager and was able to redesign the
office by investigating and selecting word processing equipment. I understand that
your opening includes responsibilities for supervising and coordinating word processing procedures with your home office. I was able to reduce my firm's operating costs
over 30 percent by selecting the best equipment for our purposes.

THE THIRD PARAGRAPH SHOULD INDICATE YOUR PLANS FOR FOLLOW-UP
CONTACT AND THAT YOUR RESUME IS ENCLOSED.

SAMPLE
ENTRY

I am excited about the opportunity of discussing with you the information I have gathered about your company and why I feel I would be a valuable asset. For your examination, I have enclosed a resume indicating my education and work experience. I will
call your office early next week to determine a convenient time for an appointment to
further discuss employment opportunities.

Sincerely,

Your first and last name
Enclosure (or Attachment)

EXHIBIT 9.0
Cover letter for community health worker position.

June 4, 1992

Mr. Harvey J. Finder
Executive Director
Lung Association of Alma County
1717 Opportunity Way
Santa Ana, California 92706

Dear Mr. Finder:

I am interested in the position of Community Health Education/Program Coordinator with the Lung Association of Alma County. I feel that my education, skills, and desire to work in this area make me a strong candidate for this position.

My education has helped me develop sound analytical abilities and has exposed me to the health care field. My involvement with health care and community organizations has provided me with the working knowledge of various public and private health institutions, which has increased my ability to communicate effectively with health care professionals, patients, and the community at large. This combination of education and exposure has stimulated my interest in seeking a career in the health field.

Please review the enclosed resume and contact me at your convenience regarding a personal interview. If I do not hear from you in the next week, I will contact you.

Sincerely yours,

Denise M. Hunter
18411 Anticipation Drive
Northridge, California 91330
(213) 555-0217

Encl.

EXHIBIT 9.P
Cover letter for a teacher with some business background.

532 Glendora Avenue
Anytown, CA 90000
April 1, 1992

Ms. Joan Addeman
Director of Personnel
ABC Corporation
Anytown, CA 90000

Dear Ms. Addeman:

I am applying for the administrative assistant position currently available at your firm. I have been impressed for some time with the outstanding reputation that ABC Corporation holds in our community.

As you read my resume, please note that my twelve years of business experience directly relate to the needs of your company. One of my greatest assets is seven years in motivational psychology related to personnel management and public school teaching. I am aware that strength in business and management is considered important in your firm, and I would like the opportunity to discuss with you, at your earliest convenience, how we might work together for our mutual benefit.

Enclosed is my resume for your review. I will telephone your secretary next week to see when we might set up an appointment to further discuss the administrative assistant position and any other ways that I could serve your corporation.

Sincerely,

Gerald Burnes

Encl: Resume

EXHIBIT 9.Q
Cover letter for electronic technician position.

412 Melbrook Avenue
Westlake Village, CA 91361
June 17, 1992

Mr. Lloyd Price
Sonar Technical Supervisor
Lear Electronic Company
1229 Van Owen
Rosemead, CA 91770

Dear Mr. Price:

I am interested in working for your company as an electronics technician in the field of systems installation and calibration.

During my tour of duty in the service, I became acquainted with many of your electronic systems aboard ship and was extremely impressed with your systems' design and documentation. I have since pursued a course of studies at Moorpark College to increase my competence in the field of electronics. For these reasons I feel I would be an asset to your company.

I am planning to contact you by telephone next week to set up a meeting to discuss employment opportunities with your company.

Sincerely yours,

Emilio Reyna

EXHIBIT 9.R
Cover letter for public relations position.

1234 Evanston Avenue
Cambridge, IL 61238
June 17, 1992

Mr. Harrison MacBuren
Director of Personnel
North Hills Mall
Cambridge, IL 61238

Dear Mr. MacBuren:

I am very interested in the position that is currently available in your Public Relations Department for an assistant to the director of public relations.

As you can see by my resume, my previous administrative experience would be a definite asset to your company. I feel that a vital part of any public relations job is the ability to deal with people. This is a skill I have acquired through many years of volunteer work.

I would like to meet with you to discuss how we might work together for our mutual benefit. I will be contacting you within the week to arrange a convenient meeting time.

Sincerely,

George Herounian

EXHIBIT 9.S
Cover letter for marketing manager position.

1736 D Street NW
Washington, D.C. 20006
(202) 555-8192
May 1, 1992

Ms. Emma Major, President
Vendo Corporation
1742 Surf Drive
Fort Lauderdale, Florida 33301

Dear Ms. Major:

I was intrigued by the writeup about your new portable vending centers in <u>Sales Management</u>
magazine. Frankly, I think it is an extremely good idea.

As you will note from the enclosed resume, my marketing, planning, and sales management
experience could be of great assistance to you at this early stage in your project. Enclosed are
some specific marketing ideas that you might like to review. I would like to make arrangements
to meet with you in Florida during the week of May 15 to discuss some of these ideas.

Because of my familiarity with the types of locations and clients you are seeking, I am sure that
if we were able to work together in this new venture, the results would reflect my contribution.

I am looking forward to meeting with you and will call next week to arrange for an
appointment.

Very truly yours,

Janet Perrill

EXHIBIT 9.T
Letter of introduction.

TO WHOM IT MAY CONCERN:

This will introduce Mary Smith, a trusted and valued member of my staff for the past two and a half years.

During this time she has held a key position, performing a variety of secretarial tasks, as well as having full charge of the ordering procedures, maintenance work, and updating in our career resources library. She is keen at spotting deficiencies and was instrumental in developing a more efficient system of updating our materials.

She has been recognized by other members of the staff, including the counselors and our program director, the dean of student personnel, as being outstanding in poise, appearance, and reliability. Additionally, and probably most important, she has been exceptionally effective in working with the students, faculty, and professionals who use the resources of our center.

Mary is a good organizer, capable of dealing with concepts and goals and devising systems approaches to problem solving. She is loyal and discreet in dealing with unusual situations and those calling for confidentiality.

If there is anything more you feel you would like to discuss regarding Mary's qualifications, please feel free to contact me.

Very truly yours,

Her Past Employer

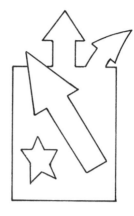

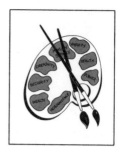

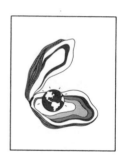

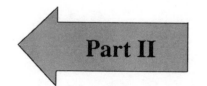

Part I

Selling Your Product 10

The person who gets the job isn't always the person who
is best qualified but rather the person who is best prepared
to find potential jobs and interview for them.

LEARNING OBJECTIVES   AT THE END OF THE CHAPTER YOU WILL BE ABLE TO:

Understand the art of interviewing

Learn how to prepare for an interview

Develop guidelines and techniques for good
interviewing

THE JOB INTERVIEW

Once you begin to feel comfortable with the notion of networking and practice
interviewing, you are ready to begin preparing for the "Olympic Finals"—the
interview.

Before the Interview

Here are some tips to take into consideration as you approach your first interview
or refine your current interviewing style.

Some of the best preparation for the interview occurs when you research the
prospective employer. You must be able to show the employer why you will be
the best person for the job. Relate your personal strengths and past accomplishments to this particular enterprise. Specifically, tell how you can help with current
problems or function as a valuable member of the organization.

Before the interview, or at least early in it, try to find out what the essential
responsibilities of the job are. Make a mental note of them, and throughout the

interview feed back the kind of information from your background that shows that you can handle these responsibilities.

Don't let a formal job description disqualify you for a job. Remember that job descriptions are only guidelines, and, once in a job, you are allowed to imprint your own style. Additionally, it is expected that over 50 percent of the work in any job is learned on the job. Thus, your ability to express what your skills are, how you can contribute to the company, and your willingness to learn new skills is as important as being able to do each task listed in the job description. In fact, if you already can do each task described, you might be labeled as overqualified and not get the job!

Consider non-traditional jobs

Your resume and cover letter become the written and mental outline upon which you elaborate to translate your skills into potential benefits to the employer. Use your resume as a point of reference; write on index cards the key points you want to convey and remember during the interview. It's appropriate to bring these cards with you to your interview.

In applying for jobs, a male increases his chances by trying to enter a field that has previously been primarily a female domain (e.g., nursing). Similarly, a female increases her chances if she applies for a position that has previously been primarily a male domain. However, it must be remembered that it will not always be easy to be the "first one" in any position.

Don't be afraid to reapply and reinterview at the same company. Your interview skills will probably have improved in the meantime, and different people may be interested in you.

Be creative if you are applying for a creative job (advertising, design, sales, art), but be conservative if you are applying for a conservative job (banking, insurance, accounting).

Before the interview, verify the particulars. Write down the interviewer's name, the location, and the time and date of your appointment. Last-minute nervousness can block such details from your memory. Plan on arriving 15 minutes early.

Ask for feedback

Apprehension, tension, and anxiety are a normal part of the preinterview jitters. Relaxation techniques, deep breathing, and chatting with the receptionist may help.

If you are turned down, consider calling to get information to improve subsequent interviews: "I realize that this is a bit unusual and I am aware that you've chosen someone else for the job, but could you spend a few moments giving me some ideas as I continue my job search?" You could end up with some valuable leads; it's worth a try!

Interviewing becomes easier as you gain practice. Don't be overly discouraged if you don't get the first job for which you interview. Interviews and even rejections are actually invaluable opportunities to reassess and reaffirm your qualifications, strengths, weaknesses, and needs.

In the competitive job market of today, you can maximize your chance of successful interviewing by doing practice interviews and being prepared to answer an employer's typical questions. Always be prepared to support your general answers with specific examples from your experience. Your interviewers will remember your examples! Consider using a video recorder to sharpen your interviewing skills. Ask a friend or classmate to be the interviewer. Using the questions below and those found on pp. 238–239, practice your responses. Then replay the tape and use the interview critique form on p. 243 to evaluate your performance and improve your answers for the next interview.

Below are several sample questions that are representative of the types commonly asked in an employment interview. Review these, and be prepared beforehand to answer such questions.

1. *Tell me about yourself.*

   Refer mentally to your resume; do not assume that the interviewer has even read it! Briefly recap your skills and experiences as they relate to this particular job.

2. *Why do you want this job? Why did you apply here?*

   Refer to information about this job and this company or institution that makes it particularly appealing to you. Do not give the impression that you're here just because the firm has a job opening. Refer to the company's history, products, and services. Let your interviewers know that you have researched the organization.

3. *Why should I hire you?*

   "Because I, with my skills, experiences, positive attitude, and enthusiasm, am obviously the best person for the job. I agree with your philosophy and feel that I will fit in. I will be an asset to your enterprise." (Reemphasize your strengths.)

4. *What are your career plans? Where do you see yourself five years from now?*

   Employers generally like to think you will be with them forever; you can't make any promises, but you can indicate you would like to be with a company that allows you to grow, asks you to assume more responsibility, and challenges you continuously. That challenges them to be that kind of place!

5. *Are there any questions?*

   You might ask just what kind of person the interviewer is really looking for. Then show how you fit the bill. You may need clarification on salary. "When can I expect to hear about the position?" "Oh, yes, I forgot to mention earlier that. . . . " "I would like to reiterate that. . . ." (See Exhibit 10.B.)

   Leave the interviewer convinced that you are ready and able to do the job.

   Never answer a question with a no without qualifying it positively. "Have you operated a cash register before?" "No, but I have good finger dexterity and I won't have any problems learning." "Can you type?" "No, I didn't realize it was part of the job description. If it is necessary, I can learn. Just how much typing will be involved?"

6. *What salary do you expect?*

   If you have done your homework, you should have an idea of the general range for the position. Find out whether this company has a fixed salary schedule. You may want to defer the matter until you know more about what the job entails.

7. *Don't you think you are too young/old for this position?*

In either case, phrase your answer so it is an advantage. Example:

Too young: Show how the job best lends itself to a young person—one who can face the challenges with youthful vigor and a fresh point of view.

Too old: Point out how your years of experience and previous success give you the confidence and wisdom to carry full responsibility with the mature judgment required by this position.

8. *Why did you leave your last job?*

If asked why you left your last position, avoid mentioning a personality conflict. Rather say, "I felt I had gone as far in that company as possible and I was ready for more responsibility, challenge, hours (etc.)." If your work history reflects many job changes, explain how you have transferred existing skills and learned new skills that can now benefit these employers.

Interview Guidelines

The interview is the goal of your job search strategy. Generally, people who are interviewed are assumed qualified to do the job; the question becomes one of appropriate meshing of personalities. Both the interviewer and interviewee are relying on their communication skills, judgment, intuition, and insight. It is a two-way process. While you are being evaluated, you should be evaluating the position and the people offering it. Remember that a good interview is a dialogue, an exchange of information.

An interview is a two-way process

Take a good look at yourself. Employers are becoming increasingly broad-minded about clothes and hair, but few are totally "liberated." If you are serious about getting a job, then you had better look and dress the part. No interviewer will tell you what you are supposed to wear, but the person will measure your maturity and judgment partially by your appearance. Remember that the first impression is often a lasting one. It's often not the best-qualified person who gets the job but the one who makes the best impression. *You never get a second chance to make a good first impression!*

There are some trick or stress questions that you may have to handle; be prepared beforehand with a response that feels comfortable to you. (See sample questions that follow.) If a question seems inappropriate, you may ask: "How does this information relate to or affect my employment here?" This may prompt an employer to express the real concerns, such as your record of stability on the job, age, child care needs, or commitment to the job and company. You may even consider bringing up these relevant issues. Often seemingly unimportant conversation is an attempt to put you and the interviewer at ease or to assess your ability to socialize.

Remember that many interviewers are just as nervous about the process as you. Feel free to make the first attempts to break the ice; when you try to relieve another's anxiety, yours becomes secondary. Note the office decor, the cordial welcome, whatever makes sense. If you are nervous, you will find that focusing on the question "What would it be like to work here?" rather than "How am I being perceived by them?" will relax you. Relax in the chair; a rigid posture reinforces your tenseness. Actually, a slightly forward position with head erect indicates interest and intimacy. Maintain eye contact. In answering questions, use your knowledge of yourself to transmit the idea that you are the best person for the job; allow strengths such as goodwill, flexibility, enthusiasm, and a professional approach to surface. Bring samples of your work if they are related. On an index card, note your strengths or key selling points in addition to the questions you may have and some cue words like "smile, speak up, relax"; review them from time to time, especially just before you go into the interview. Forthright statements about what you do well, with examples of accomplishments, are of key importance. Talk with pride, honesty, and confidence about your accomplishments and your potential, your interest and commitment, and your readiness to learn on the job.

Body language can speak louder than words

Express yourself *positively*. You are selling yourself; allow your personal *energy* and *enthusiasm* to surface.

Segments of an Interview

Although every interview is different, most follow a general pattern. A typical half-hour session can be roughly divided into four segments.

Establish initial rapport

1. The first 5 or 10 minutes are usually devoted to establishing some rapport and opening the lines of communication. Instead of wondering why the interviewer is taking valuable time chatting about the weather, your parking problems, etc., relax and enjoy the conversation. He or she will get to deeper subjects soon enough. The interview begins the moment you introduce yourselves and shake hands. Don't discount the initial period. Your ability to converse, expressing yourself intelligently, is being measured.

2. The adept interviewer will move subtly from a casual exchange to a more specific level of conversation. The second part of the interview gives you a chance to answer some "where, when, and why" questions about your background—to supply information that does not appear on your resume.

   Now is the time to describe some extracurricular activities or work experience that may explain your less-than-perfect GPA. Or to talk of changes you effected as president of a campus organization or community group. This is your chance to elaborate on your strong points and maximize whatever you have to offer. Don't monopolize the conversation; let the interviewer lead. But don't confine your statements to yes or no answers.

   The interviewer will be interested not only in what you say, but how you say it. Equally important as the information you communicate will be the demonstrated evidence of a logical organization and presentation of thoughts.

The interviewer will be mentally grading your intelligence, leadership potential, and motivation.

3. Part three begins when the interviewer feels your skills and interests have been identified and can see how they might fit the organization. If a good match seems possible, he or she will discuss the company and the openings available.

Ask questions

4. At the end of an interview, try to find out where you stand. "How do you feel I relate to this job?" "Do you need any additional information?" "When can I expect to hear from you?"

After you leave, take 10 or 15 minutes to analyze how you did. What questions did you find difficult? What did you forget to say? How can you improve on the next interview? You might even keep a diary or log with written notes on each of these concerns as well as a list of the specific interview questions asked and a note about how you responded. Also list any specific things that you can do in following up with an employer to increase your chances of getting the offer you want. If you feel you forgot to mention something or there was a misunderstanding, correct or elaborate on these points in a letter or telephone call. Type a thank-you letter to the interviewer, recalling a significant fact or idea of the interview that will set you apart from the other applicants. Write the letter while the interview is still fresh in your mind. One paragraph is usually sufficient.

Practice Questions

The following are questions that have been asked during interviews, intended to create a *stress* response. They are asked out of pattern, designed to throw you. The interviewer sometimes is more interested in *how* you respond than in what you say, so as to determine how you react and how you think on your feet. Decide which of the following questions are likely to be asked of you in your situation. PRACTICE!

1. What kind of job do you expect to hold five years from now? Ten years? Twenty years?
2. Why do you want to work for this company?
3. Why did you choose your particular field of work?
4. What do you know about this company?
5. Do you feel you have a good general education?
6. What qualifications do you have that make you feel you will be successful in your field?
7. What are your ideas on salary? Don't you think you would be dissatisfied with a job paying less than you were previously making?
8. What determines a person's progress in a good company?
9. Do you prefer working with others or by yourself?

10. What kind of supervision do you prefer?
11. Can you take criticism without becoming upset?
12. What interests you about our product/service?
13. How long do you expect to work?
14. Do you like routine work?
15. What is your major weakness? (What are three of your strong points? Three of your weak points?)
16. Have you had any serious illness or injury?
17. Are you willing to go where the company sends you? Travel? Relocate?
18. What kinds of people annoy you?
19. What are your own special abilities?
20. Do you object to working overtime?
21. What arrangements do you have for child care?
22. How would your spouse feel about your accepting this job if it were offered?
23. What is your philosophy of life?
24. Do you have any objections to a psychological test or interview?
25. Don't you feel a little too old (or young) for this position?
26. Will you take an aptitude test?
27. Tell me about yourself.
28. What are your personal goals?
29. In what ways will this company benefit from your services?
30. If you were me, why would you hire you?
31. Have you ever been fired?

Illegal Questions

There are certain hiring practices, employment application form questions, and specific interviewing procedures that are now illegal under the Fair Employment Practices Act. Review Table 10.A on the following pages to familiarize yourself with the subject matter and specifics of this legal issue.

TABLE 10.A
Preemployment inquiries: Lawful and unlawful.

SUBJECT	ACCEPTABLE PREEMPLOYMENT INQUIRIES	UNACCEPTABLE PREEMPLOYMENT INQUIRIES
Photograph	Statement that photograph may be required after employment.	Requirement that applicant affix a photograph to application form. Request that applicant submit photograph at applicant's option. Requirement of photograph after interview but before hiring.
Race or Color		Complexion, color of skin, or other questions directly or indirectly indicating race or color such as color of applicant's eyes and hair.
Citizenship	Request that applicant state residency status. (a) U.S. Citizen (b) Legal right to remain permanently in the United States. Statement that, if hired, applicant may be required to submit proof of citizenship.	Of what country are you a citizen? Inquiry whether an applicant or his or her parents or spouse are naturalized or native-born U.S. citizens; date when applicant or his/her parents or spouse acquired citizenship. Requirement that applicant produce naturalization papers or first papers.
National Origin	Inquiry into applicant's proficiency in foreign language must be job related.	Applicant's nationality, lineage, national origin, descent, or parentage. Date of arrival in United States or port of entry; how long a resident of the United States. Nationality of applicant's parents or spouse; maiden name of applicant's wife or mother. Language commonly used by applicant: "What is your mother tongue?" How applicant acquired ability to read, write, or speak a foreign language.
Education	Inquiry into academic, vocational, or professional education of an applicant and schools attended.	Any inquiry asking specifically the nationality, race or religious affiliation at a school.
Name	Inquiry about having worked for the company under a different name. Maiden name of married female applicant, assumed name, or change of name, if necessary to check education or employment records.	Former name of applicant whose name has been changed by court order or otherwise.
Address or Duration of Residence	Inquiry into place and length of residence at current and previous addresses.	Specific inquiry into foreign addresses that would indicate national origin.

continued

TABLE 10.A (continued)

SUBJECT	ACCEPTABLE PREEMPLOYMENT INQUIRIES	UNACCEPTABLE PREEMPLOYMENT INQUIRIES
Gender		If not based on a bona fide occupational qualification. It is extremely difficult for gender to be considered a lawful preemployment inquiry.
Birthplace	Requirement that applicant submit after employment a birth certificate or other proof of legal residence.	Birthplace of applicant's parents, spouse, or other relatives.
Age	Requirement that applicant submit after employment a birth certificate or other document as proof of age.	Requirement that applicant produce proof of age in the form of a birth certificate, baptismal record, or employment certificate or certificate of age issued by school authorities.
Religion		Inquiry into applicant's religious denomination, affiliation, church, parish, or pastor or which religious holidays observed. Applicant may not be told, "This is a Catholic/Protestant/Jewish/atheist, etc., organization."
Work Day and Shifts	Request that applicant state days, hours, or shift that applicant is available to work.	It is unlawful to request applicants to state days, hours, or shift that they can work if it is used to discriminate on basis of religion.

How to Handle Illegal Questions

If the question is on an application, you always have the option to put N/A in the blank. If you are asked illegal questions in an interview, you should anticipate what concerns a potential employer might have about hiring you and bring them up in a manner that is comfortable for you.

Example:

Interviewer: "Do you have any children?"

Interviewee: "I guess you are wondering about the care of my school-age children. I'd like you to know I have an excellent attendance record. You are welcome to check with my past employer, and, besides, I have a live-in sitter, etc. Additionally, I have researched the needs of this position and can assure you that I have no family responsibilities that will interfere with my ability to do this job."

Not only will employers appreciate your sensitivity to their concerns, but your statement provides you with an additional opportunity to sell yourself and to evaluate whether this position is one that you want to consider. It is often advisable for you, the interviewee, to bring up any issue that may be on the employer's mind but that, because of legal concerns, will not be addressed unless

Anticipate concerns and address them

you mention it. Such issues as age, children, spouse's feelings about this position, gender, disabilities, and qualifications can all be addressed by you in such a way as to enhance your chances of getting the job. Basically, you want to show how your age, qualifications, gender, or disability will be an advantage to your employer. This requires some thinking on your part before the interview, and the payoff—getting the job you want—is well worth the effort.

Body Language

Present yourself assertively

Your body language speaks just as loudly as your words. Eye contact is crucial. Remember that at a distance of five or six feet from another person, you can be looking at the person's nose or forehead or mouth and still maintain the feeling of eye contact. Try it with friends.

Voice tone, volume, and inflection are important. A soft wispy voice will seldom convince another that you mean business; a loud or harsh voice tends to be blocked out. Listen to yourself on a tape recorder or, preferably, on videotape. How do you sound to yourself? Ask others for their comments. Lessons in voice and diction are available in most schools. Try varying your voice pitch and volume while reading something into a tape recorder. You may find a range that sounds better.

Gum is a sticky subject—throw it out!

Try accenting your words with appropriate hand gestures to gain emphasis.

Before the interview, analyze your practice interviews. Consider the option of being videotaped during a practice interview. The instant feedback is very helpful, particularly if you use the format laid out in Table 10.B to critique your performance. If you are in a class, practice with one or more classmates, evaluating your own and your classmates' interview techniques according to the critique form.

Learning from the Interview

As much as they are interviewing you, you are in turn interviewing the representatives of a company. In fact, you will do only about 40 percent of the talking. In the remaining time, you can listen and assess whether or not you want to work for that company. Although an interview tends to be rather formal, you can still gain a feeling about the climate of the organization. Entering the building, you can observe the receptionist, support staff, people talking or not talking in the hallways. The colors or decor of the building should generate a positive or negative impression.

Take note of the punctuality of the interview—assuming you are on time or early, the arrangement of the seating in the interview room, and the dress of the interviewers. The entrance and handshake are important first impressions. Some companies deliberately set up awkward or uncomfortable situations to observe your response. They may ask tough questions just to see how well you think on your feet. If you can maintain your composure and enthusiasm in the interview, they will probably think that you are able to work equally as well under stress.

TABLE 10.B
Interview critique form.

Name _____ (individual being interviewed)	Very good	Satisfactory	Fair—could be better	Needs Improvement	Comments
1. Initial, or opening, presentation (impression).					
2. Eye contact.					
3. Sitting position.					
4. General appearance: grooming (hair, makeup, shave, beard, mustache, etc.), clothing.					
5. Ability to describe past work experiences, education, and training.					
6. Ability to explain equipment, tools, and other mechanical aids used.					
7. Ability to explain skills, techniques, processes, and procedures. Ability to stress how skills are related to job.					
8. Ability to explain personal goals, interests, and desires.					
9. Ability to explain questionable factors in personal life (functional limitations, frequent job changes, many years since last job).					
10. Ability to answer questions or make statements on company or job applying for.					
11. Ability to listen attentively to interviewer's questions and to notice his or her body language.					
12. Manner of speech or conversation understandable (voice, tone, pitch, volume, speed)?					
13. Physical mannerisms (facial expressions, gestures).					
14. Enthusiasm, interest in this job.					
15. Attitude (positive?), confidence.					
16. Overall impression? Would you hire this applicant?					

In selecting your own questions, you might ask who was the last person in the position and what happened to that person; if the person resigned, you may ask why. Another related question would be "Given the current economy, how have careers at my level been affected?" You may also ask about the background of your potential supervisor and professional mobility within the company. Although you want to emphasize your interest and commitment to the position for which you are interviewing, these questions can illustrate your interest in a future with the company.

What is the corporate culture?

A final bit of information that you should gather or confirm about the company relates to its *corporate culture*. Corporate culture refers to the personality of the potential employer. Primarily you want to seek employment with a firm that is likely to meet your personality needs. Do you need a competitive environment in order to thrive? Most likely a job in a high school or a government position won't satisfy those needs. Do you need security? The aerospace field may be a bit too unsteady for you. The prime question that is related to corporate culture and that you may ask during an interview is "Can you explain the management style or philosophy of your company?" If you want to have the opportunity for input into management, you might also ask about the use of quality circles or the potential for the use of total quality management in the organization. If you are hoping to enter the field of business but have little relevant background, it might help to take a college class or read a book on the world of business so that you can ask intelligent questions about business practices.

EXHIBIT 10.A
Sample questions to ask at the interview.

Going one step further than just *answering* the interviewer's questions, you should be prepared to take the initiative in *asking* several questions.

☐ Could you describe the duties of this job?
☐ Where does this position fit into the organization?
☐ What type of people do you prefer for this job?
☐ Is this position new?
☐ What experience is ideally suited for this job?
☐ Was the last person promoted?
☐ Whom would I be reporting to? Can you tell me a little about these people?
☐ What have been some of the best results you have received from these people?
☐ Who are the primary people I would be working with?
☐ What seem to be their strengths and weaknesses?
☐ What are your expectations for me?
☐ May I talk with present and previous employees about this job?
☐ What are some of the problems I might expect to encounter on this job, i.e., efficiency, quality control, declining profits, evaluation?
☐ What has been done recently regarding. . . ?
☐ How is this program going?
☐ Can I tell you anything more about my qualifications?
☐ What is the normal pay range for this job?
☐ If you don't mind, can I let you know by *(date)?*
☐ What kind of on-the-job training is allocated for this position?

FACTORS INFLUENCING HIRING

There are many things to consider in preparing for an interview. There are some factors over which we have control; other considerations are beyond our control. Look over this list to distinguish between the two.

Factors We Can Control Or Guard Against

- □ A poor personal appearance.
- □ An overbearing, overaggressive, conceited attitude; a "superiority complex"; being a know-it-all.
- □ An inability to express oneself clearly; poor voice, diction, or grammar.
- □ A lack of career planning—no purpose or goals.
- □ A lack of interest and enthusiasm—being passive, indifferent.
- □ A lack of confidence and poise; nervousness, being ill at ease.
- □ An overemphasis on money—interest only in best dollar offer.
- □ A poor scholastic record—just squeaking by.
- □ Being unwilling to start at the bottom—expecting too much too soon.
- □ Making excuses—evasiveness—hedging on unfavorable factors in record.
- □ Lack of courtesy—being ill mannered.
- □ Condemnation of past employers.
- □ Failure to look interviewer in the eye.
- □ A limp, fishy handshake.
- □ A sloppy application form.
- □ Insincerity; merely "shopping around."
- □ Wanting job only for short time.
- □ Lack of interest in company or in industry.
- □ Emphasizing who you know.
- □ An unwillingness to be transferred.
- □ Intolerance—strong prejudices.
- □ Having narrow interests.
- □ Being late to interview without good reason.
- □ Never having heard of company.
- □ Failure to express appreciation for interviewer's time.
- □ Failure to ask questions about the job.
- □ Being a high-pressure type.
- □ Offering indefinite responses to questions.

OUT
OF
OUR
CONTROL

Too many applicants.

Cannot pay you what you are making.

Indecisiveness on part of business owner.

Only trying to fill a temporary position.

A current employee changed
plans and decided not to leave.

Introduction of new personnel policies.

Death of a company management employee.

Looking for a certain type of person.

Lack of experience on part of interviewer.

Accepting applications only for future need.

Looking for more experience.

Looking for less experience.

Your skills are more than are needed for the position.

Company management decided that morning on a

temporary freeze on hiring—for many business reasons.

Illness of interviewer.

Change in management.

Further consideration of all applicants.

A more important post must be filled first.

Finally, experts in the field agree, for the following six reasons, why applicants may not be offered the job (Johnson, 1981).

1. Lack of clearly defined career goals.
2. Little or no knowledge of basic business principles.
3. Inability to see (and describe) how their skills and training can serve the company desired.
4. Lack of information about the firm.
5. Failure to convey a solid sense of self-awareness and confidence.
6. Lack of assertiveness and dedication.

More and more firms will be requiring a college degree. A degree will be required primarily because so many people have degrees. Even your liberal arts degree can compete with a specialist degree in business if the following factors are taken into consideration.

1. You have an excellent grade point average.
2. You have a record of extracurricular activities (club or community involvement). It's especially good to have had leadership positions.
3. You worked your way through college (it helps even more if the work was at the company with which you seek full-time employment).
4. You've made some contacts within the firm who can serve as positive references.
5. You either minored in business or, at least, selected business courses as electives (e.g., accounting, economics, marketing, information systems).
6. You have some defined goals, exude enthusiasm and confidence, and can verbalize these characteristics in an interview.

For example, AT&T employs 6,000 new college graduates a year; more than one third are liberal arts graduates.

Generally attributed to all college graduates, but especially to liberal arts graduates, are intellectual ability (verbal and quantitative) and skills in planning, organizing, decision making, interpersonal relations, leadership, and oral communication.

SUMMARY—REVIEWING THE INTERVIEW PROCESS

Preparation

- ☐ Resume—contacts—letters of reference.
- ☐ Interview log—contacts—initial contact letters written.
- ☐ Thank-you letters—contacts—know your resume.

- ☐ Letters out—make appointments—contacts.
- ☐ 3″ x 5″ cards on each interview.
- ☐ Attitudes—"You can do it"—visualize that you have the job.
- ☐ Dress the part.
- ☐ Know your resume—bring extra copies to the interview.
- ☐ Know something about the company *(Dunn and Bradstreet—Moodys—Standard & Poor—Fortune 500*—annual report—magazine articles).
- ☐ Have five or six good questions—know when to ask them.
- ☐ Keep control.
- ☐ Be on time! ! !

The Introduction

- ☐ Good posture, shake hands, breathe.
- ☐ Use good eye contact and posture.
- ☐ The first four minutes are key—establish rapport—generate the proper chemistry.
- ☐ What can I do for you?—major strengths question—tell me about your background.
- ☐ Be positive—convert negatives to pluses.

The Interview

- ☐ Smile.
- ☐ Supply information, refer to your resume.
- ☐ Seek the next interview (or the job).
- ☐ Overcome any objections—try to anticipate objections.
- ☐ Keep answers brief.
- ☐ Ask questions about the field.
- ☐ Know the rules—when a decision will be made.
- ☐ Ask for the job if it exists.
- ☐ Be positive.
- ☐ When would you like my answer?

After the Interview

- ☐ Debrief yourself—write notes (name, address, phone, impressions; if a panel of interviewers, write down names and positions of all panel members).
- ☐ Formally thank the employer or panel chairperson by letter. See Exhibit 10.B.
- ☐ Plan a follow-up strategy—if you don't hear from them, call and ask if a decision has been made.
- ☐ Don't be defeated—keep interviewing!

Use the sample thank-you letters (Exhibit 10.B) as a guide and write your own to an imaginary or real interviewer.

EXHIBIT 10.B
Sample thank-you letters.

19574 Delaware
Detroit, MI 48223
February 8, 1992

Ms. Dorothy Smith
Michels' Manufacturing Corporation
1928 North Berry Street
Livonia, MI 48150

Dear Ms. Smith:

Thank you for the time you spent with me this morning. I was certainly impressed with the efficiency, friendliness, and overall climate of Michels' Manufacturing Corporation.

Now that you've told me more about Michels' recent contract with the U.S. Tank Command, I feel my degree in industrial engineering and my two years of part-time work in task force analysis should really be of value to you.

I hope you will consider me favorably for the position of junior project engineer.

Sincerely,

Steven B. Boyd

1010 Yourstreet Avenue
Simi Valley, CA 93063
July 12, 1992

Mr. John Jones
Widget Manufacturing Company
345 Widget Avenue
Los Angeles, CA 90217

Dear Mr. Jones,

Thank you for an interesting and informative interview on July 12, 1992. The position of manufacturing representative as described is of considerable interest to me, as I am most impressed with Widget's excellent growth record.

One point was not brought out in our interview that may be of interest to you. In my previous position with Ferrals Manufacturing, I took ten weeks of intensive training in billing and credit, skills that would directly relate to the position as you described it.[*]

Again, thank you for the time you spent in interviewing me.

Yours truly,

(Ms.) Rosario Ortega

---

[*]NOTE: This is your chance to mention anything helpful to your campaign that you forgot to tell the employer in the interview. However, the point should be brief and precise.

?? WRITTEN EXERCISES

The written exercises that follow serve to prepare you for a job interview. Exercise 10.1 asks you to review and be ready to answer sample questions. Exercise 10.2 asks you to practice and critique an interview.

10.1 QUESTION REVIEW

Review the interview questions listed under Interview Guidelines, and be prepared to answer all of them.

10.2 PRACTICE INTERVIEW

Arrange a practice interview with a friend, colleague, career counselor, or potential employer (someone you've met during your information interviewing). If possible, have the practice video-taped so you can review your performance. Use the Interview Critique Form (Table 10.B) to evaluate your practice session.

EXERCISE SUMMARY

Write a Brief Paragraph Answering These Questions

What did you learn about yourself? How does this knowledge relate to your career/life planning? How do you feel?

_____

_____

_____

_____

_____

_____

_____

_____

_____

_____

_____

_____

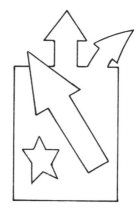

Part I

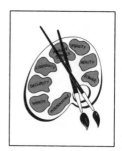

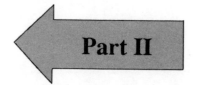

Part II

Future Focus **11**

It is a very funny thing about life; if you refuse to
accept anything but the best, you very often get it.
W. Somerset Maugham

LEARNING OBJECTIVES AT THE END OF THE CHAPTER YOU WILL BE ABLE TO:

Recognize the role of the future in your current
career-planning efforts

Understand the philosophy of personal
empowerment and career flexibility

Because the world is changing so rapidly, the future is unpredictable. Once, career
counselors could guide clients into the growth areas predicted by the U.S. Bureau
of Labor Statistics. However, such statistics were based on the assumption that
past trends would continue at the present and into the future; this assumption
proved to be totally mistaken. In the late 1960s, teaching and engineering were
still being promoted as growth fields for the 1970s. The overexpansion in hiring
teachers and engineers was not expected. Next, career counselors turned to
futurists to predict the future. We heard about robotics, genetic engineering,
telecommuting, and scenarios that depicted most people working 30 hours per
week, many working at home, with flexible working hours.

For some of us, this vision of the near future offers enough guidance to begin
our planning. For many others, these predictions are still too far-out to be useful
at this time. Selecting a major or pursuing a career just because it's the current
trend can be disillusioning: You may enjoy neither the course work nor the job
you get later. The careers in demand when you are a freshman in college may not
be in demand when you graduate, because factors that influence job market
demand are frequently unpredictable, and because new career fields and jobs
emerge every year as a result of changes in technology, public policy, and
economic trends.

The only predictable future is the one that you create for yourself! The authors
hope this book has assisted you to identify who you are, to define what you want
to do, and to research, identify, and develop your skills and create a context in

*Predicting your
future career*

*Create your own
career future*

which you are able to seek work which is meaningful for you. Following the book's guidelines puts you in full control, for you are creating your own possibilities instead of spending time preparing for the "predicted future" only to find that it does not exist.

Your future is determined by the choices that you make in the present. For this reason, this book has emphasized the development of your decision-making skills. This takes the focus away from predicting your future and puts the emphasis on creating your future. The world is changing, and you are continually changing, so why shouldn't your career be changing as well? No longer are people staying in one job until retirement. Unfortunately, however, it is human nature to resist change. Thus, many people do not turn to career counselors or books about career change until they are terminated from what had supposedly been a secure job. If you are among the fortunate who are seeking change before it is forced upon you, you have a head start. The time to seek the career of your choice is while you are already employed or still in school!

Unemployment all by itself can lead to desperation and a closed or confused mind. The anxiety and confusion generated by a life crisis makes career planning difficult, if not impossible. If you are unemployed or underemployed, you are likely to feel depressed, lethargic, and hopeless about the future. It is precisely during this time that you need to totally immerse yourself in the career-planning process rather than get stuck in your depression.

Exercise your options! In the course of evaluating your personal strengths and skills, your self-confidence will blossom. You will regain a sense of purpose and direction by setting some reasonable and achievable goals. Through networking, information interviewing, and volunteering, your interaction with people will enable you to confirm or change your current goals, and you will be energized and inspired by people who are doing the kind of jobs you find challenging and rewarding.

Exercising your options may take more effort than crystal ball gazing, but we believe the results are worth it. As you can see from your workout, finding a career is a full-time job. We hope you have pulled, stretched, and grown in the process.

RISKING
To laugh is to risk appearing the fool
To weep is to risk appearing sentimental
To reach out for another is to risk involvement
To expose feelings is to risk exposing your true self
To place your ideas, your dreams before the crowd is to risk their loss
To love is to risk not being loved in return
To live is to risk dying
To hope is to risk despair
To try is to risk failure
But risks must be taken because the greatest hazard in life is to risk nothing. The person who risks nothing does nothing, has nothing, is nothing. One may avoid suffering and sorrow, but one simply cannot learn, feel, change, grow, live, or love. Chained by certitude and safety, one becomes enslaved. Only the person who risks is free. Anonymous

References

CHAPTER 1

Gould, R. 1978. *Transformation: Growth and Change in Adult Life.* New York: Simon and Schuster.
Levinson, D. J. 1978. *The Seasons of a Man's Life.* New York: Knopf.
Sheehy, G. 1976. *Passages.* New York: E. P. Dutton.
Super, D. E. 1957. *The Psychology of Careers.* New York: Harper.

CHAPTER 2

Gelatt, H. B., et al. 1973. *Decisions and Outcomes.* College Entrance Examination Board.
Kauffman, Draper L., Jr. 1976. *Teaching the Future: A Guide to Future Education.* Palm Springs, Calif.: ETC.
Kreigel, Roger and Kreigel, Marilyn. 1984. *The C Zone.* Garden City, N.J.: Doubleday.
Murphy, Michael. 1978. *The Psychic Side of Sports.* New York: Addison-Wesley.
Samuels, Mike and Samuels, Nancy. 1975. *Seeing with the Mind's Eye.* New York: Random House.
Success Magazine. October, 1983.
Sunshine, Leo. 1975. "Affirmations: Fundamentals of Prosperity." Seminar.
Waitley, Denis. 1984. *The Psychology of Winning.* Chicago: Nightingale-Conant Corp.

CHAPTER 3

Herzberg, F. 1966. *Work and the Nature of Man.* New York: World Publishing Co.
Maslow, Abraham. 1970. *Motivation and Personality.* 2nd edition. New York: Harper and Row.
Raths, L., Simon, S., Harmin, M. 1966. *Values and Teaching.* Columbus, Ohio: Charles E. Merrill.

CHAPTER 4

Bolles, Richard Nelson. 1979. *Quick Job Hunting Map* (Advanced version). Berkeley, CA: Ten Speed Press.
Elliott, Myrna. 1982. *Transferable Skills for Teachers.* Moorpark, Calif.: Statewide Career Counselor Training Project.

CHAPTER 5

Basta, Nicholas. 1991. *Major Options.* New York: Harper Collins.
Bodner, Janet, et al. 1987. "Your Brilliant Career." *Changing Times.* November, pp. 26–33.
Braden, Paul. 1987-88. "The Impact of Technology on the Work Force." *Community, Technical, & Junior College Journal.* December/January, pp. 24–29.
Cetron, Marvin. 1983. "Getting Ready for the Jobs of the Future." *The Futurist.* June.
Jones, Robert. 1987-88. "Influence Beyond the College Gates." *Community, Technical, & Junior College Journal.* December/January, pp. 21–23.
National Forum Foundation. 1984. *Guide for Occupational Exploration.* Distributed by the American Guidance Service, Publications Building, Circle Pines, MN 55014.
U.S. Dept. of Labor, Women's Bureau. 1989. "20 Facts on Women Workers," *Statistical Abstracts of the United States.* Washington, DC: U.S. Bureau of the Census, pp. 24, 69, 134, 393, 419.

CHAPTER 6

Hispanic Times, 6355 Topanga Canyon, Suite 307, Woodland Hills, CA 91367 (818) 889-3281.
National Forum Foundation. 1984. *Guide for Occupational Exploration.* Distributed by the
    American Guidance Service, Publications Building, Circle Pines, MN 55014.

CHAPTER 7

Kauffman Jr., Draper L. 1976. *Teaching the Future: A Guide to Future Oriented Education.*
Lakein, Alan. 1979. *How to Get Control of Your Time and Your Life.* New York: NAL-Dutton.

CHAPTER 8

Bolles, Richard N. 1992. *What Color Is Your Parachute? A Practical Manual for Job Hunters and
    Career Changers.* Revised edition. Berkeley, Calif: Ten Speed Press.

OTHER REFERENCES FOR STRESSFUL CIRCUMSTANCES:

Allan, Jeffery G., J. D. 1986. *Surviving Corporate Downsizing: How to Keep Your Job.* New York:
    Wiley and Sons.
Hirsch, Paul. 1987. *Pack Your Own Parachute, How to Survive Mergers, Takeovers and Other
    Corporate Disasters.* Menlo Park, N.J.: Addison-Wesley.
Moreau, Daniel. 1991. *Take Charge of Your Career: How to Survive and Profit from a Mid-Career
    Change.* New York: Kiplinger Books.

CHAPTER 9

Brennan, Serard, & Gruber. 1990. *Resumes for Better Jobs.* New York: ARCO.
Coxford, Lola. 1991. *Resume Writing Made Easy.* Scottsdale, Ariz.: Gorsuch Scarisbrick.
Parker, Jana. 1988. *Resume Catalog, 200 Damn Good Examples.* Berkeley, Calif.: Ten Speed Press.

CHAPTER 10

"Career Planning." 1982. *CAMReport.* February 1.
Johnson, David. 1981. "Employability," *The Collegiate Career Woman.* Spring, p. 21.

Bibliography

American College Testing Program. *Career Planning Program Handbook,* 1077, p. 12, 1981.

Planning Your Career, ACT Adult Booklet, p. 14, 1981.

Appalachia Educational Lab., Inc. *Worker Trait Group Keysort Deck.* Bloomington, Ill.: McKnight Publishing Co., 1980.

Black Collegian: The National Magazine of Black College Students. New Orleans, La.: August/September 1982.

Bolles, Richard N. *What Color Is Your Parachute? A Practical Manual for Job Hunters and Career Changers.* Revised edition. Berkeley, Calif.: Ten Speed Press, 1991.

_____. *Quick Job Hunting Map.* Berkeley, Calif.: Ten Speed Press, 1979.

_____. *Newsletter.* January, 1982.

CAM Report. *Career Planning.* February 1982.

Career Opportunities News. Garrett Park Press, Garrett Park, Md.

Careers: Doubling Up on Degrees. *U.S. News & World Report,* Oct. 22, 1990.

Carter, Carol. *Majoring in the Rest of Your Life.* New York: Noonday Press, 1990.

Cetron, Marvin. *The Great Job Shakeout: How to Deal with the Coming Crash.* New York: Simon & Schuster, 1988.

Cetron, M., and Davies, O. *American Renaissance: Our Life at the 21st Century.* New York: St. Martins Press, 1990.

Crystal, John, and Bolles, R. *Where Do I Go from Here with My Life: The Crystal Life Planning Manual.* New York: Seebury Press, 1974.

Elliott, Myrna. *Transferable Skills for Teachers.* Statewide Career Counselor Training Project. Moorpark, Calif.: 1982.

_____. *Transferable Skills for Liberal Arts Graduates.* Statewide Career Counselor Training Project. Moorpark, Calif.: 1982.

Gelatt, H. B. *Decisions and Outcomes.* College Entrance Examination Board, 1973.

Herzberg, Fredrick. *Work and the Nature of Man.* New York: World Publishing Co., 1966.

Hill, Napoleon. *Think and Grow Rich.* New York: Fawcett Press, 1987.

Holland, John. *Making Vocational Choices: A Theory of Vocational Personalities and Work Environ-ments, 2nd ed.* Englewood Cliffs, N.J.: Prentice Hall, 1985.

Interest Checklist. Developed by U.S. Department of Labor, Employment and Training Administration, U.S. Employment Service, 1987.

Irish, Richard K. *Go Hire Yourself an Employer.* New York: Doubleday.

Johnson, David. Employability. *The Collegiate Career Woman,* p. 21, Spring 1981.

Jones, John E., and Pfeiffer, William J. *A Handbook of Structured Experiences for Human Relations Training.* Vol. VI. California: University Association Publishers and Consultants, 1977.

Kauffman Jr., Draper L. *Teaching the Future: A Guide to Future Oriented Education.* Palm Springs, Calif.: ETC Publishing Co., 1976.

Kreigel, Robert, and Kriegel, Marilyn. *The C Zone.* Garden City, N.Y.: Fawcett, 1985.

Lakein, Alan. *How to Get Control of Your Time and Your Life.* New York: New American Library, Inc., 1973.

L.A. 2000, Final Report from L.A. 2000 Committee, 1988.

Levinson, *The Seasons of a Man's Life.* New York: Alfred A. Knopf, 1978.

Loughary, John W., and Ripley, Theresa M. *Career and Life Planning Guide: How to Choose Your Job, How to Change Your Career, How to Manage Your Life.* New York: Cambridge, 1988.

Markus, Marian. *The Working Woman Success Book,* "Your First Job: How to Find a Good One." New York: Ace Books, 1981.

Maslow, Abraham. *Motivation and Personality.* 2nd edition. New York: Harper & Row, 1970.

Murphy, Michael. *The Psychic Side of Sports.* Reading, Mass: Addison-Wesley, 1978.

Naisbitt, John. *Megatrends 2000: Ten New Directions for the 1990s.* New York: Avon, 1990.

National Business Employment Weekly: Managing Your Career, College edition. *Wall Street Journal,* Winter/Spring 1990.

The New America. *Business Week,* September 25, 1989.

1990 Career Guide. *U.S. News & World Report,* September 25, 1989.

1991 Career Guide. *U.S. News & World Report,* September 17, 1990.

Occupational Outlook Quarterly. 1991–92. U.S. Department of Labor, Bureau of Labor Statistics.

Outlook '90 and Beyond. *The Futurist,* November–December 1989.

Phelps, Stanlee, and Austin, Nancy. *The Assertive Woman, A New Look.* San Luis Obispo, Calif.: Impact Publishers, 1987.

Samuels, Mike, and Samuels, Nancy. *Seeing with the Mind's Eye.* New York: Random House, pp. 166–167, 1975.

Simon, Sidney B., Howe, Leland W., and Kirschenbaum, Howard. *Values Clarification.* New York: Hart Publishing, 1972.

Stair, Lila B. *Careers in Business.* Ill.: Richard D. Irwin, Inc., 1980.

Sunshine, Leo. *Affirmations: Fundamentals of Prosperity.* Seminar, 1975.

Super, Donald E. *The Psychology of Careers.* New York: Harper, 1957.

Trzyna, Thomas N. *Careers for Humanities and Liberal Arts Majors: A Guide to Programs and Resources.* Ohio: R. M. Weatherford, 1980.

Waitley, Denis. *The Psychology of Winning.* Chicago: Nightingale-Conant Corp., 1984.

Waltz, Gary, and Libby, Benjamin. *Life and Career Development System.* Mich.: Human Development Services, Inc., 1975.

Other books to consider for general interest:

Basta, Nicholas. *Major Options.* New York: HarperCollins, 1991.

Career Decision Making, Walsh, W. Bruce, and Osipow, S., eds. Hillsdale, N.J.: Lawrence Erlbaum Associates, 1988.

Career Information System Conference Report: Looking to the Future. Proceedings of the February 1988 Career Information System Oregon Conference. Eugene, Oreg.: National Career Information System.

Career Opportunities News. Garrett Park, Md.: Garrett Park Press. Six issues annually.

Career Planning and Adult Development Newsletter. Twelve newsletters and four journals annually. San Jose, Calif.: CPAD Network.

Chusmir, Leonard. *Thank God It's Monday.* 1990.

The Executive Moonlighter. New York: John Wiley & Sons, 1990.

Feingold, S. N., and Atwater, M. H. *New Emerging Careers: Today, Tomorrow and in the 21st Century.* Garrett Park, Md.: Garrett Park Press, 1988.

Ferguson, Marilyn. *The Aquarian Conspiracy.* Los Angeles: Tarcher, 1980.

Fox, Marcia. *Put Your Degree To Work.* 2nd edition. Ontario, Canada: Penguin Books, 1988.

Harman, Willis W. *An Incomplete Guide to the Future.* San Francisco: San Francisco Book Co., 1980.

Helmstetter, Shad. *The Self-Talk Solution.* Pocket Books, 1987.

Herr, Edwin. *Counseling in a Dynamic Society: Opportunities and Challenges.* American Association of Counseling and Development, 1989.

Jaffe, Dennis T., and Scott, Cynthia D. *How to Change Your Work Without Changing Your Job.* New York: Simon & Schuster.

———. *Take This Job and Love It.* New York: Simon & Schuster, 1988.

Jeffers, Susan. *Feel the Fear and Do It Anyway.* New York: Fawcett Columbine, 1987.

Journal of Career Development, ed. Gysbers, Norman. New York: Human Sciences Press.

Kennedy, Marilyn Moats. *Career Knockouts—How to Battle Back.* Chicago: Follett, 1980.

Moreau, Daniel. *Take Charge of Your Career: How to Survive and Profit from a Mid-Career Change.* New York: Kiplinger Books, 1991.

Morin, William J., and Cabrera, James C. *Parting Company—How to Survive the Loss of a Job and Find Another Successfully.* New York: Harcourt Brace Jovanovich, 1984.

Pedras, K., and Pedras, R. *Jobs '90.* Englewood Cliffs, N.J.: Prentice Hall, 1990.

Peters, Tom, and Austin, Nancy. *Passion for Excellence.* New York: Random House, 1984.

Petras, Ross, and Petras, Kaffign. *Inside Track—How to Get into and Succeed in America's Prestige Companies.* New York: Vintage Books (Random House), 1986.

Sheehy, Gail. *Pathfinders.* New York: Bantam, 1982.

Snelling, R., and Snelling, A. *Jobs! What They Are, Where They Are, What They Pay.* Revised Edition. New York: Fireside Publishing (Simon & Schuster), 1989.

Strumpf, Stephen A. *Choosing a Career in Business.* New York: Simon & Schuster, 1984.

Task Force Report on Self Esteem. Toward a State of Esteem. Sacramento, Calif.: California State Department of Education. 1991.

Toffler, Alvin. *The Third Wave.* New York: Bantam Press, 1984.

Index